Deadlines

Mike Curtis

Matador
9 Priory Business Park,
Wistow Road, Kibworth Beauchamp,
Leicestershire. LE8 0RX
Tel: 0116 279 2299
Email: books@troubador.co.uk
Web: www.troubador.co.uk/matador
Twitter: @matadorbooks

ISBN 978 1788033 381

British Library Cataloguing in Publication Data.
A catalogue record for this book is available from the British Library.

Printed and bound by CPI Group (UK) Ltd, Croydon, CR0 4YY
Typeset in 11pt Aldine401 BT by Troubador Publishing Ltd, Leicester, UK

Matador is an imprint of Troubador Publishing Ltd

Dedicated to the memory of

Pilot Officer Colin Hubert Curtis
Royal Air Force Volunteer Reserve
101 Squadron
Bomber Command

www.deadlines101.com

Contents

Chapter 1

Picture in a Frame

The Voyager is making its serene way north east on a course of 070 degrees, heading for the North Sea. Glimpsed in between the puffy white stratocumulus, I catch it flying at 14,000 feet over the East Midlands, on a mission to provide a petrol station in the sky for the next few hours.

A military version of the Airbus A330, the Voyager belongs to No. 101 Squadron and has taken off from RAF Brize Norton in Oxfordshire at 13.50 on a Monday afternoon. With a call sign of 'Tartan One One', it has trailed up over Worcestershire before turning right north of Wolverhampton. It then entered the Lichfield Radar Corridor – one of several dedicated routes in the sky that are established to get military aircraft from one side of the country to the other. Somewhere over the Nottinghamshire villages of Cropwell Bishop and Colston Bassett, the Voyager emerges from the 'corridor' and calls for clearance for a direct course to Air to Air Refuelling Area 8 off the Lincolnshire coast.

People largely ignore the Ryanair Boeing 737 as it heads off to some European city or Mediterranean island. There is no interest in the regular rumble of another north-bound airliner, streaming a white contrail, as it heads for Edinburgh, Reykjavik or long haul to Seattle or Chicago. Under the

1

Lichfield corridor, I quietly curse the clouds when a less familiar roar indicates that the source is something more interesting heading for the low level training areas in Wales.

Sometimes I catch the Voyager returning, its navigation lights and white strobes piercing the dusk as it heads for home after spending hours in a racetrack pattern over the North Sea. It reflects a poignant link with the RAF's 101 Squadron that has been with me since childhood when I first got to hear about the Uncle I never knew and whose photograph helped inspire a life-long interest in aviation.

The first air crash that I covered as a young newspaper reporter involved a Vulcan from 101 Squadron – a fireball missing a school by 500 yards. The first earth-shaking four ship 'scramble' by Vulcans that I witnessed in the mid-1960s were crewed by 101. In 1992, I joined a 101 crew on their VC10 for an air refuelling mission over the Malaysian jungles. I recorded a long radio interview with the test pilot who delivered the RAF's first jet bomber, the Canberra, to 101 Squadron in 1951.

My Dad always kept a photograph of his brother on his study desk at the Vicarage. This faded photo witnessed the full names for the christenings (Robert Andrew Scarborough Ferris, anyone?), the couple's bliss of the impending wedding banns, and the undertaker's latest list of departures. In newspapers, we called this triumvirate of life and death in the classified adverts section 'the hatches, matches and despatches'.

There was the discussion with the stonemason about a deceased's request to have 'That's all folks!' on his headstone. Do we *sell* Mrs Pugh-Critchley's donated rock cakes in aid of the church restoration appeal or do we actually *use* them in the stonework? The photograph of Colin was there for the confessions and confusion of the atheist who had changed his mind as death approached, and the concerns of the twin-set and pearls of the parish about an outbreak of late night lust on the cliffs near St Oswald's.

The picture in a frame showed a handsome young man with a boyish smile, his RAF peaked cap resting at a slightly jaunty angle. Above the left breast pocket of his jacket, he wore his RAF aircrew brevet – his 'Wings'. When the photograph was taken, he was about to join 101 Squadron.

Pilot Officer Colin Curtis
– the picture in a frame on his brother's desk

Pilot Officer Colin Hubert Curtis was 22 when his Wellington bomber was shot down over the North Sea. The aircraft and the six crew members have never been found. Their names are recorded on monuments and memorials but they have no final resting place other than the sea somewhere off the Dutch coast. The man who shot them down suffered the same fate a year later.

Some 125,000 aircrew served with Bomber Command during the Second World War. Colin Curtis was one of 55,573 of those men who were killed. That was a death rate of nearly half – 44.4 per cent. More than 8,000 were wounded in action and nearly 10,000 became prisoners of war. A Bomber Command crew member had a worse chance of survival than an infantry officer on the Western Front in 1916. Aircrews posed in black and white photographs, the stress of war etched in expressions on their young faces, old before their time.

My mother's father survived the Great War, serving as a medic in the trenches at the Somme and Passchendaele. Now a generation which had survived that carnage was seeing its sons and daughters, lovers, friends and relatives going off to fight yet again. My mother's cousin died at the controls of a Sunderland flying boat two weeks after Colin was killed. Her brother had the responsibility of clearing unexploded German bombs from the north of England after the war before being badly injured in yet another conflict – Korea.

When Colin was the age to fight, he was training to be a teacher. He had no plans to join the armed forces but the threat from Hitler changed his direction in life. He joined the RAF Volunteer Reserve and disappeared without trace on his third mission, leaving behind his fiancée Doris and a recently widowed mother and four siblings.

Colin's family lived in hope that he had baled out or had been taken prisoner but, as the months passed, they had to come to terms with the evocative empty place at the family dinner table and the ghostly gap in the church pew. In the following months, his two brothers joined the Army and were posted abroad. Having lost one son, Colin's mother spent the rest of the war worrying about the other two.

—⁓—

The photograph on my father's desk, along with an exciting ear-shattering experience as an eight year old beside the runway at Farnborough, inspired a lifelong interest in aviation. Predictably failing to impress the RAF selectors as a vague aimless 16 year old, I tumbled off into a career in local newspapers and radio in which I was lucky enough to pursue my passion for planes.

Being a journalist opened doors to many new worlds and experiences. It gave young reporters glimpses into the lives and circumstances of people that we would never have met outside our own social circles. You had to be open-minded and broad-minded, and learn quickly about things you had never heard of or had no interest in. Where you *did* have an interest, you got the chances to indulge it.

In the day-to-day trawl of local news, I got the opportunity to travel abroad and fly with the RAF. My hardback 'contacts' books were full of names and numbers associated with the service and with others in aviation. There were station commanders, community relations officers, Command media men and women, specialists, retired officers, aviation experts, display pilots, enthusiastic restorers and low flying complainants.

Like all young reporters of my era, my book of contacts also reflected the wider variety of tales that we told of lives lost and unpicked, injustices highlighted, charities supported and councillors called to account. There were links to other journalists, royalty, comedians, musicians, priests, publicans, politicians, postmistresses, factory workers, ghost hunters, racehorse trainers, football managers, hand puppets, exotic dancers and a US President.

There were the reminders of real heroes like the 1981 crew of the Penlee lifeboat or the young fisherman who jumped into the dirty, murky, ice cold winter seas to rescue a drowning airman who had just ejected from his exploding jet. Way before legislation on data protection, our contacts books had the private numbers of senior military figures, well-known politicians and famous TV personalities. Even when we all went digital, I hung onto my contacts books which now spark fond flashbacks of my youthful adventures working out of noisy smoky newsrooms in the 1970s and 1980s.

The novelist Graham Greene wrote of 'tasting the pleasure of remembering'. In the preface of one of his autobiographies, Greene quotes the 19th century French writer Gustave Flaubert who, aged only 28 and about to start on *Madame Bovary*, wrote to his mother: 'As my body continues on its journey, my thoughts keep turning back and bury themselves in days past.'

Flaubert is also credited with the quote: 'I know nothing more noble than the contemplation of the world'. What did Colin Curtis contemplate as he killed time in the hours before he was killed? Some say don't look back but we do. I am with Graham and Gustave, especially if dwelling on the past sheds light on the present and the future.

My middle name is Colin. It could have been Hubert, Harold, Eaton, Launcelot, Percy or Medway but probably not Aubrey or Gerard. I could have been Michael 'Fitz Wilfrid' indicating 'son of' Wilfrid. My father was a 'Fitz Harold' but he did not land me with that patronymic prefix. 'Fitz' was a Norman word from the 11th century and, at times, was used to name illegitimate children of royalty and nobility. This may have gone over my grandfather's head but might not have ended well for me, the son of yet another clergyman in the family tree.

The name Colin seems to be one of those forenames forever chosen for comedic effect, despite the achievements in my lifetime of Firth, Farrell, Bell, Sell, Todd, Cowdrey, Montgomerie, Dexter, Welland, Baker, Jackson, Blunstone and Powell. When Edmund Blackadder set up Sodoff Baldrick as his candidate in the by-election in the rotten borough of Dunny-on-the-Wold, his party had to convince the small population of 'three rather mangy cows, a dachshund named Colin, and a small hen in its late forties.' In *The Fast Show* comedy series, the irritating office joker was called Colin who took his work colleague Doreen to the Seychelles on his computer's flight simulator. In real time.

I was given the name Colin in memory of a young man whose career as a teacher was interrupted before it even took off. Instead he literally took off into what was often described as 'the jaws of hell'. His young life was turned upside down and brutally ended by deadly lines of machine gun bullets streaming out of the night sky. I am proud to bear his name.

Chapter 2

Gods of Olympus

My young ears could detect it very early. A dull far off rumble that gradually and relentlessly grew and grew. Was it one or four this time? As it reached its peak, it was as though the Gods had descended from Mount Olympus to spread their fire and wrath across the Lincolnshire countryside.

The cacophony could last for twenty minutes, rolling round the sky and drowning out conversations, radios, and the black and white televisions. The effects were more breathtaking when the drama unfolded in the dead of night. People shivered and glanced upwards fleetingly – or went to stand in doorways to savour the experience more closely and feel the earth move rather than just the windows rattle.

On Sunday evenings in winter, the priest and his congregation would recite the Lord's Prayer and strain to hear the organ chords to lead them through 'The Day Thou Gavest, Lord is Ended' as the rolling thunder billowed and subsided. Hardly anyone complained. The farmer on his tractor barely looked up as the peace of a summer's day was swept away by the mighty roar and belching smoke. The noise was comforting and familiar, expected and welcomed and a sign that God was in his Heaven and England's green and pleasant land was safe and sound. Unless of course, it was for real.

As the rumble faded beyond the horizon, those in the know mused that the cacophony was indeed from Olympus. Indeed sixteen of them – made by Rolls Royce and bolted in to the engine bays of four Avro Vulcan nuclear bombers. Sometimes it was just one or two or three being launched. Other times the full deck of four would 'Scramble' from the operational readiness platforms at the end of runways at airfields in eastern England.

These huge delta-winged aircraft were at the forefront of the nuclear deterrent. The five crew on board each one were trained to fly east to the Soviet Union and bomb its cities in response to a nuclear attack on the UK. The bomber crews of the Second World War knew that they had something to come home to if they survived a mission. The V-force crews knew they would probably have nothing to come home to other than a scorched land.

The Cold War of the 1950s and 1960s led to an exciting outburst of aircraft designs as the government urged companies to come up with plausible platforms for delivering nuclear weapons. Vickers, Handley Page and Avro won contracts to produce the V bombers – the Valiant, the Victor with its menacing look, and the Vulcan. The Lincolnshire bases that had hosted another Avro design, the Lancaster, in the war only twenty or so years beforehand welcomed the first 25 Vulcans in 1957. Waddington and Scampton, the home of the Dambusters, became synonymous with Vulcans. The other UK bases were Coningsby which had three squadrons in the early 1960s, and Finningley and Cottesmore not far beyond the Lincolnshire county boundary.

I do not remember where I was on the day that President John F Kennedy was assassinated in Dallas in November 1963. I have no recollection of the Cuban missile crisis some 12 months earlier (not long after my Farnborough debut) when Kennedy stood firm against the Russian leader Nikita

Khrushchev and demanded that Soviet missiles be removed from Cuba. The RAF's Vulcans were dispersed around many airfields in the UK waiting for a signal that could send them to war. If they really went off in anger, there might be nothing much left of the UK by the time they reached the Baltic states. I was eight and blissfully unaware how close the world had come to Armageddon.

—◊◊◊—

Working on my newspaper in Lincolnshire, the first call on a major story inevitably came from Bob Whitaker, the local freelance TV cameraman and a photographer. A combination of good contacts and listening to police radios ensured that Bob was at the forefront of local news and gossip – and a young journalist like me could learn a lot from him. This was years before mobile phones. Bob would ring me at the newspaper or the pub. Stan, landlord of the long gone Falcon round the corner from the newspaper office in Boston, would answer the phone at the bar and shout: 'Mike. Bob. Urgent.'

The conversation was brief. 'Outside the office in three'. Persuading my editor that something significant might be up, I would be where Bob wanted me within minutes. Sure enough, shortly afterwards a Mini Clubman 1275 GT would hurtle into view with Bob, a big man for a Mini, at the wheel. If he had been at home in his slippers, so be it. There was no time to change. He just grabbed the cameras and hit the road.

On the afternoon of Monday 17th January 1977, I was at my desk in the offices of the *Lincolnshire Standard* in Boston, tidying up some magistrate court stories from the previous Friday. Reception buzzed through with Bob on the line. 'Pick you up front of the office. Looks like an aircraft down Spilsby way.' Although Spilsby was out of my patch in Boston, the newspaper group covered the whole county so the Editor was happy to let me go and support the elderly reporter who had worked that beat for decades. More to *my* point, I also pulled together the words to go with Bob's news film for Yorkshire Television's *Calendar* and *About Anglia* in Norwich for which I got paid £2.50 per story.

After a white knuckle drive up the A16 with Bob's GT Mini on the wrong side of 70 miles an hour, we came through the centre of the small market town of Spilsby and out the other side towards the village of Halton Holegate. Suddenly we came across police officers, some of whom we knew and who could start to fill in the gaps in our knowledge.

When we discovered that it was a Vulcan that had come down, there was a sharp intake of breath all round. First speculation had suggested something much smaller. The crash site was only half a mile from the centre of Spilsby where it was Market Day. I got a quote from a senior police officer who said that half the population of Spilsby could have been 'wiped out' if the V-bomber had landed half a mile further to the north west.

Miraculously (an over-used word but unquestionably appropriate in this story) no one on the ground was hurt. Bob got through the police cordon to fire off a few shots of the wreckage but there were no discernible large pieces. To add to the unreal and eerie atmosphere, an afternoon mist was developing quickly into a thicker fog, giving the crash scene an 'end of the world' feel. It was all so quiet. The headline in our weekly paper five days later read simply: 'Disintegration....into a hundred thousand fragments' which was a quote from one of the first people on the scene. The wreckage was scattered over 20 acres.

Front page of the Spilsby edition of the
Lincolnshire Standard *21st January 1977*

It appeared that the captain of the Vulcan did indeed stay with his aircraft for as long as he could before ejecting. The bomber belonged to Colin Curtis' old squadron, 101, which was now operating out of Waddington near Lincoln. XM600 had taken off on a training exercise a few hours earlier and was heading home from the North Sea when a fire broke out in the number two engine. A routine test involving the deployment of the emergency generator created electrical problems with some sparking near to a fuel pipe. A fire broke out which the extinguishers failed to douse.

A Phantom crew who were airborne from Coningsby made a visual check of the back of the Vulcan and confirmed that the fire was intensive. The captain ordered the back three crew members to bale out at somewhere around 10,000 feet and the co-pilot to eject.

One of the crew struggled to get out as his oxygen tube got caught up in the mechanism designed to hold the hatch open against the rush of air. Helped by a colleague, he eventually fell free as the Captain struggled with the increasingly unresponsive V-bomber. The problems encountered while getting the three out the hatch lost more time for the Captain and he had to abandon his plan to turn the Vulcan back towards the North Sea. He finally lost control at around 3000 feet and ejected himself. All five landed safely, swinging on their parachutes into the gathering mist and gloom.

The weather meant that not many people saw the Vulcan come down in a field at 3.45pm. Those who did said it was in flames. One watched the Vulcan coming in from the coast with a fierce fire and a trail of black smoke. Suddenly he was counting parachutes. The huge explosion when it hit the ground rocked Spilsby and the surrounding area. Parents ran to the nearby primary school to scoop up their children. The farmer who owned the field had been there only an hour beforehand. Local fire fighters dealt with a number of magnesium fires and Anglian Water came to check that aviation fuel had not polluted the nearby stream.

In another extraordinary twist to the story, the first person that the Vulcan captain met after parachuting down was someone he knew. Michael Baker had been an Air Electronics Officer on Vulcans and had retired four years earlier to open a nursery garden near Spilsby. He had been in Spilsby town centre when he heard the explosion and rushed home.

As he reached his house, he saw a man in full flying gear walking along the grass track past his house. This ghost-like figure emerged from the fog and suddenly looked familiar. 'Hello Mike said the man from the sky' was another *Lincolnshire Standard* headline that week. Michael Baker described his old friend as badly shaken but unhurt – and very concerned about whether his Vulcan had hit anybody or any property. He took him into the house and made him a cup of tea while the Captain phoned Waddington to tell them what had happened.

One of the first people at the crash site said the Vulcan crashed near to where a Lancaster had come down in the war. His father and sister had been first on the scene then and had looked after three survivors. In those days aircraft crashes were commonplace. Many crews died in training accidents or as they tried to recover their battered shot-up aeroplanes back to base. In 1977, there were still many people in the Spilsby area who remembered the wartime crashes and the formations gathering in the Lincolnshire skies before heading off to Germany. There was always a lot of affection for the RAF in the county, even when a pilotless fiery Vulcan skimmed over your town and exploded in a nearby field.

The first big event I remember was the funeral of Winston Churchill in January 1965. I watched the grainy shots on a black and white television, mesmerised by the bowing of crane jibs along the Thames and the flypast by 16 silver Lightnings of the Royal Air Force. I remember the terrible sadness of a school assembly in October 1966 as our head teacher told us about the Aberfan disaster when a colliery spoil heap in south Wales slid into homes and a school, killing 116 children and 28 adults.

Before both of these events, I remember the shock of a Vulcan crash in the dark not far from my own bed. On 7th October 1964, a 9 Squadron crew was practising an asymmetric approach into RAF Coningsby. This involved shutting down two of the four engines to idle. As the bomber pilots piled on the power again as it overshot the runway, its engines were effectively unbalanced and control was lost. It developed a spin and crashed, killing all five on board. The sense of shock and loss in the local community where the crew lived with their families was palpable and deeply poignant even to a ten year old boy with no direct connection to the tragedy. More than 50 years later, a plaque was unveiled at Coningsby to remember the five men on XM601.

There were 111 accidents involving UK military aircraft in 1964. The RAF was then spread throughout the world (Aden, Borneo, Singapore, Malaysia, Gibraltar, Hong Kong, Libya, Cyprus and Germany for starters) and it had many more aeroplanes and helicopters. The Navy had aircraft carriers and air stations on shore. Not all the accidents were fatal but the Coningsby Vulcan tragedy made me look at Uncle Colin's photograph on my father's desk in a new light.

Thousands upon thousands of people turned out to see the final flights of the last airworthy Vulcan in the autumn of 2015. They lined roads near airfields and landmarks as XH558 went on its 'farewell tours' around the UK. Like some great diva of the stage, the 'Tin Triangle' waved its wings to its adoring fans and gave vent to its familiar howl. One sunny October afternoon that year, I watched the Vulcan from a farm gate as it took one turn over the nearby East Midlands Airport and then powered off eastwards to continue its farewell tour, with East Midlands tower warning it away from the parachutists over Langar airfield and advising that a vintage Jet Provost had lifted off behind it.

The smoke trails of its four engines as it vanished from my sight that Sunday afternoon evoked once more the four ship scrambles that so often proved the highlight at RAF 'At Home' days. As a 14 year old, I watched transfixed at the Royal Review at Abingdon in 1968 when the flypast to mark the RAF's 50th anniversary included no less than 24 Vulcans and Victors. Now the last Vulcan has lost the wind beneath its wings and is grounded forever, restricted to the taxi-ways and runway of Robin Hood Doncaster Sheffield Airport which, for me, will be forever Finningley.

Just after the war, test pilot Roly Falk was injured in an accident involving a Wellington bomber like the one in which Colin lost his life. Falk recovered to lead Avro's delta wing programme. Usually dressed in a pin-stripe suit and a tie, he was alone at the controls of the Vulcan prototype on its maiden flight in 1952 and three years later amazed the crowds at the Farnborough air show by barrel-rolling the huge bomber. He was banned from repeating the manoeuvre which the Flying Control Committee deemed was 'not the sort of thing that a bomber should do.' The clip can be found on-line with commentary by a BBC legend with one of the most familiar voices across my young lifetime – wartime Spitfire pilot Raymond Baxter.

In the V-force era, a photographer from the *Lincolnshire Echo* newspaper landed an assignment to go round the world via New Zealand in one of Waddington's Vulcans. It was not the most comfortable journey, being perched on the jump seat behind the pilots, next to the three other rear-facing crew. However the Vulcan went unserviceable in Hawaii, and the crew and the photographer had two weeks in the Honolulu sunshine while a spare engine was flown out on a Hercules. Of all the places to 'go tech'......

The first official public mobile phone call was made in a publicity stunt by Ernie Wise in 1985. Up until then, reporters on newspapers and in local radio fought for public phones or bribed people to 'occupy' red call boxes to enable them to 'file their copy' or record radio voice pieces back to the studios. Urine, vomit and vandalism invariably added to the phone box experience.

The morning after the 1977 Vulcan crash, the *Daily Express* ran the story with the headline 'Vulcan crew defy flames to save town'. It was written by long serving Express journalist David Thurlow, using some of the eyewitness quotes that I had telephoned around the nationals as well as filing copy in support of Bob's films for *Calendar* and *About Anglia*. Beaverbrook Newspapers Ltd sent me a cheque for ten pounds for that bit of work.

When I sent stories to regional television or the nationals, I usually did it away from the newspaper office. I did not want my news editor getting a false impression that I was doing more for the *Express* or the *Telegraph* than the columns of the *Lincolnshire Standard*. If you were lucky, the national would accept a transfer charge call from 'Curtis of Boston'. If not, you would be shovelling pennies into the black box beneath the handset after pressing button A, sometimes while someone was knocking on the glass and asking if I was going to be long. Some youth desperate to talk to his girlfriend would just have to wait while I filed my story.

Once you got through to 'Copy' on the nationals, you waited to hear what sort of copytaker you would be dealing with on that occasion. Would it be some chirpy, flirty East End girl who kept saying 'Go on, darlin' or would it be some curmudgeonly grump who was nearing the end of his shift and probably his life, and would keep saying 'Is there much more of this?'

The late national newspaper reporter and author Derek Lambert tells this story in one of his books about life as a young newspaper reporter. A national colleague with his paper's copy phone number imprinted on his brain rang in with what was described as a long and eloquent piece. After finishing his dictation, he was transferred to the newsdesk to receive his plaudits. 'A great piece. There's only one thing....' The reporter asked if they wanted more. '*We* don't,' said the Editor, 'But your new paper might. You left us last week. Remember?'

Chapter 3

Filth and First Times

The Camp Chaplain had spent part of the day studying saucy seaside postcards. Now he was in the death hold of a diminutive comedian while campers in the Gaiety Theatre howled with laughter. How had it all come to this?

For the first two summers of my life, Dad was a Camp Chaplain. He also had a stage routine with Charlie Drake (catchphrase: 'Hello, my darlings!'). The 'Camp' was Butlins holiday enclave at Filey on the Yorkshire coast where Charlie Drake was a newly-arrived Red Coat. Once a week the young Drake, an expert in wrestling and Jiu Jitsu, would send the Chaplain 'to heaven' with a hold on the shoulders called 'The Laughing Death'. He would then bring him back to life, to the shrieks of mirth from campers crowded into the theatre awaiting the weekly 'Glamorous Grandmother' competition. Charlie Drake, who was a rear gunner with the RAF in the war, went on to fame and fortune as a slapstick comedian, writer, singer and actor.

One of the star visitors to Filey Butlins in the second summer was the American cowboy hero 'Hopalong Cassidy' who gave me a silver luck token and his autograph. 'Hopalong' was a huge star in the first half of the 20th century, first appearing in 1904 as a creation of the writer Clarence E Mulford. He unsurprisingly got his name after being shot in the leg. From 1935, he was played in films and on television by William Boyd. There was a lot of 'Hopalong' merchandise including a radio and wrist watches. God knows what Boyd was doing at Butlins on the Yorkshire coast in 1955. Aged one and a bit, I had no idea who he was but I still have the token, inscribed with 'Good Luck from Hoppy'. You can buy one on-line for about ten quid now.

Billy Butlin's slogan was 'A week's holiday for a week's pay' and he set up the Butlins empire after seeing miserable holiday makers in the rain in Skegness in the 1930s. He had a puritanical streak and wanted to ensure that each of his establishments had someone looking after the spiritual side. Hence there was a Chaplain on each camp as a symbol of propriety and abstinence amidst the perceived increasingly 'smutty' comedians and the drunken fumblings of the unmarried in the chalet rows after dark. He once upbraided a comedian who told a joke about people not all being in their own chalets after the lights went out.

The Rev Wilf Curtis explains the postcard policy to happy campers, Butlins Filey 1954 (Photo: Butlins)

One of Billy Butlin's concerns were the racks of saucy seaside post cards, usually depicting enormous breasted young women and small shrivelled bald headed gents exchanging lines like 'You've got a couple of nice handfuls' or 'Fancy being jealous of the milkman – he's in and out in five minutes.'

The 'Camp Chaplain' was asked to ensure that none of the postcards, synonymous with the master of the art Donald McGill, were too risqué or downright filthy. One afternoon Dad, with his clerical collar in clear view, was studying a rack of these postcards outside one of the shops on the camp when he became aware of two little old ladies staring at him with shocked expressions on their pinched faces. 'It's alright,' he said breezily. 'I'm only looking for the *really* rude ones.' The outraged ladies scuttled off, convinced that the clergy were going to Sodom and Gomorrah and that the end really was nigh.

Colin Curtis spent his school holidays working on the farms of south Lincolnshire. In my teens, I was back at Butlins in Filey as a 'barrow boy'. They did not pay you but gave you a barrow and a white jacket with the *Butlins* logo across the back. You then spent as long as you liked moving people's luggage around on changeover day and relying on tips alone. Some just used it as an excuse to get onto the holiday camp and spend the day in the swimming pools or amusement parks. Others like me used it as a way of earning money to supplement what I was getting for shelf stacking at Liptons or, later, from Filey Urban District Council for dispensing the deckchairs and the crazy golf putters.

Usually it was arrivals who gave bigger tips, flushed with money and high expectations of their week or fortnight in Filey. Best customers were invariably gangs of lads down from

Newcastle or across from Leeds who, apart from having their cases moved to their optimistic love shacks, wanted the inside information on the best pick up bars and where the lusty lassies lurked. The public toilet blocks at the end of each chalet row were signed 'Lads' and 'Lassies' rather that Gents and Ladies.

My younger brother Chris also served his time as a barrow boy. Collecting the outgoing luggage with a friend from one chalet, the destitute occupant apologised that he had no cash left but said 'you can have all these pills instead.' Chris' barrow buddy enthusiastically accepted the alternative, prompting a horrified Chris to remonstrate that they had no idea what all the drugs might be for, that they could be dangerous and illegal, and it would be monumentally foolish to accept them under some shady deal in lieu of cash. He was then introduced to the German lager Pilsner.

You had to get in early to get a decent barrow. Many suffered from supermarket trolley syndrome with wonky wheels. Routine maintenance involved just dumping a load of grease over the mechanism. I was landed with one of these bastard barrows on the arrivals day for a major ballroom dancing competition. Sure enough, someone's elaborate floor length ballgown dress slipped from the top of the cases and got mangled by the dirty greasy wheels of my hopeless handcart. Ruined. Much weeping exasperation and a reduced tip.

The worst tippers were those who were departing, having had a wet week with ungrateful children or having failed to pull anything other than the end of a rope in the knobbly knees Tug of War. And then there were the Christians who took over the holiday camp for a couple of weeks at the end of the season and closed all the bars. I have never forgotten a huge, red-faced barrow-less barrow boy lurching up to a group of us waiting for trade outside Reception one Saturday and yelling in a rage at the sky: 'Some f**kin' Christian's nicked me barra!'

'Lordy Plonk,' as my mother would say. Or if she was in a particularly profane mood, 'Crikey Moses!'

—〰—

Thirty two years after Colin Curtis first flew to Germany and just a year younger than he was, I followed him under vastly different circumstances. He was flying into war in an uncomfortable slow bomber with no certainty that he would ever return. I was in a sleek Boeing 737 of Britannia Airways, not going to war but off to meet those who were keeping the peace. One afternoon in February 1974, I reported to the Joint Services Air Trooping Centre at Euston before being bundled on a coach to Luton for the flight to RAF Gutersloh. The *Lincolnshire Standard* had been offered a media facility trip to visit the Royal Anglian Regiment at Munster and had despatched their young reporter to find Lincolnshire people to talk to about life with BAOR (British Army of the Rhine) as the Cold War continued.

Disembarking from the 737 at RAF Gutersloh at dusk, I noticed the line-up of camouflaged Lightnings on the ramp and wistfully wished I was visiting 19 or 92 Squadron instead of the 'Brown Jobs' (RAF slang for the Army). A couple of days later I was sticking out of the top of an Army Personnel Carrier on the Dorbaum training range when a Phantom flew low overhead. Following its progress, I failed to see the low branches of a trees heading towards me and got zapped across the face. On my return, the subs headlined my reports: 'Mike Curtis joins BAOR and gets injured – by a branch!'

A few years later, BBC Radio Oxford sent me to talk once more to the British Forces in Germany. Another Boeing 737 from Luton took me into Dusseldorf from where four of us were bussed to a hotel in Weeze, not far from what was then RAF Laarbruch. This time it *was* an RAF trip, visiting the

Buccaneer and Jaguar squadrons and some of the 5,500 people living there at the time. The overall impression of my time with the Army at Munster were the reflections, particularly in the Officers' Mess in the evenings, of the recently completed tour of Northern Ireland at the height of The Troubles. At Laarbruch, it was the constant reminder of the Cold War and the border with East Germany just a few minutes flying time away.

In an article for the local radio page of *Radio Times* about my reports, I wrote somewhat dramatically: 'Every day Buccaneer and Jaguar strike jets thunder into the air to train for something that everyone hopes they will never have to do for real. I found it a very imposing place with an underlying sense of tension. Everything, including the runway, is painted a dull green, all around there are rolls of barbed wire and armed guards are everywhere. One senior officer told me he had tried to ensure that as many men as possible actually saw the border with East Germany. That, he said, usually convinces them that, over here, we are not playing games.'

I spent the first years of my teens in Surrey before escaping back to the north-east and the relative sanity of Bridlington Grammar School. I was sent to St John's School in Leatherhead, a school established for sons of the clergy with generous discounts in the fees to match their scant stipends. One of the alumni was David Hatch who visited us at Radio Lincolnshire at the end of the 1980s in his capacity as the top man in BBC Radio. His dad was a Yorkshire vicar and he also shared my birthday.

An enthusiastic member of The Tufty Club in my childhood, I dodged organisations like the Cubs and the Scouts and joined the RAF section of the Combined Cadet

Force. Junior Corporal Curtis M was a second class shot (correct), passed exams in Principles of Flight, Navigation, Flying Engines and Meteorology. The note in the Cadet's Record of Service said that it should be stated if a Pass was 'With Credit' or 'With Distinguished Pass'. There was no need in the case of Cadet Curtis.

Our group visited RAF Lyneham in Wiltshire in February 1969. I have a scribbled note to say I had a 13 minute flight in the Comet simulator at Lyneham which was the RAF's main air transport hub at the time. I sat in the Captain's seat of a Hercules (I actually wrote 'Pleasant flightdeck') and the Flight Engineer's seat on a Bristol Britannia (my review stated: 'Dingy aircraft inside passenger compartment. Flight deck not much better'). Pulitzer Prize, anyone?

There were a few flights in Chipmunk trainers with No. 6 Air Experience Flight at White Waltham airfield. On the 13th February 1969, I was strapped onto a parachute and waddled out to Chipmunk XP776. We were up for 40 minutes and, after a full loop, barrel roll and stall, the (worryingly old looking) pilot let me take the joystick for 10 minutes.

The routine for the pilot to hand over control of an aircraft to someone else is quite formal. In the front seat of the Chipmunk, the pilot said over the radio; 'You have control' and put his hands in the air for a moment. Grinning in the back, Cadet Curtis responded: 'I have control.' It was a phrase that I had the privilege of using several times over the subsequent years but, like most things, you never forget the first time.

My very first flight had been a last-minute birthday treat. Asked if I wanted to do anything special, nothing came to mind until a light aircraft droned overhead a short time later and a light went on. We went over to the small aerodrome near the Skegness Butlins holiday camp to look at prices. Dad could only really afford a short circuit around the airfield but there was someone else there who really wanted a longer trip and offered to pay the difference. So we let him have the front seat next to the pilot while Dad and I squeezed in behind aboard the high wing Auster.

The 'long' flight took us up the coast towards Mablethorpe. Being a weekday afternoon, the pilot called up the control tower at RAF Strubby to tell him we were around and where and at what height he ought to be to avoid their Varsitys, Canberras and Meteors. Further up and inland, there were also the Jet Provosts at Manby, any one of which would upset our Auster. The flight lasted about 20 minutes and seemed to be over in a flash, but I had now seen the earth from the sky for the first time. Dad did his local vicar act and got us a tour of Strubby one afternoon, hosted by a Canberra pilot who had been up to Norway earlier in the day. His main hobby was flying Austers at weekends – 'real flying' he called it.

Some five years on from the Auster, I was now Cadet Curtis in the Chipmunk, clattering around above east Berkshire at 5000 feet. I felt fine throughout the flight. However, on the coach journey back to school, I was suddenly moved to fill my beret with the contents of my lunch. As we got off the coach, the officer barked: 'Beret on, Curtis.' He declined visual proof that my headgear was not fit for purpose at that precise moment and nobly took it into custody.

I had vague ideas about joining the RAF but I was a teenager in the late 1960s. I did not want a 'short back and sides' and did not want to march up and down and salute people. However I quite fancied flying Phantoms.

I got an appointment at the Officers and Aircrew Selection Centre at Biggin Hill but they were clearly unimpressed with this slightly long-haired, rather dubious specimen. Off to a pessimistic start, the RAF optician told me I had unbalanced eye muscles and therefore could not be a pilot. It was still another 20 years before I started wearing glasses. I was utterly useless at physics (1 per cent in a mock 'O' Level), unconvincing in discussing world affairs ('What should the RAF be doing East of Suez?') and frankly not the sort of chap that they would let anywhere near the RAF College at Cranwell.

As a journalist, I did sneak into Cranwell on a few occasions. Rather like the BBC's Broadcasting House, I was always in awe of its place in history. College Hall is an imposing and impressive building which had echoed to the footsteps of Sir Douglas Bader and Sir Frank Whittle. Under the assumed name of Shaw, T.E Lawrence (aka Lawrence of Arabia) was stationed at Cranwell in the 1920s where he finally completed his epic *Seven Pillars of Wisdom*, having lost most of the original draft when changing trains at Reading station.

Unrecorded in the history of this illustrious institution is a collision between myself and the mobile phone stuntman and wartime Merchant Navy seaman Ernie Wise. While working at the Sleaford office of the *Lincolnshire Standard* in 1977, I went to Cranwell to cover a Lord's Taverners cricket match on a very warm sunny Sunday where the celebrities were playing an RAF eleven. Willie Rushton, Nicholas Parsons, *Z-Cars* James Ellis and Ernie Wise were among those who gave their time to the charitable cause. As I turned sharply with a beer in my hand, I knocked into Little Ern. He graciously accepted my profuse apology and said it was a good job he was wearing cricket pads, which looked enormous on him. It gave me an in-road to a brief conversation garnering a few quotes for the newspaper. That was it really. Sorry. 'What do you think of it so far?' (Rubbish!)

While working for BBC Radio, I did reports over the years for BFBS – the British Forces Broadcasting Company. Sometimes these were reports or documentaries done for the BBC which had an RAF angle. Others were two monthly summaries of life in Lincolnshire for their programmes like 'Sit-Rep' which brought an audio earful of life in the UK for people serving in the Falklands, Germany, Cyprus or other far flung postings around the world.

A Radio Lincolnshire presenter called Ed Lacy switched on BFBS in Hong Kong and was wistfully surprised to hear a familiar voice from home unpicking a story about officer cadets from Cranwell selling seagulls on the seashore at Skegness. In the name of charity, they got members of the public to pick out a seagull they liked and then pay a pound for the privilege of owning it. It was a bird-brained idea and plenty of people were gullible enough (and charitably inclined) to fall for it. Lord Hugh Montague Trenchard, Father of the RAF and the man who founded Cranwell, would surely have been proud.

One of the best known aviation journalists in the 1960s was John W.R. Taylor whose name was on many articles and books including the definitive *Jane's All the World Aircraft* which he edited almost single-handed for some 30 years. He could deduce the performance of new Soviet technology by examining blurred photographs. In 1961, Western intelligence experts feared the new Tupolev Tu-22 bomber could reach a speed of Mach 2.5 but Taylor said the shape of the engine intakes made the top speed more like Mach 1.4 which proved to be the case.

My Dad actually wrote to JWR in 1971 for advice about his directionless son and to ask about ways into aviation journalism. To his great credit, Taylor wrote a long reply and invited me to drop in and see him at his home in Surbiton. Trying to get your foot in the door with one of the established aviation journals like *Flight International, Air Pictorial* or *Flying Review* was one challenging way in. Taylor's advice was rather different though. He had begun his own career by spending 15 years in the aircraft industry with Fairey and Hawker, where he worked on the development of the Hurricane. He said his years on design and aviation technical writing gave him a knowledge and experience of aircraft engineering which proved invaluable and fairly unique in his profession.

I did not tell him about my career-defining one per cent mark in the physics mock 'O' level. I was quite obviously going to skip aircraft engineering and technical writing. I thanked him for his time and went away somewhat chastened. My aeronautical and artificial horizons were looking very limited and I spent the summer working on Filey sea front looking after crazy golf, archery, motor boats and the deck chairs (all sound tracked by Radio One), with the occasional Saturday at Butlins. I aspired to work in a record shop.

Have you heard the story of the Vicar's son, the teenage girl, a bow and arrow and the nearly slaughtered nun? Looking after the archery in Filey's Glen Gardens one late September day, my range was swamped by a bunch of girls from a boarding school in the nearby village of Hunmanby. In their squealing excitement which my 17 year old self tried to contain and inject some order, one slipped and her arrow shot way upwards over the canvas matting behind the targets and disappeared. The following day, a nun appeared with a broken arrow in her hand and, with her voice aquiver, asked if it was mine. With the targets to the front of me and a rack of bow and arrows behind me, she had me bang to rights. (Coincidently 'Broken Arrow' is US military slang for an accident involving nuclear weapons which does not create the risk of nuclear war).

The elderly devotee of Catholicism had been staying in a seaside holiday nunnery way behind the archery range. She had been sitting at a right angle to her window and was reading the Bible (but of course) when the errant arrow sailed through the window in front of her, scattering glass around her room. God was with her that day – and with the council and its youthful Head of Archery Entertainment.

Looking after the deckchairs, the crazy golf or the motor boats was considerably safer. There was a way of tweaking the motor boat engines to make them cut out after a minute or so. Strangely this seemed to happen only when the boat had been hired by girls of my age, meaning the gallant boatman had to stride out in waders to rescue the damsels in distress, fire it up again and give them a longer session. No need to come in yet, Number 9.

Archery, nuns, camp chaplains, luggage, seagulls, knobbly knees, saucy seaside postcards, deck chairs, a boating lake, romance, holidaymakers and Hopalong – all the ingredients surely for a sequel to Jacques Tati's comic masterpiece of 1953 that is *Les Vacances de Monsieur Hulot*?

The late reporter shift at BBC Radio Oxford. What glamorous assignment awaits me today? Some famous actress visiting Oxford who has agreed to speak to the local radio station in her suite at the Randolph Hotel? An interview under the dreaming spires in the quiet of a senior academic's study? Progress on the Joint European Torus project at Culham? The school closure plan at Charlbury? British Leyland? Great Tew? Blenheim Palace? The Ashmolean? Thatcher's newly appointed Minister for Europe (Mid-Oxfordshire MP Douglas Hurd)? A long overdue feature on the Jaguar jet maintenance unit at RAF Abingdon? Please God, not the Vale of White Horse planning committee.

No, I was despatched down the Cowley Road to interview a group of protesters gathered opposite Oxford's new sex shop and get the other side of the argument from the manager. 'Can you get down there quickly, Mike, before they go off!' urged the producer. 'Bring us back a goodie bag,' said another.

To interview the manager, I would have to go into the shop in front of all the mainly female protesters. There was a photographer from the *Oxford Mail* loitering with intent who was also ready to get a snap of a BBC reporter entering the sex shop, if only for their newsroom notice board. There did not appear to be a back door way in so it was the front door or nothing. I decided to 'vox pop' the protesters first and then exclaim in a loud voice that I was 'going in' because I had to get the other side of the story.

There was no one in the shop apart from the manager who was on the phone. He motioned for me to go into the back room where I waited, sitting on a box full of 'explicit videos' and facing stacks of magazines of *Readers' Wives*. (I was of course only looking for the really bad ones, Dad).

The same producer sent me to a sex toys party in Abingdon at 11 o' clock in the morning. I bowled up to a semi-detached dwelling on a suburban housing estate to be greeted by a disappointingly soberly dressed hostess in her late 30s with a soft Geordie accent. They were two other women there in their 20s who were customers and had agreed to talk anonymously. The peg for this cutting-edge journalism was how this sort of thing had taken over from Tupperware parties and no one was embarrassed or fazed by it in the early 1980s.

After a demonstration of exhibits with me recording the whirring sounds of a couple of battery-operated devices, I started my interviews. These sessions were for women only, the customers wrote down what they wanted to buy and put their list into a brown envelope, and the goods were duly delivered to their home in plain packaging a few days later. 'The girls are a bit nervous at first when they come to the parties but they would never want to go into a sex shop to buy these things,' said our hostess. Especially if there was a bunch of demonstrators and an *Oxford Mail* photographer outside and a BBC reporter with a tape recorder inside, I thought.

The customers ran through some of their purchases including a bewildering range of underwear and revealing night attire, with me mentally editing everything as I went along. How much of this lot could I actually broadcast to the good people of Oxfordshire and beyond as they dipped their soldiers into their boiled eggs and munched on their *Sugar Smacks* and *Apple Jacks* tomorrow morning? 'This is Sex Sugar – a couple of spoonfuls of this in his late night cocoa and he will come alive!' one purred. Another had bought a special mug for her mother-in-law. As you drank the tea or coffee within, something started to emerge in the middle of the mug which looked as though the Sex Sugar had worked. More tea, Vicar?

Chapter 4

Son of a Preacher Man 1941

The long straight roads of the south Lincolnshire fenlands follow the dykes and drains, breaking up the fields full of sugar beet, barley, wheat and oil seed rape. Electricity pylons stand out against the huge skies, joined now by more and more wind turbines. Above these acres of agriculture, military jets dogfight with each other or line up to run into the Holbeach weapons range on the edge of The Wash.

Ancient churches with steeples are scattered across the landscape. Some lean noticeably, sinking in to the soft earth over the centuries. The names of the villages and hamlets embrace Fen, Bank, Deepings, Marsh and Drove. The visitor searches in vain for the rising land called Gedney Hill. The locals joke that the village was named after a slight ramp within one of the now closed pubs.

The Greenwich Meridian separating east and west runs through this landscape. It dissects the village of Holbeach St Johns where, seven months after the Armistice was signed to end the Great War, Colin Hubert Curtis was born. Like all his siblings, he was delivered in the upstairs bedroom of the vicarage of Holbeach St Johns, next to the relatively recent house of God built in 1840. The Vicarage had no electric lights or gas. The family relied on candles and paraffin lamps.

His father was the Rev. Harold Eaton Curtis, vicar of the parish and, fleetingly, a professional footballer. His mother was Lillian Estella Curtis. Harold was one of seven sons of the Rev William Fitz-Harry Curtis and his wife Martha Allner Spere who were living in South Africa when he was born in 1866. His brothers were Launcelot Charles Edward Curtis (born 1868) who managed a tea plantation in Assam in north east India, Hugh Sorre Curtis (1870) who went into the Royal Navy and died young in an accident, and Hubert Percy Curtis who managed a rubber plantation in Malaya.

Another brother, Colin Medway Curtis (1880), ended up in Malacca state in Malaysia, working in insurance. In 1914 he wrote to Harold saying he had been done 'a very great harm' but does not elaborate. This may have been a bad marriage. He came back to the UK for military training with the Army. He later wrote of his wife 'ruining his future' and it was 'now his one ambition to get to the Front' in France.

Gerard Fels William Curtis (1864) joined the Royal Inniskilling Fusiliers and married an actress, something that did not go down well within the ecclesiastical circle (the actress, not the Fusiliers). The second youngest was Aubrey Cole Curtis (1872) who went one better than marrying an actress by getting a young girl pregnant while he was training to be a priest. Naughty Aubrey was banished to Australia where he became a teacher for a while before working on the land out in the bush and then selling books door to door. He seemed to be constantly short of money and beseeched his brother Harold for loans. He was written out of his parents' wills. He never married and died in 1943.

It is clear that the Rev Harold Eaton Curtis named his second son after two of his brothers, hence Colin Hubert Curtis. There was a fervent hope that Colin and *his* brothers would not succumb to temptation and the pleasures of the flesh by marrying an actress or getting one of the congregation in the family way.

So could I have been given any of those names? My parents chose Michael, an Archangel no less, with Colin as my second forename, in memory of my father's fallen brother. So we were never to hear: 'Now the news with Launcelot Curtis' or 'This report by Medway Curtis'.

—⟋⟋—

The fecundity of William and Martha with their seven sons was exceeded by Anthony Veall and his exhausted wife Emily. Anthony was the schoolmaster at Moulton Chapel in south Lincolnshire and died in 1915. Emily produced no less than ten daughters, with Anthony presumably hoping if not pleading that the next one might just be a boy. One more try then? Minnie was the first to appear in 1879 followed across the next 18 years by Agnes, Lillian, Effie, Jessie, Gertie, Zetta, Maud, Kathleen and Phyllis.

The sheer volume attracted some publicity in the gossip columns of the day. The magazine 'Illustrated' (every Wednesday, 3pence) did a double page spread on the sisters in its edition of 22nd September 1945, which featured General Douglas MacArthur on the cover. By now, some were married and the remaining spinsters 'haven't given up hope yet.' A couple were governesses and another was a housekeeper. The reporter wrote that Effie 'looks just what she is – a farmer's wife.' Phyllis married Harold's brother Launcelot.

The third Veall sister Lillian – usually abbreviated to Lillie – was courted by a new south Lincolnshire vicar Harold Eaton Curtis and the couple married. Colin was their third of a disappointingly low count of only five children and arrived on 23rd June 1919. He was baptised into the Anglican church of his father a month later.

The ten Veall sisters gather in Scunthorpe sometime after the war. Colin's mother Lillian is seated far left, next to her is Gertie… no Effie… or was that Maud…? (Photo: F. Bowen of Scunthorpe)

The Curtis children (Hugh, Joyce, Colin, Mary and Wilfrid) all went to local schools, often cycling the seven miles each day to Moulton Grammar School in the summer term. There was also a school bus in which Colin first set eyes on Doris Fines. Doris' younger sister recalls that she first met Colin when she was eight. She had been fishing with one of her other sisters and had fallen into the river. She rushed home to find Colin at the house, calling on her elder sister. 'This handsome young blond man stood me by the fire and wrapped a towel round me,' she said.

The Fines family all liked this young son of a local vicar. Doris and Colin became childhood sweethearts and after leaving school, they got engaged. The local paper carried the announcement that Colin Hubert Curtis and Doris May Fines, eldest daughter of Mr and Mrs C. Fines of Broadgate House, Sutton St James, were now betrothed. They were looking forward to a life together. Within four years he would be dead with no body to bury or grave to visit.

Walter Hilliam was a schoolboy in Holbeach St Johns in the 1930s and knew the Curtis family. The Vicar, who was 53 when Colin was born, was regarded as a stern man but the children were a lively bunch. The eldest Hugh was a bit of a tearaway and a lot of fun while Wilfrid, the youngest and a contemporary of Walter, was imaginative and besotted by motorbikes and the dance bands of the time fronted by leaders like Henry Hall.

Walter was eight years younger than Colin. He remembers him as 'down to earth', modest, calm and sensible. He could be heard singing around the Vicarage. He worked on local farms in the school holidays, loading wheat onto the horse-drawn carts.

Colin wanted to be a teacher and started his career with a three month placement at the end of 1937 at Holbeach Boys School. The head teacher, Mr English, said he promised to develop into a first class teacher with his Maths pupils getting high percentages in their exams. He had earned the respect of the pupils and was punctual, pleasant and courteous. A few weeks at Fleet Fen Council School earned him similar plaudits, being described as a young man of the highest character.

The next move was enrolling at a formal teacher training course at Borough Road College in Isleworth in Middlesex (£60 fee for the full year from September 1938). He went with a hand-written reference from two head teachers. Mr E.A.G Marlam wrote: 'Colin Curtis has been a pupil of this school for the last eight years and I can write his testimonial with pleasure. He is (to) me one of the best type we turn out, always keen, interested and loyal as well as being thoroughly reliable and trustworthy.

'He is a painstaking and industrious worker, last year he matriculated by obtaining credits or better in English, History, Maths, Geography, French, Physics with Chemistry and Botany in the Cambridge School Certificate. In addition he is a school prefect and a good sportsman being a 1st colour in cricket, football and hockey. I might add that I shall be pleased to answer any further questions about him at any time.'

J.G.Westmoreland said Colin entered wholeheartedly into every phase of school life and 'was endowed with sterling qualities which contribute to success in teaching. I shall watch his career with interest for I feel sure that he will develop into a very successful teacher.'

In letters to his sister Mary in November and December 1938, Colin explained his lecture timetable which meant it was difficult to get across London to see her. He was playing Bridge and had been invited with some of his colleagues to a Bridge evening with the College Principal and his wife. He wanted to know if Mary 'had seen Hickson at all or if there was any news of Buzzer and whether old Beattie's love affairs were flourishing.'

Mary, who was addressed as 'Old Girl', obviously thought he was not making an effort to catch up with his sister who was training to be a nurse in London. Her last letter to him had included some 'sarcastic remarks' about finding time to go to dances. Colin insisted he had lectures in the evenings. 'I know I keep putting you off but you can see for yourself it can't be helped and if you don't believe me, come and ask the Principal.' I think Mary passed on that one.

The letter concluded with the weather (rain) and a hope that they will meet when he 'gets the hang of things around here a bit better – I'm not climatised yet.' There's a P.S which adds: 'There's a nice Welshman here who wants to see you.'

In a letter to his mother in July 1939, he ran through a list of questions and observations about family life. How did

Mary seem – and did she talk about her young man? When will brother Wilf's exams start and is he still trying to find work? Had his other brother Hugh said any more about going for a holiday? His fiancée Doris has just had a week at Great Yarmouth with two friends and had sent him some seaside rock in the shape of bloaters, an innovative if unusual love token.

In the months before the Second World War was declared, the Rev Harold Eaton Curtis gave up the living of Holbeach St Johns after 30 years and moved the family to a new home at Wyberton near Boston. They called it 'Cherry Holme' in homage to the 'magnificent' cherry tree at the old vicarage.

Colin hoped that the lupins from the old house had been taken to the new garden and wondered if there would be any strawberries left by the time he got home in just over a week's time. He thought he might go halves with someone and buy some in Isleworth as they were now about 8 pence a pound. Day-to-day trivia lapped up by a doting mother.

Colin ended the letter by hoping that the new house was suitable for 'such an ideal vicar's wife' and paid tribute to his mother. He agreed with a Mr Mawby (whoever he was) that his mother had been and still was a good wife and mother and 'we couldn't have had a better one. But I am afraid we don't always realise how good you have been.'

The first few months of the war were relatively quiet compared to the hell to come – it was called the Phoney War. Prime Minister Neville Chamberlain announced on the radio at 11am on 3rd September 1939 that Britain was at war with Germany following the Nazi invasion of Poland. In view of what was happening in the world, a limited form of conscription into the military had been introduced in April with men of Colin's age (20 to 22 years old) being liable for call-up. After the declaration of war, the National Service (Armed Forces) Act widened this to all men aged between 18 and 41 unless they had medical issues or were employed in certain vital occupations.

Colin passed his driving test in January 1940. He was called up later in the year, reporting to 10 Signals Recruiting Centre in Blackpool on 10th September 1940. He was enlisted as number 1311049 and given the entry rank of Aircraftsman Second class (AC2). It was a long train journey across to Blackpool where the new recruits were met by a shouting Corporal. They were marched to their accommodation – a bed and breakfast establishment near the sea front. There was a 10.30pm curfew enforced by the RAF Police.

Like so many, Colin was allocated to training as a wireless operator. The new recruits were marched everywhere, up and down parade grounds and back and forth to meals. The uniforms scratched and irritated. The buttons had to be polished repeatedly. They were given cotton, spare buttons and sewing needles to ensure everything remained spick and span. There were medical examinations and lectures on sexually transmitted diseases.

With a character described as 'Very Good', Colin decided that, now he was in the RAF, he wanted to be a pilot and volunteered for aircrew as a member of the RAF Volunteer Reserve. That summer and into autumn, the Battle of Britain raged in the skies over London and the south east.

His next posting was to No.10 Initial Training Wing which had requisitioned the famous Grand Hotel on Scarborough's South Bay. This six week training programme, starting just after Christmas in 1940, was designed to improve discipline, physical fitness and mental alertness, and provide a sound basic understanding of the RAF. He learnt to recognise rank badges so that he saluted the right people. The syllabus included guns, engines, hygiene, discipline, administration, maths, meteorology, navigation, signals and Kings Regulations (Air). At the end of the course, he was promoted to Leading Aircraftsman.

It was now time to see if he could fly and he was sent to No 20 Elementary and Reserve Flying Training School for ten weeks early in April 1941 as a pilot 'under training' (U/T). This was based at RAF Yeadon, the airfield that eventually became Leeds/Bradford Airport. At five feet four and a half inches, it must have been a challenge to operate the foot pedals of the Tiger Moth training bi-plane but Colin showed a natural aptitude for flying and qualified for the next step. Pilots generally had 15 hours instruction on the Moths and most were expected to fly solo before reaching 10 hours.

Much of the early time was spent in the circuit around the airfield, following the instructor's orders bellowed down the Gosport tube which was a thin pipe connected to the headphones in his flying helmet. Colin had to master the skill of 'rounding out' as he came into land, perfecting the three point landing with his main wheels and the tail skid settling on the grass runway at the same time. As with all small tail-draggers, he learnt how to weave from side to side on the ground as the engine obscured the view forward.

He did have one mishap early in his flying training. On the 10th April, his brand new Tiger Moth (serial number N5446) made a crash landing on Hazlewood Moor near Bolton Abbey, some 15 miles north west of Yeadon. Colin and his instructor in the back seat, Sgt John Edwin Midgley, were slightly injured. It seems that Colin did not trouble his family or his fiancée with news of this accident.

The Tiger Moth was dismantled at the crash site and sent for repair. It spent some years being used by the Fleet Air Arm until it was put into storage in 1944. Seven years later, it was flying again until its UK registration was finally cancelled after another accident in 1957 while being used by the Edinburgh Flying club at Turnhouse. It later turned up in the United States, being photographed at John Wayne Airport in Orange County near Los Angeles in 1969. More than 75 years since it was built, N5446 is still being flown by a private owner in Carrollton in the state of Georgia.

Nine months after Colin was killed, Sgt Midgley was commissioned into the RAF Volunteer Reserve. He survived the war and came out of the RAF in 1946.

The British government did a deal with the Canadian authorities to train many of its aircrew away from the war in Europe and in the wide open and safe skies of North America. It had around 20 training bases including Medicine Hat in Alberta, home of the RAF's No. 34 Service Flying Training Unit. It opened only a few months before Colin Curtis was sent there in 1941. It trained over 2000 airmen before it was closed in November 1944. Across those three and a half years, 48 airmen lost their lives in accidents and most were buried at the Hillside Cemetery nearby rather than being repatriated.

Colin Curtis was billeted in Hut 14A at Medicine Hat. The journey to his new base took two weeks with 10 days at sea in a convoy. He watched as escort destroyers zigzagged around the convoy and nervously pondered the threat from German U-boats. Docking at Halifax in Nova Scotia, he boarded a troop train for a four day roll across Canada. He wrote home about a very good and quiet crossing and said the train journey was 'very interesting'. The food on the ship was very good and was excellent at Medicine Hat where there were eggs for breakfast every day if you wanted them.

'It really is a great treat to see all the lights at night again, to see all the shops full of goods and to be able to get apples and oranges once more. We get plenty of butter, cheese, sugar and milk and we have some good canteens on the camp,' he wrote, reflecting on the contrast back home with wartime rationing and the nightly blackout. The weather was warm and they had been issued with cotton khaki outfits. The war in Europe was a world away.

Colin did his training on the Avro Anson, a twin-engine aircraft which first flew in 1935 and was originally designed for the maritime reconnaissance role. However it proved unsuitable for this task but was ideal for crew training for the twin-engine bombers that were in RAF service such as the Whitley, the Hampden, the Blenheim, the Battle and the Wellington. Avro stopped building them in 1952 but they continued in RAF service until 1968. It was the first RAF aircraft to have retractable undercarriage although it required 140 turns of the hand crank by the pilot to benefit from this new idea.

While Colin was at Medicine Hat, the base was visited by the Duke of Kent. There was a picture of Colin with some of his colleagues – Scottie, Bill, Alf, Roddie and Ted. They got the opportunity to go horse riding on the prairie surrounding the airfield. There is another picture of Colin with nine other trainees gathered round an Anson, some of them wearing their leather flying helmets. They were getting used to a hard runway instead of grass. On the back, the photograph is dated August 1941 with a list of 'Fags, Silks, Post, Cotton.'

Fags – well everyone smoked in those days including Colin and his two brothers. In many photographs of them as young men, they invariably had a fag between their fingers. The phrase 'hitting the silk' meant baling out of an aircraft and descending to the ground under a parachute canopy. Silk maps were devised by the Americans and used by aircrew for escape purposes if they landed in enemy territory. Colin's mention of 'silks' was probably simply a reminder to get some real silk stockings for his fiancée back in the UK. Cotton too was on the ration. 'Post' was all important – the only way to communicate between loved ones.

—w—

Back home his mother was wondering if he was getting her letters. On August 6th, she wrote that this was the sixth letter from home but she had only had one cable and one letter from him up to now. 'I keep looking out for another from you; we think of you and talk of you and pray for you every day,' she wrote.

'Father is very well for him, but cannot get his pipe to go but he will not leave go of it. I have put a little hedge all round the lawn at the back, I hope it will be growing nicely by the time you come home. Oh when that time comes, how thankful we will be.' This letter revealed that Joyce was off for an interview at the Ministry of Labour the following day. Auntie Gertie had gone to Stratford-upon-Avon that week to meet her future mother-in-law and Lillian was wondering how she was getting on there.

There were dancing lessons on the wireless and Wilf was trying them out. Colin's young brother was now 17 and spending his nights up the top of Boston Stump as a 'firewatcher', reporting by phone to the fire brigade if he saw any fires from German bombing. Mary was on a month of night nursing duty. Mr Barrand had not finished painting the house yet as he had hurt his thumb rather badly (regrettably history does not record how).

Father was having his supper and Joyce was 'washing her head'. When she had finished writing the letter she would not seal and post it until the morning to see if a letter from Colin arrived. She was going to ring Doris and see if she wanted to come for the weekend again. Amidst all this domestic tittle tattle, the wireless reminded everyone that the country was at war.

Thursday morning at 9.15am and still no letter. Doris was out when she rang the previous evening but her father said 'she had received four or five letters from you so where is mine?' In his last letter to Doris, Colin had written that he had not received any letters or cables from home. In another letter on 21st August, three marrows are reported cut and marrow and fig jam is being prepared. Beans are growing slowly because it has been too wet. There are five tomatoes on Colin's plant and hopes of five more soon. Joyce had dug up most of the potatoes and they were now going to plant more cabbages and cauliflowers for the spring. Keep up!

At least two letters to Colin from his mother appeared to have arrived at Medicine Hat long after he had left. One which was posted on 7th August 1941 was stamped as 'Unable to Deliver in Canada. Return to Sender on Air Ministry Instructions'. It seemed to have gone 'round the houses', being stamped with dates of 28 October, 27 November 1941 and even 31 January 1942 – ten days after Colin was killed. Another letter about the same time suffered the same fate, ending back at the RAF Records Office in Ruislip before being opened and stamped 'Return to Sender.' (Elvis Presley was six in 1941).

The Wings Dinner of Number 21 Course at Medicine Hat was held on Friday 29th August 1941. The venue was the Canadian Legion Club's banqueting hall, and the menu featured fruit juices, roast beef with roast potatoes and green peas followed by apple tart or ice cream, cheese and biscuits and tea or coffee. Group Captain Ellis CBE proposed the loyal toast to His Majesty the King. Colin and his colleagues were now eligible for their Wings and, two days later, started the journey home to fight for King and country. How many would live to see the end of the war? How long would they each survive – months, weeks or days?

Chapter 5

Binbrook Ghosts

The old airfield at Binbrook sits high on the Lincolnshire Wolds, surrounded by an Area of Outstanding Natural Beauty. The hills belie the perception that Lincolnshire is a flat and featureless land. The remaining hangars of this once busy and exciting aerodrome can be seen for miles around. The skies above were suddenly quieter from June 1988 when the last two Lightnings took off. The pilots staged a memorable low level fly past over the now empty dispersal in front of the control tower before powering away into the summer sky.

During the Second World War, engineers nevertheless found enough flatness to construct the main runway running south-west to north-east. This was extended even further to 7,500 feet to accommodate the Cold War jets of the early 1960s. Its geographical position did leave it vulnerable to the weather – notably wind, fog and snow. In the big freeze of 1947, it was cut off by snow for more than a week and the RAF arranged air drops of food, drink and 'essential' cigarettes for its beleaguered base.

In the 1960s, Binbrook was a very exciting place for a youngster in the initial throes of passion about military aeroplanes. I pestered my parents to take me up there if only for an hour to watch the comings and goings of a cavalcade of

British military ingenuity. One airfield but what a collection within! Operational squadrons and the Central Fighter Establishment were based at Binbrook with Meteors, pointy-nosed Canberras, high-tailed delta winged Javelins, sleek Hunters and shiny silver supersonic Lightnings which trailed billowing parachutes when they landed.

Approaching Binbrook on a murky day, silent prayers were offered that something would be 'happening'. A lone Javelin in the circuit slipped tantalisingly out of the low cloud and disappeared again. I was out of the car and running to Crash Gate 2 to the west of the threshold of Runway 03. Every lover of the Lightning has stood on that desolate spot before 1988, waiting in hope for the distant whine and roar that told you something was starting up across the other side of the airfield. At the north-east end of the runway, Crash Gate 3 acquired its status as another Lightning lovers' legendary location, just up the dead-end track from the village of Thorganby.

After one fruitless trip (probably a Friday afternoon), my Dad was inspired to write to the top man at Binbrook to ask when was usually the best time to visit to see some flying. Assuming that the address including the word 'Rectory' indicated that he was not dealing with the Soviet Embassy, Group Captain Ian MacDougall DFC replied on 8th January 1964 that we could come and tour the station accompanied by one of his chaps. I have still got the letter. I did not know it then but Ian MacDougall was a Pilot Officer in the Battle of Britain. He died in 1987 – the year before the Lightning was retired from RAF service.

—๛—

No longer was I at the Crash Gate, peering in. I was in an RAF Land Rover being driven down Binbrook's runway after a Canberra of 85 Squadron confirmed to the control tower that it had 'vacated' after testing its compass. The Land Rover had F/11 on both ends, indicating in this case 11 Group of Fighter Command. I was in the Control Tower as a couple of Hunters were 'talked down' by the radar controllers. I saw a crew room and had my photograph taken next to the Spitfire gate guardian, dressed in my short-trousered suit and new slip-on shoes with aspirations to look like the ten year old epitome of cool, just two months after the Beatles first album was released.

That same year, the RAF left RAF Middleton St George near Darlington. Up in the north east on grandparent parade, we saw an article in the *Northern Echo* about the Lightnings of 226 Operational Conversion Unit flying out the following day. The Rev. Curtis rang the base and was told there was no public event but 'come along anyway and use my name at guardroom.' Such relaxed informality. We were there to watch as all the Lightnings started up, taxied out and took off for their new home at Coltishall in Norfolk. Another ear-shattering, exciting episode for a ten year old convert to aviation and more fuel on the fire of a life-long love of the English Electric Lightning.

I returned to Binbrook numerous times over the years as an airshow attendee or as a working journalist. If I was heading up to see my parents on the Yorkshire coast via the Humber Bridge, I would sometimes make a small detour to the Crash Gate, even after the Lightnings had gone and the airfield gradually returned to farmland. The control tower was demolished but the hangars and the two Quick Reaction Alert sheds at the end of runway 21 remained – final evocative symbols of a once busy airfield and a reminder of the many men who disappeared into the dark skies, never to return.

The aerodrome lost many bomber crews during the Second World War and many pilots afterwards, including those at the controls of Lightnings.

Binbrook had its share of ghost stories. One concerned a figure often seen at the end of the runway as dusk fell. He appeared to be signalling furiously to something, almost raging against the dying of the light. The story was that he was one of the ground crew who suddenly realised that the bombs loaded onto a bomber that was about to take off had been fused (normally done just before being dropped). As he tried to flag down the bomber on its take-off run, it exploded killing all the crew and him.

Another story came from the Canberra era when, after some night flying, the ground crew working on one of the aircraft noticed that an airman was still around and had not joined the others on the crew transport. A group of them saw this figure, who looked sad and disorientated, wander off and fade into the darkness. They all realised they had seen a ghost.

On another night, the man on duty in the Station Armoury did his final checks, ensuring he was the only person in the building. He secured all the doors and locked himself into the inner office and lay down on his bed to read a book. Not long afterwards, he heard all the light switches in the corridor outside being switched on and off. No footsteps – just switches. He stayed where he was, utterly convinced that he was the only human in the building and very reluctant to challenge this ghostly presence.

A few miles away, there was another wartime airfield straddling the Lincolnshire Wolds. Kelstern was also home to Lancaster bombers and closed immediately after the war, leaving few traces of the airfield apart from some concrete hard standings and a small memorial to the lives lost on 625 Squadron. The road from Binbrook to the market town of Louth cuts across the bleak old airfield. Local people tell of drivers being flagged down by a mysterious airman wanting to be taken to RAF Kelstern, only for him to vanish before their eyes.

One misty autumnal morning, a driver passed a lone piper playing by the memorial. It looked so eerie that the driver did not dare stop. Local enquiries could find no trace of a piper who had turned out that morning. More common stories relate how people have heard the sound of Lancaster bombers on the airfield years after it was closed. If you stop your car at dusk at Kelstern or Binbrook or indeed any long deserted wartime airfield, get out and contemplate the world. You can sense the sadness and loss, and maybe it is not too great a leap for the mind to imagine the sounds of Merlin engines, dance bands playing 'Moonlight Serenade' or to glimpse the outline of a man in a flying jacket and thick boots gazing into the far distance before fading away.

One summer in the mid-1980s we had a temp secretary in the Radio Lincolnshire newsroom called Rosie who expressed an interest in visiting one of the RAF bases that regularly featured in the stories that were dictated to her over the phone by our news team out and about. I had a long standing invitation to have another look at Binbrook from the new Community Relations Officer so took her with me one afternoon.

It was very busy with the Lightnings of 5 and 11 Squadrons, and the Lightning Training Flight, up and down all afternoon. We watched as the fighters swung in to the flight line, were refuelled and checked over and lurched off again to the runway. Lightnings were notoriously thirsty aircraft and, if there were no air-to-air refuelling tankers available over the North Sea, they had to be back at Binbrook for more fuel often well within the hour.

The presence of a young woman on the flight line did have one immediate implication for the Lightning pilots during the quick turn-round on the ground. While their aircraft was being attended to, some of them would take the opportunity to unstrap, climb down the ladder and run over to the grass and relieve themselves. Rosie's appearance had them instead scurrying back to the hangar to answer nature's call. We looked at the flying boots nailed to the ceiling in the Officer's Mess – a traditional reminder of the people who had safely ejected from a problem aircraft. Back in the crew room, Rosie fell into conversation with one of the pilots whose nickname was 'Spock' after an incident with a Vulcan. Logical, (Group) Captain.

Ahead of the closure, I interviewed the last station commander at Binbrook, Group Captain John Spencer. He was a Lightning man through and through, having joined the RAF in 1958 just before the interceptor entered service. He had flown them for years and had led a squadron before commanding the last ever RAF Lightning base. He had a personalised aircraft with 'JS' on the fin. Lighting a cigarette in his office in the Station Headquarters, he mused that in certain circumstances, the now obsolete Lightning could still out-manoeuvre modern American jets like the F15 and, at high altitude, go faster than the Tornado F3 which was replacing it.

However its avionics and hopeless endurance rendered it out of date. It was born of an age when it was required to climb high and fast to shoot down Soviet nuclear bombers heading to the United Kingdom to attack cities and V-bomber bases. John Spencer conceded there would be regret at the end of the Lightning but it would be more from the heart than the head. Years later, I realised that it was at that point I should have put in a request for a media facility trip in a T-Bird – the two seat training version. Why on earth did I not do that with the top man?

At 'The Last, Last Lightning show' – the final air display at Binbrook in August 1987 – John Spencer flew 'JS' in the middle of a Diamond Nine formation led by the boss of 11 Squadron. He left the RAF as an Air Commodore and died in 2014.

An early Lightning F1A in the markings of 226 Operational Conversion Unit at Coltishall, seen at the Finningley air show 1966. XM192 has been preserved at Tattershall Thorpe in Lincolnshire (Photo: MC's dad)

Eleven Lightnings were launched at the show, two as spares for the Diamond Nine. The weather was awful with driving rain but the Lightning reminded everyone that it was an 'all weather' fighter. The formation did a stream take-off from the northerly end of the runway, banking sharply right at the other end and turning almost a full circle to fly straight towards the crowd back over the runway while the stream was still taking off.

Kicking in full reheat, each pilot pulled back on the stick to push the Lightning into a steep climb over the hangars. The condensation shockwaves shimmered around the wings as each one thundered away into the 'clag' – an aviation term for grey, drizzly low cloud that started life as meaning 'Cloud Low Aircraft Grounded'.

The Diamond Nine returned for a few fly-pasts and a solo

Lightning gave a spirited 'flat display', keeping the aircraft below the cloud base. The following spring and summer, the Lightnings left Binbrook for good. Some went to museums but too many ended up near that south west Crash Gate awaiting the scrap merchant's cutting equipment. The domestic site became a new large village, given the name Brookenby, and the buildings behind the hangars formed a new trading estate.

Revisiting Binbrook airfield on a damp, foggy November morning in 2015, I took in both ends of the old runway. It was silent except for a far away tractor in a field across the valley. The taxi-way had been narrowed by the creep of vegetation and indeed much had been dug up or had just disappeared. A memorial to a young lad who died young and who 'loved Lightnings' had been established near the north-east end of the old runway and surrounded by a wooden fence. There was now no trace of this tribute to a life cut short.

You can drive along the old flight-line and see the fading flash of 5 Squadron on a hangar wall. There is a shell of a Sea Harrier and the shape of a Lightning awaiting renovation. The old guardroom where I had an altercation with a overbearing Warrant Officer who insisted I parked the other way round as I checked in seemed to be falling into ruin. The fog that wreathed around the Wolds that morning enveloped Binbrook and amplified the sad sensations of times past and the lingering ghosts of men and machines.

After the Lightnings had gone, World War Two bombers briefly returned to Binbrook in July 1989 and took it back in time. The film *Memphis Belle*, starring Matthew Modine, Eric Stoltz and Harry Connick Junior, was partly shot on the airfield and five real B-17 Flying Fortresses were rounded up from the USA, France and the UK and flown in. The movie, about the 25th and final mission of a B-17 and its American crew in 1943, was co-produced by David Puttnam who stayed in a Lincoln hotel and was amenable to interviews with Radio Lincolnshire. During filming at Binbrook, one of the B-17s crashed on takeoff but the ten people on board all escaped without serious injury.

—ɯ—

When the Lightning came into service at Coltishall in Norfolk in 1960, it became the 'poster plane' for RAF recruiting. I collected the glossy brochures with names like 'Flying and You' and 'Aircrew – a flying career in the Royal Air Force'. They featured Lightnings from squadrons like 74 (The Tigers) and 56 (The Firebirds) with fresh-faced young pilots clutching their helmets and gazing away from the camera to the skies beyond. One advertisement read: 'What are they like to fly today?' and ran a report by a journalist as he joined what was then called The Ten Ton Club which presented you with a special tie if you had flown at more than 1000 miles an hour.

The writer had joined Flt Lt Malcolm Moore in a two seat Lightning for a sortie from Wattisham in Suffolk. *'Beneath us Wattisham falls away. The enormous power of the two Rolls Royce Avon jet engines hurl us above the clouds. ....I scan the sky and realise the intensity of its colour at such a height. Overhead, the deepest azure through the canopy; in the mid-distance, Air Force blue.'* Ok, I'm convinced. The RAF adverts urged me to become an 'aerocrat' and to send off my application form to Adastral House in London WC1 which dealt with RAF recruitment. There was nothing *there* about being good at physics.

Those brochures enthused about the new aircraft heading for RAF service. There was the HS801 which morphed into the Nimrod, the Andover, the VC10, Dominie, Belfast, Basset, Hercules, the Phantom and the Kestrel jump-jet, later called the Harrier. The V-bombers would be joined by the TSR2. RAF officers were pictured perpetually smiling off-duty in Cyprus, Singapore (which had three RAF airfields), Gibraltar, Brunei, Sarawak, Germany and Labuan.

Allan Smethurst wrote a song about the noise that Lightnings made and called it 'Sound Barrier'. Smethurst was known as The Singing Postman and had one big hit in 1966 with a song called 'Hev Yew gotta loight, Boy?' He appeared on one episode of *Top of the Pops* along with The Rolling Stones. He was a real postman who wrote songs about living in East Anglia. The studio that he used for recording was under the flight path in and out of RAF Wattisham where two squadrons of Lightnings were based at the time. Every time one went over, he had to stop the recording and start again which prompted the song.

There was a photograph of him next to an old red and blue road sign pointing to RAF Wattisham. After his big 'Loight' hit, things fell apart. He had a mild heart attack, developed arthritis which affected his guitar playing and four years later was unemployed and broke. He spent the last 20 years of his life in a Salvation Army hostel in Grimsby, a few miles north east of Binbrook.

In the early 1990s, British astronaut Michael Foale flew on three Space Shuttle missions. Radio Lincolnshire sort of adopted him as we could precede every story about him with the phrase 'Lincolnshire-born'. His father Colin, who retired as an RAF Air Commodore, was a fighter pilot serving at Binbrook when Michael was born in 1957. There is now a road named after the astronaut in Louth – Michael Foale Lane.

Uncertainty about the future of RAF Binbrook had bubbled along for a few years after it was confirmed that the Tornado F3 would replace the Lightning (and Phantoms) as the RAF's air defence interceptor. The new Tornados were going to Coningsby, also in Lincolnshire, Leeming in North Yorkshire and Leuchars in Fife. Bases were closing all the time as the RAF got smaller – and there were fears that Binbrook would become superfluous.

Sometime in 1985, the Secretary of State for Defence Michael Heseltine was invited to a Conservative constituency event in Louth. I discussed the visit with the BBC Radio Lincolnshire reporter for East Lindsey which included Louth and Binbrook and worked out some questions that were relevant to the district and to Lincolnshire. One of these was obviously the future of Binbrook and the implications for jobs and the local economy if it closed. The BBC representative duly asked the Defence Secretary and was met with a quizzical 'What's **a** Binbrook?'

'Er, it is still one of your frontline air defence bases, Secretary of State!' The Defence Secretary had not been briefed very well at all. 'I don't know about that. Can't talk about that.'

Michael Heseltine was an occasional visitor to Radio Oxford over the years. He was MP for Henley-on-Thames and lived in a village near Banbury. He would drop into the Radio Oxford studios on his way to London to do an interview 'down the line' with the *Today* programme and indeed with us – his local station.

One morning when I was the early newsreader, he came in for a *Today* interview. I got him a coffee and the newspapers and left him in Reception, saying I would come and get him at the appointed time and hook him up to Radio 4 in London. When I returned to Reception, he said: 'Oh by the way, I have signed for your post.' Thanks very much.

The following morning, Postman Pete reappeared with our delivery requiring another signature. I asked him who had signed for it the day before. 'I dunno – there was some blond geezer that let me in.' That, my friend, was the Secretary of State for the Environment of Her Majesty's Government of the United Kingdom. 'Whatever. Sign 'ere.'

Chapter 6

Life Short Call Now

Another call from Bob Whitaker, another air crash and another nerve-wracking ride in his car – this time an old Jaguar. New York, Scrub Hill and Dogdyke flashed by as we headed towards the village of Coningsby, famous for its one handed clock and its RAF base. Coningsby had been full of Vulcans before closing for refurbishment to prepare to handle the next generation of expensive hardware – the all-British tactical strike reconnaissance aircraft which never lasted long enough to be known as anything other than the TSR2. Harold Wilson's new Labour government scrapped the project in 1965 because of rising costs and inter-service disputes over where to spend the available budget. Ten years later, Coningsby was home to the American-built Phantom which had been bought partly to fill the gap left by the cancellation.

There was a tale about a family who wanted to take legal action to restrict or even close down RAF Coningsby because of the noise. When they moved in to their new house a few miles south of the base, they were upset by the noise of the Coningsby Phantoms in the southern circuit. It was pointed out that the air base had been there a long time and that even a cursory look at an Ordnance Survey map would show that their new dwelling was not far away. It transpired that, during the whole of the buying process, the family had come up to Lincolnshire from London only at weekends. Therefore they had no idea of the Rolls Royce roar that could be unleashed overhead from Monday to Friday.

Just before 3pm on the 3rd March 1975, a Phantom FGR2 of Treble One (111 Squadron) was returning to Coningsby after being fogbound elsewhere over the weekend. As it climbed away from Runway 25 after an overshoot, there was a big bang followed by flames shooting out of one of the engines. Both the crew ejected safely at 400 feet with the pilot trying to point the aircraft straight down into a field. However the jet had other ideas and banked to the right and headed north and downwards at about 180 miles an hour.

When Bob and I got to the scene of the crash at Tattershall Bridge about a mile west of the end of Coningsby's runway, there was nothing to see. Where was the crashed aircraft with its wreckage smouldering in a field? There were a few policeman and fire officers walking along the bank of the River Witham. Our first question was answered by a policeman pointing at a house down the track beside the river. 'If you look at it carefully, you will see something's missing,' he said.

What was missing was a corner of the house. Part of the roof and some of the surrounding wall had gone. Incredibly it was the only sign that a supersonic military jet had crashed. There had surely been another 'miracle' to reflect in a newspaper headline.

The pilotless Phantom had sliced the corner off this house and gone straight into the River Witham. It sank out of sight with the water immediately extinguishing any explosion on impact, leaving a few bits of hot metal to set off a couple of small grass fires. Before ripping off the roof, it had shaved the tops of some trees and narrowly avoided another house where a mother and her two young children were watching television.

Mrs Marion Warrener, then 56, was cleaning her fireplace downstairs when she heard a jet noise getting louder and louder. Living so close to Coningsby, she was used to the sound of jets. The dog barked and she rushed to a window. There was a big bang and she ran upstairs to look out the bedroom window. 'There was dust everywhere which I thought was smoke at first. I went into the toilet where it was coming from and there was a huge hole in the roof and half the wall had gone.'

Her husband Jack had been working in the farm yard nearby and his view of his house was obstructed by a barn. 'I heard a bang then there was a hell of a noise. This thing screamed over and disappeared behind the barn. I didn't realise it had hit the house until my wife shouted 'Look at our home, Jack' and pointed at the roof.' Bob and I were still with them when their 15 year old daughter arrived, having been pulled out of class at a nearby school.

The fragility of life in newspaper headlines. Tragedy and miracle
March 1975

The Warreners and the family in the adjoining house were extremely lucky. We were with them so soon after the crash that the full shock had not set in. They were happy to be photographed and talk to us, reflecting shakily on how lucky they had been. No one had died or been injured but we felt we were nevertheless intruding and wished them well. Relatives and friends were arriving to support them.

The following day I was back in the same area after two pensioners from the nearby town of Horncastle were killed when the coach in which they were travelling hit a stationary lorry on the A1 near Stamford. The luck bestowed on the Warreners was not there for the passengers of that coach, on their way to help with the catering at Huntingdon races. Apart from the two fatalities, 25 were injured, some of them seriously. The lorry had suffered a tyre blow-out and was parked on the verge. The driver had gone to find a phone to ring for help (That's right, there were no mobiles in 1975.....)

A stationary lorry parked on the verge of the A1 and two people die and 25 are injured. A pilotless out-of-control Phantom jet streaking out of the sky heading for a random rendezvous with earth and no one is even scratched. I had my name on both stories on the same front page that week. They were two illustrations of the fragility of life for a young news reporter to reflect on. Life Short, Call Now.

Back to the RAT. This is the Ram Air Turbine emergency generator that pops out the fuselage if the aircraft loses engine power. This frenetic little windmill rotates round at high speed to drive all the bits dependent on the engine such as the hydraulics and the electrics. It was a routine test of the RAT that sparked the electrical fire in the Vulcan that crashed near Spilsby.

One morning at BBC Radio Lincolnshire I took a call from the Community Relations Officer at RAF Binbrook.

'We wonder if you could help us find a rat that we have unfortunately lost somewhere,' he said. An image of rats replacing air dog Alsations as cheap security flashed for a moment before he explained all things RAT. Somehow the RAT on a RAF Phantom had fallen off that morning somewhere in Lincolnshire.

The Phantom was based at Coningsby and when it returned to base, the ground crew found that the RAT had gone awol. It had spent most of the training flight doing some general handling in the Binbrook area where it had run through some emergency procedures that included deploying the RAT. Consequently this little lump of metal had probably plummeted down somewhere over the Wolds and the RAF wondered if we could put out a public appeal to find it.

It made a short news item, giving a brief description of the missing metal and asking anyone who found it to ring the police or the RAF. It was never found and is no doubt still buried deep in the fine and fertile Lincolnshire soil. It would have been travelling at a fair rate having fallen off several thousand feet up. The RAF was lucky that it did not make another story. If it had hit a cow or a horse or a human being, it would have killed outright. If it had just gone through someone's roof, it would have made a hell of a mess. Luck meant it made a paragraph in the local paper rather than a national tabloid front page 'splash' about a bizarre fatality.

The wartime generation of course was used to metal raining out of the sky. Interviewing people who were children in the south-east during the Battle of Britain, they all spoke to me of dodging the bullets and shrapnel that fell to earth from the dogfights above them. Bullets that missed their target had to land somewhere. Bits that were shot off aircraft – and shot down aircraft – all came raining down on the people below.

—ᙡ—

It was an evening of apocalyptic proportions. The sky rained fire. The darkness of the stormy skies was turned into daylight. People who had retired for the night found their bedrooms full of light. People who had drawn their curtains got up to investigate why there was a huge brightness outside. People tentatively opened their front doors to see what was going on and nipped quickly back inside as metallic hailstones rained down onto their lawn and roof. The electric storms had engulfed a catastrophic collision in the skies above.

Where to begin? A Canberra was coming off the range at Wainfleet after several low altitude bombing runs. The crew had come across the North Sea from the RAF base at Bruggen in West Germany. They had completed the exercise and were heading away from Wainfleet on a south easterly route over Norfolk before routing back to Bruggen.

The weather was dreadful. The summer evening of 19th August 1968 ended with what was described by some as violent electric storms. Across The Wash from Wainfleet, a Victor air refuelling tanker (similar in size to a Vulcan) lifted off from RAF Marham south of Kings Lynn and headed towards the North Sea on a tanker training exercise. The weather was so bad that the limited 1960s technology of the various radar stations covering East Anglia could not make out the radar returns of the two aircraft. The controllers could not help the two crews.

It was a terrible chance in a million. They had no idea they were in the same airspace. The Canberra and the Victor collided at around 13,000 feet and exploded into the storms. The tragedy happened in the skies above the small town of Holt, a few miles south of Blakeney on the north Norfolk coast. The aftermath of the impact was seen and heard above the cacophony of the thunder for miles around. The glow in the sky as the two blazing aircraft fell to earth could be seen back at Marham – some 30 miles away.

I was 14 when this accident happened and living on the North Yorkshire coast. I read about it in the newspaper that came through the letterbox every morning. There must have been something on the black and white news on BBC1 – the channel would not broadcast in colour until the following year. I had no connection with any of the seven airmen who died and I did not know the area. However, like the Vulcan crash at Coningsby four years earlier, it pulled up this teenager and made him reflect on lives lost. I picked up my *Airfix* kits of a Victor and a Canberra and tried to conjure in my mind what it was like to fly real ones with the ever present danger of dying in one. Years later, I realized that Colin Curtis may well have flown eastwards over Holt a few hours before his death only 26 years earlier. In 1992 I flew over the same area in a Red Arrows Hawk before my pilot banked right over Cromer for a practice approach into RAF Coltishall.

Astonishingly, no one on the ground was hurt as fire and rain thundered down over Kelling Heath and the wider area. It is nearly 50 years since Holt was delivered from a place in the list of national tragedies. Early in 2017 I lit a candle in the parish church of St Andrew the Apostle in Holt in memory of the seven aircrew who lost their lives that night. There is a memorial within the church with the names of the three in the Canberra and the four in the Victor. The inscription reads: 'Indeed you did not grow old. We will remember'.

The last day of the life of Pilot Officer Colin Curtis was 20th January 1942. Exactly 35 years later, on Thursday 20th January 1977, I had been alive nearly two months longer than him. Three days earlier that Vulcan had crashed near Spilsby, missing the school by a few hundred yards. . The entry in my diary for the 20th January read 'RP News' and 'Car to Holland

Brothers' (the local Austin-Rover dealers – I had a very brief and regrettable liaison with the deeply unfashionable Allegro off the back of my insurance nightmare Mini Cooper S).

'RP News' reminded me that I had my weekly appointment to go to the Pilgrim Hospital on the north side of Boston and read the local news on Radio Pilgrim, the hospital radio station. Once the *Lincolnshire Standard* was published for that week, my bosses were happy for me to turn some of the stories into snappy paragraphs for broadcast. Apart from being very satisfying, it also gave me my first experiences behind a 'live' microphone and thus a good launch pad for my career in BBC radio.

The listeners may have been comatose, hallucinating, drowsy on drugs, fast asleep or just too weak to reach the 'off' switch but I attempted to entertain them for a couple of hours on a Sunday evening as well. For a programme imaginatively called 'Rock-bed', I took in music and comedy records from my own collection and regaled my bed-ridden audience with familiar and unusual offerings in my best 'Bob Harris' voice straight off *The Old Grey Whistle Test*.

One clear-headed patient wrote to me about one particular piece of music that he wanted to hear again, preferably having bought it himself rather than wait another week in a hospital bed. For the record so to speak, it was 'Guajira' off Santana's third album. Despite being banned by the BBC, Donna Summer's 1975 hit 'Love to Love You, Baby', with all its groaning and moaning, got an airing on my programme. In retrospect, it was probably a rather indelicate choice to tickle the ears of someone recovering from a heart attack.

You had to be careful about what you played on hospital radio. Were bits of Tony Hancock's *The Blood Donor* episode appropriate? Did patients want to hear anything by The Grateful Dead? Bob Dylan's 'Knockin' on Heaven's Door' was off-limits. Fred Astaire's 'Cheek to Cheek', which starts with the line 'Heaven, I'm in Heaven', might alarm someone coming round from the anaesthetic.

Radio Pilgrim was set up by two local electricians Melvyn Kennedy and Mike Carson who both had their own shows under the names of Killerwatts and The Weird Beard. One had a beard. Fund raising included a darts marathon and the obligatory sponsored walks. One of these was a 20 mile stroll along the coast path from Wainfleet to Boston, with most of my friends and colleagues offering one pence a mile thus handing over the princely sum of 20 pence each.

Over 250 people turned up for a fundraising 'Celebrity Sportsnight' to hear and meet eight well-known sportsmen of the time. They included Commonwealth and European shot putter and policeman Geoff Capes, a renowned budgerigar breeder who lived near Spalding, welterweight boxing champion Dave 'Boy' Green and light welterweight Des Morrison, boxing manager Andy Smith, Wimbledon's top referee Fred Hoyles who at the time was overseeing the likes of Borg and McEnroe, Nottinghamshire cricket coach Frank Woodhead, world champion stock car racer Jim Welch and local motor cycling star Derek Chatterton. It was a huge achievement for the bunch of RP volunteers and made a good photo-spread for the paper.

I used to go to the hospital for other reasons, not least parties at the nurses' residency (as they called it). There were also inquests where the pathologist would give the police and the press the most harrowing and gruesome explanations of his post-mortems before the families and the public arrived. The descriptions would never have made the scripts of *Midsomer Murders*.

Death came to school one year when I was about 15. A

friend my age and another 'Son of the Cloth' did not return for the autumn term. The head teacher told the school assembly that he had died falling off a cliff on a family holiday. He was there in the summer term, playing his beloved Tamla Motown records when he could get on the communal record player and oust the Beatles, The Stones and Jimi Hendrix. He was dead in the autumn. He was the only fan of Motown in our group and, graciously batting away the teasing, actually introduced people like me to the musical magnificence of soul stars like Otis Redding, Aretha Franklin, Smokey Robinson and Marvin Gaye.

The first dead body I saw was a seaman who had returned to his ship in Boston docks after a night on the town. He missed his footing and went head first into the water. No one knew so he was not reported as missing until the following morning when Bob Whitaker and I were sent to the docks to get the story. While we were there, they dragged out the unfortunate man and his body lay on the quayside in a pool of murky sea water until the appropriate vehicle arrived to take him away. He was about the same age as me.

Our newspaper had a female darts team which played in a league in and around Boston. One night they were due to play the team from a pub near Boston docks. Next morning I asked one of the girls how they had got on. The match never went ahead as the pub suddenly could not raise a team. A Dutch ship docked early in the evening and pitched out a load of saucy seaman brandishing wads of cash. 'No darts for tarts,' she said grimly.

Chapter 7

A Stickler for Exactitude

My first ever assignment on my debut morning at the *Lincolnshire Standard* newspaper was to contact an Air Training Corps cadet who had won a scholarship. I had to ring him up from one of the two phones in the newsroom that were on a side desk. There were no phones on any of the individual reporter desks apart from the one belonging to the Editor. My fingers were trembling as I dialled the number. There was a clicking sound and then the 'number unobtainable' signal. Please God I only want to ring a 15 year old ATC cadet and ask how long he has been in the bleedin' Corps and what he wants to do with his life. Oh and his age, address and can we take a picture of him? The phone refused to work. I dialled again and it was answered almost immediately.

It sounded like 'Low Subs'. And when I enquired if Cadet Thistlewaite was there, there was a distinct 'Never 'eard of him.' The tension was rising. The smell of the stubbed out cigarettes piled up in the ash tray between the two reporter phones made me feel nauseous.

The man on the phone was not being helpful. In fact he was being deliberately awkward and standing in the way of the Freedom of the Press. The public had a right to know about the achievements of this young cadet. It was time to assert myself. 'My name is Curtis. I'm from the *Lincolnshire Standard* newspaper. I have been given this number to contact Master Thistlewaite.'

The man on the other end of this tortuous conversation then asked me if I was new. It can't be that obvious, surely? So I said I had been around for a bit. *'Aye, but not long enough to know that you have to dial 9 to get an outside line. You've got extension 28 – the Subs.'* He muttered the words 'daft bugger' as he replaced the receiver.

I finally got through to the bloody cadet. Desperately remembering everything from my print journalism course, I grilled him on who, what, when, where and why and strung a few paragraphs together. The Chief Reporter Allan Eves, who had a column cheekily called 'Eves Droppings', tidied up a couple of things with his red biro and I was ready for the next hurdle – delivering the copy to the sub-editors.

This bunch held court in a dark and daunting room across the corridor. It was full of bearded men who did not seem to smile very much. Some of them had done their time on the nationals. It was they who could summon you – by phone or in person – to come and retrieve your miserable copy and re-write it. Sometimes you did not get as far as the door before hearing 'What's this intro?' It was they who could turn your epic into one single paragraph filler. They were also encouraging, particularly in their natural habitat – the pub. They had the power of headlines and even more important – the power to bless a reporter with his or her name at the top of the story. A by-line.

Once they had finished with your story, they stuck it in a plastic container and put it in a pneumatic system which fired it off down a tube to the compositors elsewhere in the building. This was a big leap in technology from shouting for the 'copy boy' to collect the story and take it in person. The tube shot off like a ferret up a trouser leg. The whoosh was one of those familiar sounds from the old newspaper newsrooms like the clatter of typewriters and the anguished cries of some forlorn hack desperately trying to decipher his or her scribbled Teeline or Pitman shorthand note from the previous night's council meeting.

In the corner of the subs room was the man who marshalled the village correspondents. These pillars of the community nosed around their villages and sent in sheets of snippets about mainly trivial topics that nevertheless concerned the congregations of the churches and the drinkers in the snugs of the pubs. There were sometimes volatile boundary disputes among them with simmering resentment about the nominated representative for Fosdyke submitting the local Women's Institute report when it should have come from him, the proud newsman for Algarkirk.

At the time, the Yorkshire TV soap *Emmerdale Farm* (the 'Farm' was dropped from the title in 1989) had a character called Amos Brearly who was not only the joint landlord of The Woolpack pub but also the village correspondent. He diligently covered Beckindale for the local newspaper, the *Hotton Courier*, and met his weekly deadline. Every week when the paper arrived he would go straight to his Beckindale news and see how it had been edited. 'They know nothing, those sub-editors,' he would grumble. One of the *Emmerdale Farm* scriptwriters had clearly worked in real local newspapers.

'Vicar's son on picket line' promised a titillating headline in the *Scarborough Evening News* sometime around 1980. This media morsel about industrial disruption fell out of a conversation between my father and the 'Amos Brearly' for Filey. The story read: 'Mike Curtis, son of the Rev Wilf Curtis, Vicar of Filey, was on the picket line in the British Leyland dispute at Cowley this week – as a reporter for the BBC. He was seen in television news bulletins on Monday and Tuesday interviewing strikers.'

The story implied that I was the television reporter but I was there for BBC Radio Oxford. I was indeed caught in some television news shots but the idea that I was 'interviewing' British Leyland workers was stretching it a bit. I never liked going out to do 'vox-pops' with the great British public because these brief snippets ultimately never really added much to a story. It was more difficult in newspapers as you not only had to stop and persuade people to talk to you about some issue of the day but also get their actual name and then produce the photographer, hiding in a shop doorway. You had to then convince them it would be a good idea to have a mug shot to accompany their words of wisdom like 'Something should be done' or 'It's not right, is it?'

Trying to stop BL workers in a foul mood streaming out of Cowley was impossible if not suicidal. After one mass meeting when a new pay offer was put to them, I was left with two minutes on tape of me saying 'What did you make of that, mate?', changing to 'What did you think of that, Sir?' with no other voices to be heard other than the occasional 'no comment' or 'f**k off!'

British Leyland was having a rough time at the end of the 1970s with industrial trouble at both Longbridge in Birmingham and at Cowley. When I first arrived at Radio Oxford, you could not take a foreign-made car onto the Cowley complex in case it inflamed the workers. By the time I left in 1982, BL had done a deal with Honda of Japan and was producing the joint venture known as the Acclaim.

All of us in the Oxford newsroom lost hours of our lives chasing down Cowley union officials to get their views on the latest pay offer, collaboration deal or 're-structuring initiative'. One night I tracked down the leader of the toolmakers to a pub in Garsington where he was playing 'Aunt Sally', a pub game popular in the South Midlands which involves players throwing sticks or battens at a model of an old woman's head. Another union official at Cowley somewhat surprisingly rode with one of the Oxfordshire hunts. Maybe both pastimes were euphemisms for the endless negotiations with the management.

The press officer for BL at Cowley was a crumpled figure who seemed to carry the weight of the world on his shoulders. You would ring him up and cheerily say 'Hello, it's Mike Curtis at Radio Ox……' and before you could finish your introduction, he would wail: 'What have they said about us now?'

The staff handbook for the *Lincolnshire Standard* newspaper in 1973 was required reading for a new reporter. At the front was a quote from Lord Beaverbook which told journalists to 'Use your feet and meet the people.' The handbook emphasised that 'His Late Lordship's advice is sound. A reporter doing his calls on foot or bicycle meets the people, builds up better contacts, sees life at first hand. A reporter sitting at a telephone sees only the pin-up on the opposite wall.' How quaint, from a time when girlie calendars and Page 3 pictures were routinely pinned or taped to office walls.

If you hit a wrong key on your Underwood typewriter, you should cross out the whole word and type it again. How often would a typewriter ribbon run out as you were frantically typing a story against a deadline? All names should be in capitals. Use short words and short sentences. Add 'mf' for 'more follows' when your story goes onto another sheet and always add 'ends' at the end. Never assume the reader saw last week's paper – recap the details. Do not 'blow up' a story for the sake of finding a lead. 'We live among our readers.

They can smell a phoney story before the ink is dry on the paper.'

There was a Thought for the Day. 'A man seldom dies following an accident. He dies after one.' We were discouraged from writing that fire appliances 'rushed' to the blazing house or that detectives had 'swooped' onto a night club.

'Remember that people are more interesting than things. Words are our stock-in-trade. Choose them carefully as you would a wife, a girlfriend or a motor car.' No mention there of husbands or boyfriends even though the *Standard* newsroom was about 50/50 between males and females. One of my female colleagues at the time was Mary Riddell who went on to have a successful career in national papers and became a well–known columnist.

It was *de rigueur* to enjoy 'liquid lunches' in newsrooms when I started. I was taken to the pub on my second day at the newspaper and, after one pint of fine Bateman's Lincolnshire bitter, rose to my feet with the not unreasonable line that I better be getting back. No one moved and my exit route was blocked. 'We've come out for a drink. You don't go after just one.' One more whiff of the barmaid's apron, as they used to say.

At Radio Oxford, The Dewdrop pub next door was called Studio 4 by staff and was the second home for many of the station's journalists. A couple of doors further up the Banbury Road, Raymond Blanc was building up his first award-winning restaurant and Oxfam had its headquarters. On one occasion, the brewery Courage laid on a promotional stunt at The Dewdrop offering pints of Director's bitter to lunchtime drinkers. Two pints in, it was a fine idea at the time but became a brilliant mistake, to paraphrase Elvis Costello. After a rush back to the radio station to read the 2pm bulletin, the script looked remarkably similar to the 1pm news except a little blurred and slurred at the edges. A lesson learnt.

Over the years, those pub lunches fell out of fashion as the culture changed and people remained at their desks with a lettuce leaf and a bottle of sparkling mineral water. Healthier but joyless – and stories lost and gossip gone. The Christmas bonus at the *Lincolnshire Standard Group* in my first year was two bottles of Johnny Walker whisky for each member of staff.

—⁂—

Most Wednesdays and Fridays, this young newspaper reporter would find himself at the local magistrates court as the regulars of the police parade shuffled forward. Two youths appeared one day on charges of assaulting a police officer. Their occupations were given as potato picker and cabbage cutter. Some might think that a suit and tie would help their case but, to the dismay of the legal aid solicitor defending them, the two stood in the dock wearing tee-shirts with the slogan 'Pigs are Beautiful'. To ensure there was no misunderstanding, the three words were accompanied by a charming portrait of a portly porker in police uniform. The young swains – or 'swines' as the prosecuting inspector muttered to the press bench – departed with a thirty pound fine each.

A motorist appeared on a charge of driving a vehicle in a dangerous condition in that the front right wing flapped in and out. You could see the fine double as he revealed his occupation – an automotive welding instructor.

The debates in the local council chamber dragged on as the elected representatives pontificated about the issues of the day and the area. An elderly councillor stood up at one meeting and said: 'Now what about this 'ere doings then?' and sat down again. No one had the slightest idea what he was on about and the debate moved on. One of my fellow travellers anguished over whether to fully report all direct quotes in a discussion about the lack of street lighting. 'Mr

Chairman, I've had these young women. They don't know who's around until they're on top of them,' exclaimed one ancient committee member, adding for good measure: 'They dare not use their back passages at night.'

—ɱ—

'Maxwell has agreed to talk to us,' said Roger Clark, duty producer on my first proper shift as a radio reporter, six days into my BBC career. Roger was a big man with a horseshoe moustache, heavy rimmed spectacles and a rumoured toupee. To the new reporter, he was a daunting but kindly man with a background in local newspapers and a passion for following horse-racing. When Roger was duty producer, a copy of Timeform was inevitably on the production desk alongside news releases and council reports.

The first bulletin of that Sunday morning had informed everyone that Robert Maxwell, the boss of Pergamon Press and the former Labour MP for Buckingham, had failed in his bid to be nominated to fight the seat again the following year. He agreed to talk about his failure to Radio Oxford and the new reporter was trusted with putting the questions face to face. Quite a baptism.

I parked my old blue Ford Escort between two Rolls Royce motors on the forecourt of Headington Hall on the north east side of Oxford and rang the door bell. I was ushered into the man's study and prayed that my tape recorder would work properly and, only a few days after being taught how to use it, that *I* would work properly. Maxwell had a reputation for being difficult and indeed litigious and I wondered what sort of mood he would be in after his failure to be nominated. He treated me with courtesy, answered all my questions and bade me good day. He had an extraordinary career, being awarded the Military Cross at the end of the Second World War, but will be remembered as the man who siphoned off money from his own companies' pension funds, notably the *Daily Mirror*, before drowning after falling off his yacht.

The Pergamon Press headquarters was already a 'no smoking' building in those days. One morning, so the story goes, Maxwell was striding down a corridor when he came upon a young man puffing away on a cigarette. 'Come with me,' he bellowed and headed for the Wages Office. 'How much do you earn a week?' The man duly replied that it was about £50. 'You do not flout my No Smoking rules. Take a week's wages and get out – you are fired!' Two weeks later it emerged that the man did not work for Pergamon Press at all. He was a delivery driver waiting to pick up a package whose quick drag on a fag earned him a swift fifty quid.

One of the Radio Oxford staff at the time was Timmy Mallett who later went on to become a very well-known children's entertainer, artist and one-hit wonder man with 'Itsy Bitsy Teeny Weeny Yellow Polka Dot Bikini' (1990). Being shown round the radio station on my first morning, we entered a studio to find Timmy, then a junior station assistant and a fellow 'Son of the Cloth', with his feet on the desk and wearing jeans. For some reason, I had not expected employees of the BBC to be wearing denim as we were not allowed to wear such casual attire at the newspaper.

As a Station Assistant, one of Mr Mallett's duties early each morning was to read out the livestock prices from the various markets around Oxfordshire. He livened this up by adding a wide range of sound effects underneath him as he intoned the prices of heifers, steers, hoggets, porkers and ewes. This was the equivalent of spicing up the Shipping Forecast with sounds of gales, seagulls and cries of 'Ahoy there!' Some farmers were apoplectic and rang the manager to get this 'clown' away from their baconers.

'Timmy on the Tranny Through 'til Two' became a somewhat anarchic lunchtime programme, featuring a character called 'Auntie Brickface' played by another newcomer who went on to become a very distinguished reporter and documentary maker for the BBC. You always had to be particularly alert when reading the news in a Timmy Mallett show. In the run-up to one bulletin, he went on and on about a new band called The Bodysnatchers, who were an all-girl band in the British 2 Tone Ska scene. 'That's The Bodysnatchers, kids! Remember the name – The Bodysnatchers. Fantastic – more of The Bodysnatchers later. Here's the news with Mike Curtis.'

My first three stories were all about local bodies. An accident, an inquest and a court case were deemed to be the three top stories for Radio Oxford that lunchtime. The bulletin started with a pause and a rustling of paper as I desperately delved down into my pile of stories for something to give me a bridge away from The Bodysnatchers. 'There's been renewed shelling in Beirut this morning.' On another occasion, Timmy was setting up material in an adjoining studio and inadvertently opened up a fader and put to air what he was playing. In the middle of my solemn news bulletin, I was suddenly drowned out by a Kenny Everett character. 'Hello kids, Sid Snot here!'

You were not totally sure if what you were hearing in your headphones was what the listener was getting so you carried on. Other challenges while reading the news included a freelance who, while sitting across from you in the studio to read a live report or the sport, would get out his lighter and set fire to your script. You heard yourself speeding up as the flames licked through the paper which was then dropped into the metal waste bin at your feet. During my very last news read at Oxford, two people came in to the studio and started to remove their clothing. Should I speed up for him or slow down for her?

One morning the early news reader arrived about 5am and, as he opened a door and switched on the light, he tripped over something. It was the late news producer slumped across the floor and fast asleep. It seems he had spent longer in The Dewdrop pub next door than anticipated and got no further than the radio station on his journey home. He went into the newsroom and rang his wife. 'Sorry dear. Slight delay. Could you run me a bath?'

A short time after getting home, he got a call from the early news reader, asking where he had actually put the news bulletin that he had been compiling the night before. 'Ah… let me think. Try the waste bin near the Editor's desk.' That information would be more helpful on other mornings when the early producer would be faced with a paper chase around the radio station to find the morning bulletin. The same late news prankster would leave clues on the receptionist's chair, on top of the admin cupboard or in the fridge.

—m—

A reporter went for a newsroom job at BBC Radio Cumbria. He was asked by the news editor what he knew about Vicars. He replied that priests were often very good contacts with their finger on the pulse of their community and Anna Ford's father became a vicar in the Lake District and so on. They let him go on for a couple of minutes before interrupting. 'We actually meant *Vickers*, the shipbuilders at Barrow-in-Furness and Cumbria's biggest employer.'

I had a couple of BBC interviews at 5 Portland Place on the other side of Regent Street to Broadcasting House. Like a doctor's surgery, people sat nervously waiting to be called to face the panel somewhere on the floors above. Apocryphal and possibly true stories were told of people with the same name being called to the wrong room, with an applicant for a producer job on Radio 4's *Today* programme being asked about their cleaning credentials. Other stories had candidates storming out of an interview and getting the wrong door, lurching into a cupboard instead and then rather sheepishly reversing out and fumbling for the correct handle.

Further south across Regent Street was Grafton House, then home of the Local Radio Headquarters and its Training Unit and now a luxury hotel. At the end of the working day, wave upon wave of BBC staff descended on its basement to one of the liveliest BBC bars where experienced correspondents mixed with local radio newcomers. It was the place to be for local radio gossip as the cheap alcohol loosened tongues and discretion flew out the door. It was said that my promotion to News Editor at Radio Lincolnshire from producer at Radio Cornwall was common knowledge in the Grafton bar the night before anyone told me. A Personnel Officer had let it slip but there were no mobile phones or social media to spread the word, especially to me.

A handful of my Radio Oxford packages (radio reports of about four minutes in length) were accepted for broadcast by the *Today* programme and I went and shadowed a full shift with the team to see what it was like. This involved securing a BBC bed in Grafton House which was cheaper and more convenient than a hotel. I turned up for the mid-evening briefing with the editor and the two presenters John Timpson and Brian Redhead. Later they went to get their heads down and I was led over to the Grafton bar by a senior editor who fancied a snifter or three. He went back to work and I found my room in Grafton House and crashed out for a few hours, by this time oblivious to the stories of the Grafton ghost and the snoring next door of Radio 4's early continuity announcer.

—〰—

One of my first school reports said that I was 'a stickler for exactitude'. It was the most perceptive line about me from the many agonising academic summaries over the years and served me well in my subsequent journalistic career. The final statement from Leatherhead said: 'His approach is not suited to the rigours of an academic education' which was also brutally correct. University was not for me and I went off into local newspapers instead after a print journalism course at Darlington Technical College. My last Headmaster, whom I do not recall actually meeting in a year at Bridlington Grammar School, said I had developed well. 'He has been rather retiring but his influence has been valuable. I hope he will enjoy a happy career'.

I joined the Darlington course late and did not excel. I could not crack a sustained 100 words a minute in the Teeline shorthand test and even flunked the Use of English exam. However the instructors conceded that I could write and could unpick the top angle out of a jumble of possible leads in a pile of council papers or a smoke screen press release. I was curious, inquisitive, and was told that I generally achieved fairness and balance in my reporting. I applied for a job on the evening paper in York and got my first rejection letter without even an interview.

Sir Harold Evans, one of the great campaigning journalists in British newspapers, was the Editor of *The Northern Echo* in Darlington for five years in the 1960s. Evans, who did his national service in the RAF, started his journalistic life in 1944 aged 16 as a reporter on the *Ashton-under-Lyne Weekly Reporter,* earning one pound a week. When he went for the interview, he was given a baffling test, beautifully described in his book *My Paper Chase*. The gruff old editor bundled up a half a dozen bits of paper from his desk and thrust them at Evans, shouting 'Asparagus'.

'Asparagus?' This was still a delicacy largely unknown

in Lancashire and none of the bits of paper referred to this vegetable. There were reports of whist drives, Rotary Club meetings, mourners at a funeral and church news but nothing about 'asparagus'.

Young Harold put some paper in his typewriter and actually typed 'Asparagus' in one corner and stared blankly ahead. One of the journalists looked at him and at the papers strewn on the desk. 'Ah, you're new', he said. 'Just write up those submissions as paragraphs.' Evans was overcome with relief at this timely intervention. Today it would be held up as a fine example of predictive text.

Evans was introduced to the proprietor of the newspaper company as a new boy who cycled into work. 'How many spokes on a bicycle wheel?' boomed the boss. Well, he had no idea (and nor do I). 'Find out! Curiosity is the thing in journalism!'

Chapter 8

Mind over Matter 1941

While Colin Curtis was learning to fly twin-engine aircraft at Medicine Hat in Canada, the war in Europe was intensifying. Although bombs still rained down on English cities, the significant action was in the east of the continent. That August 1941, German forces trapped the Red Army in Smolensk and closed in on Leningrad. Three months later, the Germans reached Moscow.

US President Franklin D Roosevelt and Winston Churchill had meetings on two warships off Newfoundland while Colin was still in Canada. Although America was not yet involved, the talks produced the Atlantic Charter in which the two leaders looked ahead to the world after the Nazis had been defeated.

On 1st January 1942, Churchill was back in the United States for talks in the light of Pearl Harbour. On a train travelling from Ottawa to Washington, he called his staff and newspaper correspondents to the dining car and raised his glass. 'Here's to 1942, here's to a year of toil – a year of struggle and peril, and a long step forward towards victory. May we all come through safe and with honour.'

—∭—

After the two week trip back to the UK from his flying training in Canada, Colin Curtis got back home to south Lincolnshire in mid-September to discover that his father had died on the first of the month. Harold Eaton Curtis had succumbed to senile myocardial degeneration (degeneration of the heart) at the age of 75. He had passed away while Colin was on board the troop ship heading home from Canada. He left his wife just over £2000 in his will.

—ɯ—

After the funeral and some leave, Colin was told to report to No 3 Personnel Reception Centre in Bournemouth. The function of the PRC was to orientate aircrew as they arrived back from overseas training, to organise refresher courses, arrange lectures from experienced aircrew, issue the battle dress and flying kit and to act as an agent for the Air Ministry in arranging postings. Some aircrew were frustratingly left languishing at PRCs for weeks as the war raged around them but it seems Colin was in Bournemouth for only a month.

His commission as a Pilot Officer (on probation) in the RAF Volunteer Reserve had come through. His Service Number as an officer was now 107980. Early in October, he was sent to RAF Chipping Warden, six miles north-east of Banbury where No 12 Operational Training Unit would teach him how to fly the RAF's front line bomber at the time – the Vickers Wellington.

In a letter home, Colin thanked his mother for sending him a new dressing gown and a letter from his bank. He reports that he and Doris have bought a dressing table for Mary's 21st birthday present. 'You can tell Wilf that I am flying Wellingtons now and I may be popping over Boston way soon.'

'I have only been out once since I got here and that was only for three hours last Saturday night. Actually there is very little to do if one *does* go out and the pictures are always crowded on a Saturday night.'

In his book 'Lie in the Dark and Listen', the author Wing Commander Ken Rees told how he was given a break from operations and posted to No 12 OTU as an instructor a year after Colin was there. Rees, who was later shot down and became one of those involved in 'The Great Escape' from Stalag Luft III, spoke of nights out in Banbury and cycle rides along a bridle path to a pub called the White Hart. The resentment of the local lads towards the glamorous RAF 'fly-boys' was tangible and it did not take much to spill over into scuffling and fist fights.

Flying training at Medicine Hat, Canada August 1941. Colin Curtis is at the front, second right

The training started with sessions in the Crew Trainer which was an old Wellington fuselage on a wooden stand in one of the hangars. The fabric had been removed so that all the electrics, fuel pipes and flying controls could be easily seen and explained. In the pilot's seat, Colin learned to locate every control and switch with his eyes shut. Then there were seven or eight hours in the air with an instructor before being cleared to 'go solo'.

During ground training, Colin's pay would have been around two shillings and sixpence a day. During flying training, that would have gone up to five shillings and six pence a day, plus another two bob for flying instructional pay. Once all the training was complete, someone like Colin could expect 11 shillings and six pence a day, plus allowances, as an RAFVR officer. His uniform, food, accommodation, medical and dental treatment were all provided free.

Chipping Warden was one of several airfields in the area which housed Operational Training Units. Barford St John, Bicester, Croughton, Finmere, Hinton-in-the-Hedges, Silverstone, Turweston and Upper Heyford were all busy turning out aircrew to take the war to Germany. The skies were full of Wellingtons, Hampdens, Blenheims and the American-built Douglas Bostons.

Local aviation researcher Garth Barnard has discovered that there were more than 400 aircraft losses within a 15 mile radius of Brackley during the war, many involving a loss of life. It is estimated that Bomber Command lost around 3000 aircrew in training accidents during the war, with the figure for the whole of the RAF nearly 8,000.

Back in Holbeach St Johns, 14 year old Walter Hilliam witnessed many aircraft crashes around the Fens. A few were German but most were British. Nearly all of them were on training flights as the RAF strived to get enough aircrew battle-ready for the fight against the enemy. In October 1941 alone, more than 30 RAF aircraft were reported as having crashed in Lincolnshire. The most common types involved were Airspeed Oxfords, Whitleys and Hampdens.

In the month that Colin arrived at Chipping Warden, No.

12 Operational Training Unit suffered two fatal crashes with its Wellingtons. On 20th October, one crashed into the nearby village at 23.10 while preparing for a night-time landing. The two Pilot Officers on board were killed and the two Sergeants were injured. Four nights later another Wellington, which was turning steeply to line-up with the flare path, hit a hangar and burst into flames. Ten brave ground staff went to the rescue of the seven men on board and got six of them out alive but injured. One man died in the wreckage.

One of the men who died in the crash on the 20th October was a famous England cricketer. Kenneth Farnes played in 15 Test Matches for England between 1934 and 1939 and was Wisden's *Cricketer of the Year* in 1939. The year before he died, he published his autobiography called 'Tours and Tests'. Like Colin, he did most of his flying training in Canada, joined the RAF Volunteer Reserve and was promoted from Sergeant to Pilot Officer when he was commissioned. I wonder if they ever met in the short time they were both at Chipping Warden before that fateful night landing.

New intakes would find themselves on parade in a hangar and, in a process resembling modern speed-dating, told to form themselves into five man crews. The training was relentless and often at night, preparing them for the reality of the long missions in darkness that lay ahead of them. Sometimes they would get experience of 'flak' as nervy British gunners on the ground tried to make out if the engine whine above them was coming from an enemy bomber.

On the 7th December 1941, the Japanese attacked Pearl Harbour. The following day, the United States declared war on Japan and entered the Second World War. Just over a week later, after two months learning to fly the Wellington, Colin Curtis reported to 101 Squadron, flying Wellington bombers out of RAF Oakington in Cambridgeshire. He was finally going to war.

—ᴍ—

101 Squadron was formed on 12th July 1917 at Farnborough as a night fighter unit and moved to France two weeks later. It therefore celebrated its 100th anniversary in 2017. The squadron was disbanded a year after the Great War ended but was reformed in March 1928 as a daylight bomber squadron flying the new Boulton Paul Sidestrand, named after a Norfolk village on the coast by its Norwich-based manufacturers. In 1935 the squadron converted to the Overstrand (yes, another Norfolk coastal village) followed by the Blenheim in 1938. At the start of the Second World War, it was a training unit and did not drop a bomb in anger until July 1940.

The squadron badge, approved by King George VI in February 1938, shows a rampant lion rising from the battlements of a tower. The lion indicates the unit's fighting power and spirit while the battlements symbolise 101's pioneering role in the development of power-operated gun turrets on its aircraft. The squadron motto is 'Mens Agitat Molem', translated as 'Mind over Matter'. More specifically, the purist will tell you it is 'The Mind moves the Matter' (or The Mass) and is attributed to Virgil from his Latin poem *The Aeneid*. Basically the body is guided by our wisdom and intelligence. The same motto is used by the University of Oregon.

The Wellington 1C arrived in April 1941 and the squadron began to take part in Bomber Command raids on Germany two months later. On 6th July, it moved to Oakington a few miles west of Cambridge and was transferred into Bomber Command's No 3 Group. Earlier that year the airfield, which opened on 1st July 1940, was a terrible mess. It was a mass of mud when the snow and ice thawed and a dangerously slippery site when it froze. In January 1941, it was so cold that a rum ration was issued to some approved personnel.

The Short Stirling bomber was based there but crews struggled with the muddy grass runways. Such was the state of the ground that the Stirlings had to fly the short distance to RAF Wyton to be 'bombed up' for a night's mission. Work started on the concrete runways in September 1941 although all three were not completed until the following May.

With a geodesic 'basketweave' fuselage designed by Barnes Wallis, who later came up with the bouncing bomb used in the Dambuster raids, the Wellington carried a pair of .303 Browning machine guns in the hydraulically-powered nose and tail turrets as well as guns mid-way down the fuselage. It was a strong and resilient beast and could limp home despite serious battle damage. However crews felt it was under-powered and lumbered along too much for their own good.

Vickers built more than 11,000 Wellingtons. The workforce could assemble one in 60 hours. With the arrival of the *four* engine heavy bombers like the Lancaster, it was withdrawn as a night bomber and used in other roles by Coastal Command and Transport Command. Some remained in service in secondary roles into the 1950s. The Wellington was one of two bombers named after Arthur Wellesley, the 1st Duke of Wellington and a national hero after the defeat of Napoleon at Waterloo in 1815. The other was the earlier Vickers Wellesley which was virtually obsolete by the start of the war. The Wellington was nicknamed the 'Wimpy' after the J. Wellington Wimpy character in the *Popeye* cartoons.

An Air Ministry publication entitled *Bomber Command* was issued in 1941 which highlighted the work of the aircrews. 'Their life is not that of other men – not that even of those in the other branches of the service. Its very physical conditions are different. For them nowadays much of the night is day, much of the day a time for sleep and repose. Discipline is constant yet flexible…Triumph and disaster are met and vanquished together.

'The captain and his second pilot do the actual flying, the observer navigates and drops the bombs, the wireless operator helps the navigator and with the air gunners does the fighting. The same spirit and practice of co-ordination is required of a bomber crew as a crew of a racing eight or the members of a football eleven.'

The book outlined the difference between the life of the fighter pilots, who had won the Battle of Britain over England the previous year, and the bomber pilots who were now taking the war to the enemy. The fighter pilot was in action for an hour and a half to two hours at most whereas the bomber pilot may find himself remaining for nine, ten, eleven or even twelve hours at a time over hostile territory or the cruel sea.

One visitor to 101 Squadron early in 1941 was an Air Ministry public relations officer called Herbert Bates. He was so impressed with the story of one Wellington crew who crash landed in France and some of whom made it back to the UK with the help of the Resistance that he used it as the basis for a book. *Fair Stood the Wind for France* by H.E.Bates was published in 1944.

The Wellington OTUs were producing about 20 crews plus a few spare pilots every two weeks. If crews had gone through the OTU together, they were often kept together when they were posted off to a squadron. Pilots like Colin would have done about 30 hours on Wellingtons during their training. On arrival at the frontline, they would do five trips on operations as a second pilot to get the hang of things and what was expected of them.

An inexperienced co-pilot flying with a veteran crew was often called a 'Dicky' or a '2nd Dicky'. The second pilot's perch on Wellingtons was called the 'Dicky seat' after the small third seat found in some two-seat sports cars of the time. It was usually removed to make it easier to move up and down the aircraft and indeed to get out in a hurry. Once airborne, the second pilot could be asked to fill in on any role while the incumbent was occupied elsewhere. He would monitor the petrol flow, pump oil into the engines, read the map and man the machine guns. This 'dogsbody' life gave the future captain the chance to understand what each member of his crew actually faced and the implications of his orders from the pilot's seat. After those five trips, he could be captaining his own aircraft.

—⚉—

The day after Colin arrived at Oakington, 101 Squadron sent five Wellingtons to attack the docks at Brest. All aircraft returned safely from this night raid, including one captained by a Sergeant Callender who would later be Colin's captain on his second mission. For Pilot Officer Curtis and two other new boys from the same OTU, Pilot Officers Lewis and Kennedy, the day was spent flying training missions in the Oakington area. It appears that the others that Colin trained with at Chipping Warden did not follow him to Cambridgeshire.

Flying over the next four days was seriously curtailed due to bad weather. Instead there were ground training sessions including lectures on First Aid by the Medical Officer and a briefing by the Squadron Leader who was responsible for intelligence matters at the base. On Tuesday 23 December, seven Wellingtons made a successful attack on the docks at Brest. The eighth aircraft, captained by Sgt Peter Chapman who would die along with Colin less than a month later, abandoned the mission due to an engine failure.

On Christmas Eve, there was more local training in the Oakington circuit. For Christmas Day and Boxing Day, the Wellingtons stayed on the ground but all the crews were on a two-hour standby for possible daylight missions. There were suggestions that the Germans might try to move their battleships *Scharnhorst* and *Gneisenau* from Brest back to a German port, supposedly taking advantage of a hung-over RAF. Phone calls off the base were banned. All ranks who were not on call for operations were dragged into keeping the runway and taxiways clear of snow.

The crews were not called upon but, come darkness, no aircrew were allowed off the base to celebrate Christmas. The bar at the Railway Hotel near Oakington station did not benefit from aircrew that night. They had to walk several miles from the main gate of the airfield to reach the pub until someone had the idea of cutting a gap in the perimeter fence. After that it was a short hop across the railway line from the airfield. Oakington railway station, much used by the RAF during the war, survived until the Beeching cuts in the 1960s.

Colin sent an official RAF Oakington Christmas card to his family, signed just 'Colin xxx'. With the RAF crest on the front and a red, white and blue ribbon on one side, it was placed on the mantelpiece in the main sitting room at the new family home near the Pincushion Inn at Wyberton. There was an air of sadness in the house. His mother Lillian was still mourning the loss of her husband three months earlier. The card reminded her that her eldest son was going into battle and her two other sons would be called up soon.

Colin got home for one night over the Christmas period. He sat up late with his two brothers, discussing the war and dwelling on memories of their father. Sister Joyce said: 'It's time you lads went to bed' but their mother intervened. 'Let them have a bit longer. You never know when they'll be together again.' My father wrote years later: 'We never were.'

With Christmas out of the way, 101 Squadron was ready for action again and the name of Acting Pilot Officer Colin Curtis began to appear on the daily 'Orbats' – the Orders of Battle that listed the men flying that night.

—ᴍᴍ—

Bomber Command had a bad year in 1941 with many casualties. In December, the men at the top sought the views of the Group commanders and discovered a feeling of 'hopelessness and ineffectiveness' among many squadrons. There was huge concern about standards of navigation and target marking, with targets being 'stumbled upon' largely through luck rather than judgement. A few months earlier, a civil servant called David Bensusan-Butt had been commissioned to study more than 600 photographs of attacked targets and compare them to claims by the crews. The Butt Report revealed the widespread failure of bombers to deliver their bomb-loads on the intended target. Prime Minister Winston Churchill was not impressed.

There was also a leadership vacuum at the top of Bomber Command. The Chief of the Air Staff, Air Chief Marshal Sir Charles Portal, grew increasingly dissatisfied with his successor Air Marshal Sir Richard Peirse and, prompted by the big losses and the ineffectiveness of the bombing, redeployed Peirse to another job. When Colin joined his first operational squadron at the end of 1941, Bomber Command had a 'caretaker' commander until Arthur Harris took over in February 1942.

Down the command chain, 101 Squadron was in action again on the 27th December. Five Wellingtons successfully attacked Dusseldorf but four other aircraft failed to make the target because of technical issues. One Wellington failed to return to Oakington and the six crew were posted as 'missing'.

Bad weather closed in again in the days up to the New Year. On 31st December, there was more ground training in the morning before the squadron was 'stood down' in the afternoon. The aircrew at Oakington could now be confident that they would at least see in the New Year of 1942. The unspoken question was how many of them would survive the next twelve months.

—ᨣ—

The first trips for a new pilot would be less challenging than a full raid on German targets. The crew might be tasked to drop leaflets or lay mines (known as 'gardening'). Colin's name first appeared on the 'Orbat' for 2nd January 1942 as the second pilot of a Wellington that would be responsible for any air sea rescue co-ordination. When the day came, the crew was not used.

Two days later he was briefed for an operation to the docks at Brest but it was cancelled due to poor weather over the target. The following day 154 aircraft including 89 Wellingtons *did* attack Brest where the German battleships *Scharnhorst* and *Gneisenau* were docked. A smoke screen prevented accurate bombing and the following month the two warships, along with the heavy cruiser *Prinz Eugen* and their escorts, made their famous 'Channel Dash' up the English Channel away from the heavily-bombed Brest to the relative safety of their German bases.

Colin flew his first operational mission on the 8th January against more naval targets in Cherbourg docks on the north coast of France. Twelve Wellingtons from 101 took part with Colin on board Z1095 with Pilot Officer Fooks, and Sergeants Ryan, Davies, Pollock and Spooner. One Wellington from another squadron was lost in this raid which was described by Bomber Command as a 'minor' operation compared to a separate assault on Brest involving 124 aircraft. Three Wellingtons and two Hampdens were lost in that mission.

Two days later, nine 101 Squadron Wellingtons attacked Wilhelmshaven on the north coast of Germany. Colin was the second pilot on Z1146 with Sgt Callender as captain and Pilot Officer Doig, Flt Sgt Howitt and Sgts Young and Wigham also on board. Their bomber was among 124 involved in the attack which only caused light damage and injured six people according to German records. Three Wellingtons and two Hampdens were lost but all of the 101 Squadron aircraft returned safely.

At least they were now operating under the cover of darkness. Until six months earlier, Wellingtons were used on daylight raids and many more were shot down. The man in charge of Bomber Command's No. 3 Group, Air Vice Marshal John Baldwin, said that the Wellington, 'which lacks armament, speed and handiness and especially rate of climb, is a most unsuitable type of aircraft for daylight operations.' His bosses at Headquarters agreed and declared that 101 Squadron would henceforth be used for night bombing only.

Colin did not fly operationally for another ten days due to a period of bad weather. The Met Office summary for January 1942 was cold, mainly dull with considerable snow and severe frost. On the 19th a deep depression moved across the UK with heavy rain to the west and considerable snow to the east. For the third January in succession, temperatures were below average particularly in the east of England. The Met Office said it was 'exceedingly cold' from the 11th to 22nd January. At Dunstable in Bedfordshire it stayed at 32 degrees Fahrenheit or below (in other words freezing point).

Around 19th to 21st January, there was up to eight inches of snow in the Midlands. There was no thaw until the 23rd – three days after Colin Curtis had succumbed to the heat of battle and died in the icy waters of the North Sea.

Chapter 9

Cotswold Radar

The rather imperious lady on the phone was getting irritable. She had rung the local RAF base to complain about aircraft noise and was not getting anywhere with the man responsible for soothing ruffled feathers and the aching ears of the local community. Exasperated, she finally blurted out the core of her anguish: 'Why do they have to land so low?'

When I was working at BBC Radio Oxford, the Community Relations Officer at RAF Brize Norton was Flight Lieutenant Jimmy Kenefic. Jimmy was said to be the oldest Flight Lieutenant in the RAF and was rumoured to attribute his longevity in the service due to his phenomenal skills at playing bridge. Brize Norton and indeed the wider RAF could win tournaments with Jimmy in the team.

It was Jimmy who faced the lady who asked why the aircraft had to land so low. Usually if someone complained about the noise, he would ask if they were sure it was 'one of ours'. When he was assured it was, he would say 'Thank Goodness! We have not been invaded!' It made a change from the usual retort of the Americans – 'That's the Sound of Freedom, Ma'am!'

Jimmy got me my first of several flights in a VC10 out of Brize Norton. I joined a crew training mission one winter's day during which they did several practice approaches at Prestwick and East Midlands airports. He also presented me with a national 'exclusive' early in my BBC career and top billing on Radio 4's *The World at One* on a December day in 1979.

I had made a routine call to Jimmy to see if there was any news out of Brize Norton that might give us a story on Radio Oxford. He said he did have something of interest actually – namely that one of 10 Squadron's VC10s was due to take Lord Soames to Rhodesia that very afternoon. Soames, who was in Margaret Thatcher's Cabinet as Lord President of the Council, had been named as the transitional governor for Rhodesia to oversee its progress into legal independence from the UK. It would then be renamed Zimbabwe.

I knew the story well. My colleagues and I had been reflecting the saga, including the Constitutional Conference at Lancaster House in London, in our bulletins and programmes for some time. The names of the figures associated with it were a magnificent challenge for any newsreader – Bishop Abel Muzorewa, Joshua Nkomo, Ndabaningi Sithole and Canaan Banana. So the thought of getting an Oxfordshire angle on this unfolding international epic appealed rather a lot.

Jimmy told me that the VC10 would leave Brize for Heathrow to pick up Lord Soames and his party and then fly straight on to Salisbury, now called Harare. It would depart about 2pm and he even had the name of the Captain. I thanked him very much and recorded a minute-long report for the Radio Oxford news bulletins. I also sent the story to the main BBC newsroom in London. It went out at 11am on Radio Oxford and I turned to other tales of Oxfordshire life.

About 45 minutes later, I got a call from the main BBC newsroom in London. 'This story you have sent us about Soames – are you sure about it?' They had not used it yet.

The London newsroom frequently doubted what local radio journalists told them. I said I was indeed sure. Jimmy Kenefic would not lie to me or wind me up. London's problem was that no one in the Government would confirm that Lord Soames was indeed heading to Rhodesia that very afternoon.

After the midday news, I got a call from Jimmy. 'Er, have you used that stuff I gave you earlier?' I was able to confirm his worst fears that not only had we used it on Radio Oxford but I had sent it to London. Jimmy had received a call from the Ministry of Defence asking how on earth the BBC knew all about the flight. It was then that Jimmy had noticed the two words at the bottom of his bit of paper – 'Strictly Classified'.

In the Oxford newsroom, I got a call from one of the BBC's senior foreign correspondents who had been using all the contacts in his book to try and confirm the story. Then a political correspondent rang and queried it. Nobody was talking in the government or the MOD. After more calls from the London newsroom, someone decided to go with it and I was asked to pull together and record a 45 second voice piece for them to use. If I had got it spectacularly wrong, then they made sure my name was all over it. It was given due prominence at the top of *The World at One* bulletin.

As a young reporter in my second year at the BBC, I did start to get nervous after all these calls from the BBC in London and with so many people in power refusing to confirm what I had got. I had to sweat it out until 3pm when Margaret Thatcher gave a statement in the House of Commons, confirming that, even as she spoke, Lord Soames was in the air on his way to Rhodesia. Jimmy got a 'dressing down' but survived in his role for a few more years before retiring to Lincolnshire. We mulled it over with wry amusement at a Battle of Britain reception at RAF Coningsby some ten years later.

One of the squadrons at Brize Norton was Colin Curtis's wartime unit 101, which now operated VC10 air refuelling tankers. In March 1990, I got the opportunity to fly in one of their VC10s over the jungles of Malaysia. A group of journalists and a couple of film crews were invited to join an RAF exercise for a week during a detachment to the Royal Malaysian Air Force base at Butterworth just across the water from Penang Island. It involved four Tornado F3s from 5 Squadron at Coningsby, two Tornado GR1s from 27 Squadron at Marham, a couple of 101 Squadron VC10s and various Hercules in support.

Among the aircrew we interviewed at Butterworth was the boss of 27 Squadron, Wing Commander Bill Green. Five months later, the newly promoted Group Captain Green was killed flying a Tornado on a night mission from RAF Marham. The aircraft crashed ten miles north east of Spurn Head. Like Colin Curtis nearly 50 years earlier, Bill Green's body was never recovered from the North Sea. His loss prompted his wife Jenny to set up the RAF Widows Association two years later.

In Malaysia, the VC10s were based at Bayan Lepas, Penang's international airport. One morning we boarded ZA144 (E) for a sortie across the country to Kuantan air base, refuelling some Tornados on the way. Each Tornado edged closer to the VC10, the pilot aiming the refuelling probe expertly into the 'shuttlecock' at the end of the trailing wing hoses. Up to 1000 kilograms of fuel could be transferred each minute that the Tornado hung on the line. Below, the green jungles of Malaysia could be seen between the wispy white clouds. I called my 30 minute documentary 'Tornados in the Tropics'.

The trip out to Malaysia was club class on a British Airways 747 to Kuala Lumpur followed by an internal hop to Penang. The flight back was under more austere and 'dry' conditions on an RAF TriStar. The landing back at Brize was particularly heavy with the overhead luggage rack doors all bursting open and the senior ranks and other pilots in the cabin tutting audibly. As the TriStar taxied towards the terminal, the Captain came on the intercom: 'Welcome to Brize Norton. Sorry about the landing. It had nothing to do with me.' The co-pilot must have reddened considerably and anticipated some time on the naughty chair. The TriStar apparently spent some time in the hangar having its main undercarriage and the wings bent back into shape.

A couple of hours later, I was brought back to earth from Malaysia with another bump, namely a rain-lashed rush-hour railway platform at Swindon station.

Just before I left Boston for the BBC in 1978, the town was hit by severe floods caused by heavy rain and high tides. As Chief Reporter, I wanted to mix with the people who were caught up in the deluge and, apart from gathering material for the newspaper and Bob Whitaker's news film, see if I could actually help anybody. I traipsed round the town centre nearly waist deep in waste and Wash water. On every circuit, I dropped back in to the front office of the police station to find out where the latest afflicted area was being reported.

There was no social media or local radio to update the inundated victims who were more likely to rely on folklore than technology. My dad once chaired a meeting to organise a village garden fete and everyone got bogged down planning what to do if it was wet. (Old joke: '3pm Red Arrows display. If wet, in village hall'). An even older farmer called Sam Whaler sat listening in silence to the babble before someone asked him what he thought. He paused, took his pipe out of his mouth and said: 'It won't rain, Vicar.' And it did not.

Local radio really came into its own when the heavy snows fell. It took a while for radio stations to set up a special code with the head teachers of each school to stop enterprising pupils ringing up impersonating them and closing a school which was still open. We read out long lists of school closures across the county before realising it would be simpler to read out a list of the few that remained open.

At BBC Radio Lincolnshire I took a call at the height of a snow storm from a very posh sounding elderly lady. 'Is that Lincoln Radio? I usually only listen to the Third programme but due to this blessed inclemency, I am trying to tune my wireless to you to hear if my weekly bridge club is orf. How does one dial you up?'

As the snows came down, local radio stations set up special 'snowlines' to deal with the volume of messages from their listeners. At Radio Oxford this service was subversively called Snow Hazard Information Time. Apart from schools and colleges, clubs and societies would ring to cancel meetings, bus and train timetables would be in chaos and roads would be blocked or just dangerous. Power lines would be down and people would be listening to us on battery-driven portable radios by the flickering light of candles.

Not content with trying to close educational establishments by radio messages, the pranksters would invent events that were to be cancelled due the inclemency. At Radio Oxford, one presenter read out that the Bicester and District Cottaging Society was postponing its evening gathering due to the cold. Another one that got through in the blizzard of messages was the cancellation of the Oxford Onanists team meeting. The person answering the phone just handed the note straight to the presenter who broadcast it straight-faced without a pause and moved onto the chaos faced by public transport.

—m—

I still have *The Ladybird Book of Aircraft*, published in 1964 by Wills and Hepworth of Loughborough. Against a drawing of a MIG-21, it says: 'Although not likely to be seen over Britain, this Russian single-seat fighter has often been in the news.' If it *was* seen over Britain in 1964, questions would have been asked and probably too late. *The Observer's Book of Aircraft* from 1959 carried a very grainy black and white photograph of the new MIG-21 and revealed that its NATO codename was 'Faceplate', later changed to 'Fishbed'. It was the time when breakfast cereals contained red plastic soldiers or a grey submarine that went up and down if you put some baking powder in it.

For six pence, there was *I SPY Aircraft*, number 15 in the I SPY range overseen by Big Chief I-SPY who wrote every day in the national *News Chronicle* newspaper. He told of adventures of Fleetfoot with Jack and Jill and sent secret messages in code to those of us in the Great Tribe. Jack and Jill, not content with just going up the hill to get a pail of water and falling down again, could score 1,250 points in *I-SPY Aircraft* and be entitled to an Order of Merit with the Tribal Rank of Air Observer – 2nd class.

'There it goes, whining overhead. Just another aircraft – but wait!…..'It's a jet!' said Jack. 'Look how fast it is moving'… ….'And I-SPY its twin booms!' cried Jill, really entering into the spirit of it all. 'I bet it's a de Havilland!' Well, she got the manufacturer correct but from the accompanying drawing, it was obviously a Sea Vixen prototype and she should have made that clear. Big Chief I-SPY said: 'Girls are pretty good at spotting planes and all you Redskins can join in the fun. What great fun it is too!'

I suppose I am a plane spotter although the only registration numbers that I ever noted down were of aircraft that I actually flew in or had a particular interest in. Many a time I had to disappoint an aviation aficionado who breathlessly ran past me shouting 'Did you get the number of that Herc?' as it drifted over the perimeter fence. Working in local journalism, I met many enthusiasts who were passionate about their hobbies – in aviation, railways, steam engines, bird watching, vintage car drivers, model makers, restorers, campanologists and so on. Those who sneered at such things seemed to be interested in nothing.

I took photographs at airshows for a few years, usually trying to get some context with the ground. (deadlines101. com). For years now, I have left it to the professionals and the banks of amateur enthusiasts who raise their huge zoom lens in unison and click away. Many post some very fine catches on-line. I just enjoyed being around aeroplanes and airfields. An airband radio and a pair of racing binoculars was all I ever needed at an airshow or the end of a runway.

After the early shift at Radio Oxford, I would sometimes stop off at the eastern end of Brize Norton to see if anything unusual had dropped in or just catch a couple of transports on finals. There is a hump back bridge there which obscured the traffic lights from northbound motorists. There would be a squeal of brakes and a smell of burnt rubber as an unsuspecting driver sailed over the bridge and slewed to a sudden stop for a red light as a VC10 'landed low'.

Another favourite place for a detour after the early shift was the American air base at Upper Heyford to the north west of Bicester. You slipped through the village of Ardley to find the single track road that went over the main London to Birmingham railway line and up to the perimeter fence near to the eastern end of Heyford's runway. From there you could watch the General Dynamics F-111 Aardvarks as they wound up their two engines, held the brakes fleetingly then lurched forward, flames roaring out the jet nozzles as reheat was engaged. You would also catch them coming into land, variable-sweep wings pushed fully forward with red airbrakes protruding and wheels dangling.

If you drive east along Camp Road with the now closed Upper Heyford air base on your left, you come to a fork in the road. The main road goes round to the right and the fork left takes you off to the northbound B430 towards what is now the Cherwell Services junction on the M40. There's a story about a Heyford pilot who came to grief at this junction many years ago.

The tale goes that the pilot had been on a low level training exercise in Scotland one day, flying down valleys and pulling up over hills and mountains. In the evening he went to the bar for a few drinks before driving home, heading down the straight Camp Road towards this forked junction. A few drinks in and with his mind elsewhere, he instinctively pulled back on the steering wheel like an aircraft 'joystick' instead of following the bend round to the right. He therefore went straight on, crashing into the trees, receiving minor injuries and a conviction for drink-driving.

Chapter 10

South West Approaches

Hurricane-force winds gusting up to 100 miles an hour and waves up to 60 feet high were battering the Cornish coast one night just before Christmas in 1981. Struggling through it in the dark, a ship called the *Union Star,* carrying a cargo of fertiliser from the Netherlands to Ireland, got into trouble between The Lizard and Land's End. Its engines failed and, after some radio discussion between the captain and the owners over accepting assistance from a salvage tug, it put out a distress call which was picked up by the regional coastguard station at Falmouth.

The *Union Star* was being driven across Mount's Bay toward the cliffs at Lamorna south of Penzance and Newlyn. The Coastguard scrambled a Royal Navy rescue helicopter from the nearby Culdrose Naval Air Station but the crew were unable to winch anyone off the vessel because of the weather. So the coxswain of the nearest lifeboat, Penlee at Mousehole, was called and he pulled together a crew of seven and set off into the raging sea. Despite the eagerness of all the volunteers to help, he ensured that only one person from any family joined him in case things went wrong. The lifeboat was called the *Soloman Browne* and the crew all died that night, along with the eight people on the *Union Star.*

The inquest into this tragedy was held early in 1983 by which time the BBC had opened its latest local radio stations to serve both Devon and Cornwall. I was one of the senior journalists on the Cornwall launch team who, along with one of my new colleagues, also produced the final editions of the regional breakfast radio programme, *Morning Sou' West,* which had been an opt-out of Radio 4's *Today* programme.

The Penlee inquest heard from an exchange pilot from the U.S. Navy who was the captain of the Sea King rescue helicopter that night. He described the actions of the Penlee lifeboat crew as 'the greatest act of courage that I have ever seen, and am ever likely to see.' They got four people off the *Union Star* at the first attempt and then tried to get alongside again to get the other four. The lifeboat was picked up by the huge waves and dropped onto the *Union Star* deck. The last radio message from the Coxswain Trevelyan Richards was timed at 9.20pm. *'We've got four off... there are two more...'*

As witnessed by the helicopter crew, they were going back to get the other four. With the permission of the families and the Coastguard, the last radio exchange was released to the media after being played at the inquest. I still remember the chilling, heartbreaking words played in bulletins that I was presenting on Radio Cornwall.

'Penlee Lifeboat, Penlee Lifeboat, this is Falmouth Coastguard, over... Penlee Lifeboat, Penlee Lifeboat, Falmouth Coastguard, over... Penlee Lifeboat, Penlee Lifeboat, Falmouth Coastguard, over'... silence.

BBC Radio Cornwall, BBC Radio Devon and indeed *BBC Breakfast Television*, with Frank Bough and Selina Scott, all started broadcasting on 17th January 1983. The official opening of Radio Cornwall included a flypast by one of Culdrose's rescue helicopters, persuaded to make a small diversion from a training sortie. I did some spoof *Private Eye* covers to mark the occasion, one of which featured Prince Andrew saying how thrilled he was that the BBC had come to Cornwall. One copy fell into the hands of the media relations officer at Culdrose who showed it to one of the helicopter pilots on a tour there at the time – Prince Andrew. I was informed that he was amused and that I was not bound for the Tower.

Cornwall was not used to radio news and its immediacy. Talking to one councillor before the launch of the radio station, we said we looked forward to interviewing him about council decisions. He said he would be delighted – and added seriously 'pop the questions in the post and I'll send you a reply by return.'

A local vicar came in to complain about some of the music we were playing including Cliff Richard's 'Devil Woman'. He was equally concerned about the American band Bread and its hit song 'Make it with You'. Collaring our Manager, he twitched: 'You know what *that's* about, don't you? Yes, *that*.'

On a still night at home between Truro and Falmouth, you could sometimes hear the Falmouth fog horn, booming four second blasts every 45 seconds or so through the rolling fogbanks enveloping the English Channel. Flamborough Head near Bridlington and Souter Lighthouse near Sunderland were two other foghorns whose eerie wails resonated with me over the years – old technology replaced now by satellite links and GPS. Each foghorn had a distinctive sound and timing to help sailors work out which bit of coast they were endeavouring to steer clear of.

The mournful cry of the Trevose lighthouse fog horn failed to help one tanker crew who ran aground there in the

1960s. The ship left Liverpool for a breaker's yard in Antwerp and, so the story goes from local journalists, the crew started drinking. In thick fog, they turned left around a lighthouse which they thought was Land's End and set course up the English Channel. In fact they had turned to port at Trevose Head on the north coast near Padstow and ran aground at the nearby Fox Cove. The crew initially reported that they had run aground at The Lizard so all the emergency services went there instead of Trevose.

Another evocative sound was the lifeboat maroon. When the weather was bad with gale force winds whipping up the mountainous North Sea, the maroon would often be fired in the middle of the night. The sound ricocheted round the town of Filey and everyone tensed, waiting to see if there would be a second bang. The first maroon alerted the lifeboat crew in the days before mobile phones and pagers; the second maroon usually meant the big boat, rather than the small inshore rescue boat, was being launched. The huge bangs from the maroons put the lives of the lifeboat crew at the forefront of everyone's thoughts as they lay safe in their beds and, if within range, hopefully told the person in trouble on the seas that help was on its way. *Oh hear us when we cry to Thee, For those in peril on the sea.*

One very warm sunny Saturday afternoon in July 1983, I was invited to open the village fete at Perranwell Station, a little village half way between Truro and Falmouth. I was living in the village and someone through someone else had suggested that I might like to declare it open as I was 'on the radio' and some people had heard me if not heard *of* me. After duly saying a few words and encouraging them all to listen to Radio Cornwall, I stayed for a little while before returning home up the hill.

My wife had just taken a call from the radio station. Could I ring the newsroom as soon as I got in? I dialled immediately to be told that we had a major story on our hands. A civilian S61 helicopter, in transit from Penzance heliport to St Mary's in the Isles of Scilly, had apparently crashed into the sea.

Our Penzance reporter was on the case and another of the team was on his way to help him. In the newsroom that Saturday afternoon, we pulled together newsflashes and bulletins and fed the newsrooms in Plymouth and London. As the story unfolded, it became apparent that 26 passengers and crew had been on the S61 which had come down in the sea not far from St Mary's. Thick fog was hampering the rescue operation. There had been no 'Mayday' message. The control tower at St Mary's airfield lost contact with the helicopter and raised the alarm.

Only six people survived the crash including the two pilots. They were picked up by the St Mary's lifeboat as the Culdrose rescue helicopters struggled with the bad visibility. One of the survivors who escaped from the sinking fuselage recalled floating in the sea in the fog and hearing the maroons go off as the lifeboat crew were summoned at St Mary's. The inquiry concluded that the helicopter, which had been flying low because of the fog, had gradually been flown into the sea as the pilots became disorientated.

This was another big national news story long before the days of mobile phones, social media and rolling news on television and radio. Our News Editor was in Wales on family business and out of touch with the office for the weekend. On Sunday afternoon he drove back to Truro, picked up some Sunday newspapers from a local garage without looking at them, cooked a meal and then settled in the garden in the late afternoon sun to catch up with the world. And as he scanned the main story on the front pages….fade to black.

—ɯ—

One of the entries in my Cornwall contacts book reads 'Elton John's friend – Mrs Sylvester.' No idea what that was all about. Others include the Concorde Fan Club who loved the fact that the supersonic airliner created big bangs over the Duchy as it headed for New York. There were phone numbers for the Indian branch of the Cornish National Party in New Delhi, the Panama Embassy in London, Methodist Barry Manilow fans, the manager of The Who, a Shirley Bassey impressionist, a 'Rhino woman – Miss Lugg' and 'Four Lanes Witches Row.'

There are numbers for Tim Rice, Jeffrey Archer, Defence Secretary John Nott (who was MP for St Ives), rower Chay Blyth, the writer and historian A L Rowse (proud of his Cornish roots and living in retirement at Trenarren), SDP founder David Owen (a Plymouth MP), William Golding (who lived not far from me at Perranarworthal), Daphne du Maurier (who died at her Cornwall home at Par in 1989) and Goonhilly Downs, once the world's biggest satellite earth station which, from The Lizard, connected the world with the Apollo space programme, Live Aid and the Olympics.

The former Prime Minister Ted Heath passed through Radio Cornwall for an interview, asking us in the newsroom if we had the latest shipping forecast for Plymouth, Sole, Lundy and Fastnet. Another visitor was Irish comedian Dave Allen, stopping on his way to the studio to ask what we were working on. Dave Allen started his working life in newspapers, joining the *Drogheda Argus* as a copy-boy.

St Austell-born John Nettles dropped by for interviews with us and 'down the line' to other outlets, asking if he could borrow our copy of *The Financial Times* while he waited. He was then the young Jersey detective Jim Bergerac, heading later for promotion to DCI Tom Barnaby in Midsomer via the Royal Shakespeare Company. I liked *Bergerac* with its scenes of the sea similar to Cornwall, its George Fenton 'ear-worm' theme music and the hero hiding behind a copy of *The Jersey Evening Post*. Corbière Point on the south west corner of Jersey is one of my magical places. I got a brown leather jacket like Jim Bergerac wore and held onto it for far too long.

We had voice training at BBC Radio Cornwall with well-known radio newsreaders like Laurie Macmillan, Peter Donaldson, Bryan Martin and David Dunhill, complete with cigarette holder aloft and tales of training people like Libby Purvis (who left Radio Oxford just before I arrived), Jon Snow and Jill Dando. We made sure we had the right pronunciation for the places of Cornwall. Launceston was not called 'Lawn-ceston' but 'Lawn-sun' although some of the locals insisted it should be 'Lanson'. The village of Mousehole should be pronounced 'Mow-sel' but you could still find a local who said 'Mouse Hole'.

My Dad once had to go to a hamlet called Chop Gate near the Bilsdale TV transmitter in the middle of the North Yorkshire moors. He stopped the car to ask an elderly man for directions but he did not recognise a place called Chop Gate. 'How do you spell it, Padre?' Dad pointed to a written down address and the local's face lit up. 'Ah, you mean Shoggut'.

The new Cornwall Coliseum at St Austell was very generous with free tickets for the local media in the early 1980s. It got some big names such as The Police, Eric Clapton, the newly resurgent Tina Turner and Smokey Robinson, wearing a striking pair of red knee-length boots. In the media room at one concert, I met Judi Spiers, a West Country on-screen legend and close companion of Gus Honeybun. Gus was the rabbit puppet who was the mascot of *Westward Television*, later *Television South West,* for years. He was famous for his 'Magic Birthdays' slot with the continuity presenters like Judi and Fern Britton. People would write in with details of their son or daughter's birthday and Gus would do the requisite number of bunny hops or ear waggles to mark the youngster's years on earth. Behind some of those requests for eight year olds were grown-ups, such was Gus' appeal. I believe his head flew off on one energetic occasion.

—ᴍ—

Much of southern Cornwall is designated as an 'Area of Intense Aerial Activity', mainly due to the helicopters from Culdrose. In years gone by, local people got used to the supersonic bangs echoing round the Duchy as the crews of British Airways Concordes opened up the throttles to start the supersonic run across the Atlantic to New York. To this day, there is a military air-to-air flight refuelling area (AARA 10) running along the spine of Cornwall.

For years, the most familiar fixed wing aircraft in the Cornish skies were the Shackletons and later the Nimrods, the long range maritime reconnaissance aircraft based at RAF St Mawgan up the road from Newquay. In 1992, all the RAF's Nimrods were concentrated at RAF Kinloss in Scotland and now, although there is still an RAF presence at the base, the runway is in civilian hands.

One summer's evening in 1983, I gazed straight down St Mawgan's runway 30. It was 8.20pm and I was on the flight deck of a Nimrod MR2 of 42 Squadron, joining the 11 strong crew of XV242 on a nine hour flight beyond the South West Approaches to the Bay of Biscay.

I was on an assignment to do a feature on the Nimrod crews at St Mawgan. I was the only journalist on board and was given free range to wander around the aircraft, recording interviews whenever the team had a spare moment. I could plug in my head-set in a number of places and stick a microphone between the headphone and my ear to try and record snatches of radio communications between the crew.

The Nimrod headed out to the Bay of Biscay, coming down to between 700 and 300 feet at times and using its powerful searchlight mounted on the starboard wing. They said this light was the equivalent of more than 60 million candlepower (an obsolete unit of expressing luminous intensity no less) and had a range of more than a mile. It must have been an awesome sight for the French fishermen plying their trade on the sea below. Sitting by the bubble windows when the crew were not using them, I could see the lights on these French fishing boats flashing by as the mighty Nimrod roared over the waves as its crew practised anti-submarine warfare techniques and checked out what they called 'surface contacts'.

A Nimrod piles on the power above the Lancaster,
Mildenhall circa 1988 (Photo: MC)

'Captain, we've got a problem at the back.' I did not have my tape recorder switched on at that precise moment but the remark rather grabbed my attention. Three hundred feet over the Bay of Biscay in the middle of the night and we have a problem? No one looked unduly concerned but the Nimrod went into a steep climb to gain height while the problem was assessed. One of the crew had found some hydraulic fluid slopping about in the hydraulics bay at the back of the aircraft. They decided to err on the side of caution and head for home, abandoning the last hour or so of the exercise.

Another cup of coffee and some in-flight rations were offered again as the Nimrod headed through the night back towards St Mawgan. I was told that we would be making an emergency landing but the leakage was probably not as dramatic as it sounded. The cabin may fill up with fumes in which case we would not hang around in the aircraft once we were on the ground. I felt reassured.

'By the way, do you like Yorkshire?' asked one of the crew. I did indeed, very much. I grew up on the Yorkshire coast and…oh never mind. Why? 'Well, that's where we're going at the moment.' The fog had descended overnight in Cornwall and, with about an hour to go before the final approach, St Mawgan was fog-bound. The captain was advised that his MEDA (Military Emergency Diversion Airfield) was RAF Leeming, beside the A1 in North Yorkshire where the weather was clear. My heart sank. I anticipated a potentially difficult phone call from a coin box at RAF Leeming to my news editor back in Truro.

I had left St Mawgan on a clear summer's evening on Wednesday 8th June, flying into a beautiful sunset. I was hoping some nine hours later for a 5am touchdown on the same Runway 30 on Thursday 9th June. Now I was going to be at the other end of England on one of the most significant national news days of the year. Thursday 9th June 1983 was General Election day in the United Kingdom – an election that would give Margaret Thatcher her second spell as Prime Minister and a very decisive victory due to her troops' triumph in the Falklands War, not least 101 Squadron's contribution.

The plan was for me to drive straight to Radio Cornwall from St Mawgan and edit a couple of pieces for that morning's breakfast show. On election day, you could not report very much about it all until the polling booths closed at 10pm. We thought my reports about life inside a Cornish Nimrod over the high seas would provide a welcome respite from reporting that 'polling was said to be brisk' at the launderette that was being used as a polling station and other such stories. It would give presenter Chris Blount something else to talk about – and he could talk to me as well as let me introduce the voices and sound effects gathered on the flight.

I would then go home, cast my vote and return to help with the Election Special later that evening. I was also due to be the reporter at the election count in Truro on the Friday morning. If the fog persisted all day at St Mawgan, I would be 'our Radio Cornwall reporter definitely not at the scene' but stranded by Nimrod in Yorkshire.

The Nimrod crew didn't want to go to Yorkshire either. They were ready for home after a night shift over the Bay of Biscay. Shortly before the final diversion decision, Air Traffic Control at St Mawgan confirmed a ' window in the weather' which would allow the aircraft to make a safe approach and landing. In the end the Nimrod touched down without incident and the cabin did not fill up with fumes. We made an orderly exit after all the shutdown checks. Sorry for the lack of drama again.

As I swung out of St Mawgan's main gate a short time later, the first rays of the new rising sun started to seep through the mists and the radio played 'Every breath you take'. The polling stations would open in less than two hours and the new Social Democrat Party – founded by four senior Labour politicians who were upset by calls to leave the European Union among other Labour policies – were hoping to make

an impact in their alliance with the Liberals. Those were the days when Europe really dominated our news agendas..........
Local journalists were regularly and lavishly hosted in Brussels and Luxembourg by MEPs and mandarins who were eager to help people back home make sense of the whole bureaucratic behemoth.

I experienced my most turbulent landing ever on St Mawgan's Runway 30 some months later. I had been up to London for a union meeting and it was agreed that I could fly there and back as it was quicker and no more expensive that the long train journey. The winter weather for the return trip was not good and the Dash 7 of Brymon Airways was being buffeted noticeably as it flew into south west airspace.

The little twin-prop dropped into Plymouth airport first, emptying about two thirds of the people on board including a well refreshed celebrity of the time. It then took off again for St Mawgan and the small terminal of Newquay airport in the north west corner of the airfield. As we taxied out again at Plymouth, the captain told us that the weather at Newquay was about the same as Plymouth but 'considerably windier.' As the high-winged Dash hopped over Bodmin Moor, the turbulence became significant. I was sitting next to a Royal Navy diver from Culdrose and we were both nursing Irish whiskeys, mainly trying to keep the liquid in the glass as the aircraft bumped up and down. People around us started to be air-sick.

The Dash made its approach fighting a severe cross-wind. There was a cheer as the aircraft thudded down and straightened up. At the terminal, one of the airport team that I had interviewed a few weeks earlier said she had nearly sent us back to Plymouth and they were not accepting any more civilian flights that night.

On the other side of St Mawgan, a number of Nimrods sat under the floodlights awaiting more maritime reconnaissance missions or search and rescue scrambles that could send them way out over the Atlantic regardless of the weather.

One of my earliest memories of helicopters was the yellow Whirlwind from RAF Manston clattering low along the water's edge on Margate beach. A highlight of the summer holidays on the Kent coast was the almost daily appearance of the RAF rescue 'cab', side door wide open with the winchman sat on the edge waving to everyone on the beach. This seemingly care-free existence all looked rather fun to ten year old me who was yet to appreciate the dangers that these men faced when they answered a real rescue call way out to sea on a stormy night.

One of my more glamorous colleagues at Radio Cornwall got three of us a trip on Sea King rescue helicopter from Culdrose. Vanessa persuaded a Navy crew to take us on a training exercise with a Royal Fleet Auxiliary ship in the Channel that was returning from the Falkland Islands. As we had touched down on the vessel outside British territorial waters (beyond 12 nautical miles off the coast), we had to go through Customs at Culdrose on our return. Nothing to declare but still looked and felt guilty.

The earliest television series that I recall watching was about helicopters and called *Whirlybirds*. It was produced in the same studios that gave us the perpetually cacophonous *I Love Lucy* shows and featured Chuck and Pete who owned a helicopter chartering company in California. They came to someone's rescue in every episode and the sun always shone from a black and white cloudless sky.

Another early American comedy was called *No Time for*

Sergeants which was a spin-off from a 1958 film of the same name. It featured a rather dim conscript character called Will Stockdale who joins the US Air Force and gets into various scrapes, including taking off under hypnosis in a nuclear bomber to attack the now-friendly Germany. It was somewhat eclipsed by another US forces comedy series – the iconic *Sgt Bilko*.

—ɯ—

Valerie Singleton was the reporter at the 1983 Truro constituency count for BBC Television news that morning. Despite the initial scare of being stranded by Nimrod in Yorkshire, I was there after all for BBC Radio Cornwall. Nationally the opposition vote was split between Labour and the SDP/Liberal Alliance, giving Thatcher her resounding victory. The sitting Liberal MP in Truro, David Penhaligon, unsurprisingly won again and would have done so regardless of what was going on elsewhere in the country.

David Penhaligan was a popular local figure who campaigned endlessly for all of Cornwall. Three years later he was killed in a road accident when a van skidded on ice and hit his car. It happened early one morning three days before Christmas. He was on his way to visit local postal workers at their sorting office. At one dinner I attended, he was guest speaker. He introduced himself as the Liberal spokesman on......wait for it. He produced a piece of paper and rattled through a very long list of responsibilities. There were not many Liberal MPs. He was one of the good guys in politics.

I covered the first ever news reading shift on BBC Radio Cornwall on that launch morning on 17th January 1983. After that, I was often the early newsreader on duty with presenter Chris Blount who was Cornwall born and bred. Waiting to read the headlines one morning soon after the launch, I was half listening as Chris ran through the weather forecast again. He finished with the line: 'I bet that strong one is licking round brown willy this morning. Here's the News with Mike Curtis.' I looked at him horrified for a second before stumbling off into the headlines.

What a moment to hear of Brown Willy for the first time, the highest point on Bodmin Moor and therefore undoubtedly a very windy place at the best of times.

Chapter 11

Mrs Simpson played the organ

As local newspapers closed, there were fewer journalists with gossip and anecdotes acquired from trudging round the streets, calling in at the front counter of police stations, meeting up with contacts over a pint in the pub at lunchtime, and pursuing the priest, publican and the postmaster in local villages for stories. More and more, they did their interviews over the phone and pursued their journalism through emails and social media. The mobile phone changed things considerably.

Young and inexperienced reporters had a steep learning curve in life in the 1970s. Just out of school or college, you had to be across so many subjects. You never knew what stories you would be tackling each day and could veer between covering a very complicated finance committee, a magistrates' court, a gruesome inquest or a charity marathon mad man dressed as a mongoose. You had to write carefully and try and understand every aspect and nuance of the Armed Forces as well as local government, national politics, the clergy, the NHS, the itinerant travellers, farming, business and every sport. You needed to cultivate a curious and inquisitive mind.

One morning after the paper came out, the receptionist put a call through to me. It was the Chief Executive of the Borough Council, a diminutive but fearsome public servant who insisted on being called R. Ernest Coley. The 'R' stood for Ronnie but you never called him that in the paper. My heart sank. I had written up several council stories that week and I had obviously got confused, missed the point or failed to grasp the importance of some debate within the Dog Fouling and Dustbins Sub-Committee. 'Mr Curtis, Mr Coley here. I have just rung to congratulate you on a very fair, balanced and well written report on the committee meeting. Well done and thank you.' And he was gone again. Did I dream that call?

You mixed with young and old, retired Colonels, councillors, policemen and women, social workers, probation officers, shop girls, factory workers, publicans and the recidivist youths who found themselves in front of the magistrates time and again.

One errant soul challenged me in a Boston pub once, keen to confirm that I was indeed the reporter who had covered his court case for some minor assault. He snarled: 'Why the f**k was I on Page 32?' He thought his case should be front page news. I patiently explained newspaper production processes which meant that, as his hearing was on the Friday, all the cases that day would go to fill the 'early pages' towards the back of the newspaper for the following week's edition. If he wanted to be towards the front page, he should talk to his Legal Aid solicitor about getting his case heard on the Wednesday, a few hours before the paper was 'put to bed'.

Someone else whose court case for assault appeared in the paper actually came to the newspaper reception to complain. As the journalist who was in court, I went to meet him and took him into the interview room off Reception. He promptly lost his temper and grabbed me by the throat. I asserted my full five foot six and threw him off, assuring him that he had just committed another assault and that I would get the Receptionist to call the constabulary. When I added that I had heard in court about his 'previous' (a list of earlier misdemeanours), he crumpled and apologised. The report was fair but he had lost his job after his boss found out about his criminal convictions. He shook my hand and left.

Newspaper reporters got used to many complaints in the course of their work. A story about a controversial building plan might echo to the applicant saying 'I know your Managing Director very well.' Investigating allegations that a garage was chucking away old engine oil in a haphazard and possibly illegal way would be met with 'We spend a lot of money advertising in your rag, you know.' For anyone to call the newspaper a 'rag' was a sure-fire way to irritate the journalist as it was nearly always used in the pejorative sense.

A friend of mine on another newspaper started his career in the 1960s when you had to provide your own typewriter in the office. It was also an era when new reporters were actually sent to funerals to get the names of the mourners. You would stand outside the church or crematorium at the end of the service and keep muttering in hushed and reverential tones: 'From the Gazette, could I have your name please?' At one funeral, a rather haughty lady looked at the reporter and said 'Gloucester'. This went in the funeral report as 'Mrs Gloucester', only for the Editor to get a call after publication to say it was actually the Duchess of Gloucester.

By the time I started in newspapers we did not have to go to funerals but got the undertakers to give a form to the bereaved. We would be amused by some of the spelling on these forms – the mourners included the deceased's two 'dautering laws'. There were forms for weddings as well, with predictable 'typos' slipping into our production process and thus laid out in black and white in the paper. 'The groom and his *bridge* will *love* at Drury Lane, Bicker.'

A vicar was offered the choice of two particular parishes in south Lincolnshire – the options were either to Bicker or Wrangle. Some Lincolnshire village names would not look out of place as characters in a P.G.Wodehouse book. How about Muckton Bottom and Claxby Pluckacre? Raymond Chandler or Evelyn Waugh surely had a character called Carlton Scroop after the village near Grantham? Then there is Dogdyke, Snitterby, Swineshead and Belchford. There is the happy couple in the Wolds – Mavis Enderby and Old Bolingbroke. In its early days, Radio Lincolnshire actually had a car sticker that read: 'I get it in Mavis Enderby' (Radio Lincolnshire that is…). Boothby Graffoe is a name which has been heard far and wide after being adopted by a comedian as his stage-name. 'Boothby' started his career with a weekly show on Radio Lincolnshire and claims to be the only comedian in the world named after a Lincolnshire village.

On the newspaper, I was sometimes sent out to these villages on Fridays to find stories by talking to those priests and postmasters. You stared hopefully at village notice boards before sliding into deserted pubs at lunchtime to tap up the tapster for local gossip. One landlady of ample bosom and rouged lips took a shine to me and plied me with halves of bitter and lines like 'Are you a roving or a raving reporter' and promised me an 'exclusive'. I made my excuses and left.

At the Red Lion in Bicker, I fell into brief conversation with an old man sitting at the bar and asked him if he was from round here. He looked momentarily shocked, grimaced and took his pipe out of his mouth. 'Nay lad. I'm not from round 'ere. I'm from Donington.' Two miles away. More than 40 years on, the same question would more likely elicit a reply like Poland or Romania. The Boston area now seems to be the place to go for the national media to reflect on the effects of immigration into the UK.

At BBC Radio Lincolnshire when the staffing allowed, I

would photocopy part of an Ordnance Survey map and draw a ring around several villagers excluding towns and send a young reporter out on the same mission. They surprised themselves by always coming back with interesting tales. One youngster was told by a villager that he ought to 'knock on that door over there as I'm told there is someone interesting living there.' He duly did and the occupant eyed him suspiciously before relenting and inviting him in. It was the folk rock musician Roy Harper, collaborator and friend of the Pink Floyd and Led Zeppelin, who had recently moved into the village. He gave an interview and some of his LPs to the reporter who had never heard of him. One of Harper's songs was titled 'One of those days in England.'

There is a village in Oxfordshire called Marsh Gibbon. Around 1980, its village football team scored 17 goals in a match. Reading the results on Radio Oxford's Saturday sport programme, the manager at the time Ted Gorton stumbled into this surprise result and 'corpsed', reeling off the other results while desperately and unsuccessfully trying to stifle laughter. 'Rather thrown by the Marsh Gibbon score, I fear.' Why did it have to be Marsh Gibbon and not any other team from a village with a less distinctive name?

Another near collapse occurred in a Radio Lincolnshire bulletin about the former RAF Fulbeck which was designated as a potential nuclear waste site in 1986, prompting a huge campaign against the proposal. The locals set up LAND – Lincolnshire Against Nuclear Dumping. Except in one bulletin, it came out as Nuclear 'Dumplings'. One of my colleagues read 'Brian Clough, the Forest Manager' as 'Brian Clough, the Foreign Minister' and one of my own radio bloopers made the *Today* programme one Christmas. I had said that the manager of Oxford United, Bill Asprey, would not be naming his team until a few minutes *after* the kick-off. On reflection, probably just as well.

The Inner Wheel Club was an international organisation that was founded to bring together the wives and daughters of members of the male-only Rotary Clubs. Every time it met in Boston, someone would send in a report for the paper. One week our headline read: 'Inner Wheel hears of New Zealand'. About bloody time. Did you know that, in December 1975, Bourne Conservative Women's Tea Club voted overwhelmingly to bring back capital punishment? They did, you know.

A village near Boston had its roads widened in 1974 but they did not move the telegraph poles as well. Consequently motorists were confronted with poles in the actual carriageway, hastily painted in white and given a flashing light. 'The police were particularly concerned at the situation in view of the recent fog', we reported in the paper. Bob Whitaker filmed it for local television and I provided the accompanying words but it actually made the national ITV *News at Ten*, introduced by the legendary Reginald Bosanquet with a lop-sided smile and twinkle in the eye. 'And finally.........it's enough to drive drivers up the pole'.....'We know about holes in the road – but poles?'

A topless dancer called Penny Lane worked with the Soul Time disco which had booked the council-owned Boston Assembly Rooms for one Saturday night in April 1975. A Mr Robinson, who clearly did not attend, contacted the newspaper to condemn what he called 'this degrading spectacle' and demanded to know if the council knew about young Penny. 'Am I to understand that this sort of function meets with the approval of our local body of administrators? If it was approved by the council, it would have been better if the building had been burned to the ground forever than to arise as such a tarnished Phoenix,' he said somewhat dramatically, referring to a fire in the building some ten years earlier.

He had not finished. 'In a world of lowered standards, of general lack of accountability and approaching moral morass, I think we still have a duty to cry in the wilderness and take a stand against this rot. We all know the cost of Salome's infamous dance – whose head goes on the plate this time?' This was all catnip for a local newspaper. One front page story sorted for that week.

It also read like one of the church reports that were submitted to the paper every week. One always contained the full diatribe from the visiting preacher about the world in trouble, sinful behaviour, sexual deviancy, drink, drugs, flashing flesh and the fire and brimstone that would rain down on those who turned away from God. Inevitably the Book of Revelations was drawn upon, with the Devil and the Unfaithful cast alive into a lake of fire with loud wailings and gnashing of teeth to be tormented day and night forever and ever. Sinners are all off to Fire and Damnation.

Every apocalyptic report ended with the same five words: 'Mrs Simpson played the organ.'

Young newspaper reporters were regularly expected to venture into things where they had no experience or qualifications. One such task was the 'death knock' – going to see a family who had lost a loved one to get some details about the life lost and hopefully borrow a cherished photograph for the paper. Sometime you used an intermediary like as the local priest or the undertaker. Other times, it was just you, nervously knocking on the door and wondering what kind of reception you would get from the bereaved. Nine times out of ten you were invited in, given a cup of tea and all the help you wanted. Photo albums were produced and life stories unpicked. You took it as a personal responsibility to ensure the photograph was returned.

No one taught us how to write reviews. We were just expected to deliver so many words by the entertainment page deadline. As these were usually about local people performing in front of other local people, you usually spared criticism and cranked up the compliments. A bad review of the efforts of the local am-dram society would have supporters turning up in reception saying 'How could you? It was for charity as well.'

While I was working out of the *Lincolnshire Standard*'s Sleaford office I was sent to review a play called 'Captain Carvello' at the little theatre on the base at the RAF College Cranwell. The comedy was written by the British writer Denis Cannan and first put on in 1950. I ended up praising the whole bloody lot including the man who played the Professor of Biology. He had a line stating that he did not get married because 'I would then be unable to view the tadpole objectively.' What a side-splitter. I reported incisively that he looked like Mr Brown (the actor Richard Wattis) who lived next door in Eric Sykes' television comedy of the time.

Bob Neish, a friend who succumbed to cancer at a cruelly young age, used to do the newspaper reviews for Boston Folk Club. If he was not around, I would sometimes stand in. If you were doing the review, you got in free, meaning more cash for that extra pint. Many respected musicians slogged round the folk circuit like Martin Simpson, Vin Garbutt, Jack Hudson, Dave Burland, Alistair Anderson, Richard Digance, Rosie Hardman, Brenda Wootton, Nic Jones, Wizz Jones and the brilliant 'Bolton Bullfrog' Bernard Wrigley. They always delivered a good night and never warranted a lukewarm review.

The first single I possessed was Cliff Richard's 'The Young Ones' (flip side 'We Say Yeah), given to me by an aunt after it hit the charts in 1962. It was a good song but that era, including rock and roll and skiffle, never really enthralled me. It was the soundtrack for the generation before me. So I was probably not the best person to be asked to review a Marty Wilde concert at the Regal Cinema in Boston in 1977. It was not a great evening for the organisers who lost the princely sum of £300. The turnout prompted the cancellation of Billy Fury a few months later as the promoters looked again at the Miki and Griff gig the previous year which had gone down so well in South Lincolnshire.

On the 'Wilde night', the support band arrived late and took to the stage without a sound check which meant the lead vocals were all but lost. An overlong interval led to slow hand-clapping. The delay was due to someone bringing the wrong adaptor which mean that Mr Wilde's microphone could not be plugged in. A frantic back-stage scramble eventually unearthed a replacement.

Marty Wilde (born Reginald Leonard Smith) worked his largely female audience very well. He dispensed with 'Teenager in Love' and 'Rubber Ball' quite early in the set, then surprisingly launched into Joni Mitchell's hippy anthem 'Woodstock'. A quick encore of 'At the Hop' and he was gone after clocking up about 40 minutes on stage. Photographer Bob Whitaker and I went back stage for a few comments and witnessed Mr Wilde being mobbed by a few ladies of a certain age. We ran a photograph in the paper of Marty with his daughter Kim, who must have been about 14 at the time and went on to success herself with her debut single 'Kids in America' making number 2 in the UK charts in 1981.

—w—

One of the regular assignments for the new reporter would be the Golden Wedding celebration. The newspaper would be contacted by a son or daughter to say that their parents, usually with old names like Herbert and Ida, were celebrating 50 years of matrimony. Off you would go with a photographer to ask the happy couple what their secret was and politely gulp down a sweet sherry or sweet martini with no mixer, poured into a glass that had not seen a tap for some time.

'Hello. I'm from *The Standard*', said the photographer on the doorstep. 'Congratulations on your 50 years of wedlock'. The woman gave him a look of utter disdain. 'My parents are in the lounge', she sighed.

These people were married in the mid-1920s, many with the Great War still fresh in the collective memory. Not for them the 'Roaring Twenties' and the Jazz age and the 'flappers' but a repetitive dull job for the man and babies and housework for the woman. They had stayed together through thick and thin because of a shared sense of humour and the children, even though she would say: 'I could knock his block off sometimes.' One couple told me: 'We don't fall out like that Elizabeth Taylor and Richard Burton. What's all that about then?'

They were a generation that 'made do' and were reluctant to throw things away. They kept used envelopes and old margarine containers and the elastic bands round their daily post 'just in case' they could be used again. They made new Christmas cards by recycling the ones from last year, cutting off the front and sticking it onto new card. My grandfather could barely comprehend the slogan for the new Access credit card which boasted: 'It takes the waiting out of wanting.'

Not long before I arrived at Radio Oxford, Burton and Taylor stayed at The Bear Hotel in Woodstock. Oxford journalist Colin Fenton was asked by some of the national newspapers to stake out the couple and feed any gossip into

Fleet Street. Colin became a fixture at the bar, eventually being offered a drink by Burton as Taylor stomped off to bed. It was by all accounts a long night. Richard Burton joined the RAF as a navigator at the age of 18 in 1944. Like Colin Curtis, he went to Canada for further training, but the war ended before he could gain any combat experience. He had to wait another two years before he got de-mobbed.

When the prominent Labour politician Tony Crosland fell ill in February 1977, he was taken to the Radcliffe Infirmary in Oxford. Once again Colin was asked by the nationals to hang around the hospital for updates on Crosland's condition. After five days of little or nothing to report, Colin gave up and went home. Shortly afterwards, Tony Crosland passed away. Colleagues speculated that he had clearly hung onto life, regularly asking the nursing staff 'Is that bloody journalist still outside?'

Colin's parents had both worked at the *Oxford Mail* and Colin became a freelance in the city, working for the nationals and doing shifts with us at Radio Oxford. In 1963 Colin, his brother Paton and Gordon Kitchen, who later became News Editor at Radio Oxford, got a call on the night of the Great Train Robbery. A contact in Forest Hill to the north east of Oxford had seen three vehicles speeding through the village in the middle of the night. The three jumped in the car and raced after the gang but never caught up with them. Probably for the best.

Pursuing his love of motorcycles and the TT Races, Colin retired to the Isle of Man. His daughter Alex told the *Oxford Mail* that all the years of hard drinking whiskey and smoking cigarettes caught up with him in 2013 when he succumbed to mouth and throat cancer. He was 76. Alex said: 'He was an exciting dad who was never dull or boring. He was also very kind and calm.' Colin reminded me of my early mentor in Lincolnshire, Bob Whitaker. A freelance journalist that you could learn from, not least holding your own at the bar while soaking up compelling yarns of reportage.

The Oxfordshire village of North Aston made the UK headlines for a week in July 1978 due to an armed siege involving a man and a child. The media set up camp next to the village green and awaited developments. A police sniper maintained cover above and behind the media pack. After a few days the man decided he wanted to make an appeal over the radio and Radio Oxford, under police supervision, duly obliged. Afterwards he said he meant on Radio 1. Throughout it all, a ram was tethered on the green, lazily chomping on the grass and eyeing the gathered media with an ovine insouciance.

After four or five days, the media was getting restless. The Radio Oxford radio car and a reporter was tied up at North Aston with nothing to report. Most of us put in a shift there. Suddenly on a Friday afternoon with the weekend looming, everyone decided they had had enough and packed up. The stand-off ended peacefully a short time later, with just an agency man there to record it.

The media and the police wondered aloud how many days they had wasted around the village green at North Aston. If they had packed up after a day, would that have been the end of it then? Veterans of the vigil were offered a tie designed by Colin Fenton – a ram with a rifle and a camera tripod crossed above it and the word 'NASA' underneath, standing not for the space agency but the North Aston Siege Association.

Chapter 12

Riders on the Storm 1942

Dawn on Tuesday 20th January 1942. Wellington bombers of 101 Squadron are scattered around the perimeter track at RAF Oakington, snow on their wings and cockpits. Ground crew grip mugs of hot cocoa and shiver against the icy blast. Soon they will go out to the silent bombers to clear away the snow and spark them into life again. Most of them will probably be needed tonight for a raid over Germany.

Elsewhere in the world, senior Nazi officials meet in the Berlin suburb of Wannsee to discuss the implementation of the 'Final Solution to the Jewish Question' – effectively relocation to the concentration camps and then extermination. The Japanese are invading Burma, having just taken large numbers of British troops as prisoners north of Singapore. Enemy aircraft continue to bomb Malta.

In the House of Commons, MPs discuss the idea of 'electrically recording' and then broadcasting important speeches about the war. Churchill was in favour as he had to repeat his Commons speeches for the BBC and this was an added strain. He felt the recordings at the time could then be broadcast to other countries around the world at the most convenient hours. Churchill said he would leave the idea to a free vote but the level of opposition meant that the idea never got off the ground. Permanent broadcasting of Parliament was not introduced until 1978.

Also on 20th January 1942, Churchill pays tribute in the Commons to Prince Arthur, the Duke of Connaught and Strathearn, who had died a few days earlier at the age of 91. The Duke was the brother of the King and the seventh child of Queen Victoria and Prince Albert.

On the other side of the Atlantic in Glen Ridge, New Jersey, a young lad called Edwin Aldrin is celebrating his 12th birthday. Years later the world would know him as 'Buzz' Aldrin, the second man to walk on the Moon. Four days earlier on 16th January 1942, Colin's RAF diary stated there had been a New Moon at 9.32 pm when the moon would not be visible. The news from the USA revolved around the death in an air crash on the 16th of the actress Carole Lombard. Aged 33, she had just completed work on the film 'To Be or Not To Be', a satire about Nazism and the war.

The 'Orbat' for 101 Squadron is marked 'Secret.' It is Battle Order Serial number 107 and signed by the Officer Commanding of the squadron, Wing Commander T.H.L.Nicholls, who had taken over only six days earlier. The details will be revealed at the briefing early in the afternoon.

The aircraft that will be used tonight are run up in the morning and given an air test – a brief flight in the vicinity of the airfield to ensure everything works. Once they are back on the ground, the ground crew continue to work on them as a long line of low trailers edges towards them carrying the bombs from the station bomb store. The aircraft carries the bombs in cells in its bomb bay which is now open. Each trailer is manoeuvred under the Wellington and each bomb is lifted by a hand-operated winch until the lug on the bomb engages with the hook of the bomb carrier which is then snapped shut.

For tonight's raid, each Wellington is carrying two containers of 4 pound incendiaries and six 500 pound bombs fused for a 0.025 second delay. The bombs are adjusted to ensure they do not wobble or vibrate when the aircraft gets into the air. The fusing link is connected up. This enables the bomb aimer to make the bombs 'live' before they are dropped. The fuel bowser arrives to top up the tanks. Elsewhere the oxygen bottles are double-checked and the astrodome and the Perspex canopies of the turrets and cockpit are polished. In the heat of battle, one speck of dirt in the gunner's eye-line could be mistaken for an enemy fighter. Any distraction could be the difference between life and death. The armourers fill the ammunition tanks with the long snake-like belts of machine-gun bullets.

Six Wellingtons will leave Oakington after dark tonight. The 36 men who will be on board are summoned to the station's briefing room at 2pm to hear about the target and the routes there and back. They will hear about the danger spots for anti-aircraft fire and the sort of weather they can expect, including the 'predicted winds'. They note the diversion airfields available if and when they get back to 'Blighty'. They will recall a publicity film released by the Air Ministry in July 1941 called 'Target for Tonight' about a real Wellington bomber crew facing a night time mission over Germany.

Tonight's target for 101 Squadron are the docks at Emden on the north coast of Germany. It is an important port for the German military and one of the places that builds U-Boat submarines. Twenty five bombers have been allocated to this raid. There are 20 Wellingtons including the six from 101 Squadron at Oakington, along with five Hampdens. Good visibility is reported over the target with no cloud. Once the bombers leave the British coast, the route there and back will be over the sea most of the time.

In the briefing room, there is a sign on the wall. 'It is better to keep your mouth shut and let people think you are a fool than to open it and remove all doubt.' Once the briefing is over, there is no contact with the outside world. Careless talk costs lives.

The crews pore over maps and discuss the routes. As the crow flies, the distance from RAF Oakington to Emden is about 310 miles. That direct route would take them over Texel, the largest and most populated of the Dutch Frisian Islands off the north Holland coast. However it is said to be well defended with anti-aircraft batteries and searchlights. The Wellingtons will therefore take a slightly longer route further north near Terschelling before turning south into the estuary of the River Ems and the Emden docks.

The 'Orbat' for 101 Squadron's six
Wellington crews on 20th January 1942

The 36 men troop off to their messes for the last meal before the mission. The meal was often irreverently called 'The Last Supper'. The irony was not lost on the clergyman's son from south Lincolnshire. As they are on operations, they can have an egg if eggs are available. Did anyone repeat the 'gallows humour' of asking a colleague if he can have his egg tomorrow if he fails to return?

Eggs and bacon! This luxury meal, which is rarely available to civilians, is one small consolation for the crews about to go to war. Civilians might get one or two eggs a month. It is also possibly one of the worst meals that they could have as the fried food creates gas in the human system. As they ascend into the thinner air some three miles up, they can swell up a little and feel uncomfortable. However to remove this privilege would cause an uproar among the aircrew.

They wait in their rooms for the call to action. Henry Hall's 'Teddy Bear's Picnic' and Vera Lynn's 'We'll meet again' would have been on the wireless, along with Bing Crosby and Glen Miller. Colin put 'Sospiri' on his 78 rpm gramophone player and stared at the ceiling, cigarette smoke curling up above as he contemplated the coming hours in the air. He looked forward to seeing his fiancée Doris at the weekend. 'Sospiri', meaning 'Sighs', was written by Edward Elgar as the First World War broke out. It is surely one of the saddest and most beautiful pieces of music ever written.

As dusk falls, the Wellington crews gather their flying clothing and their rations for the flight. They wear their battle dress so that, if they bale out over Germany, they can claim 'Prisoner of War' status and not be shot as spies. Over their uniform they might pull on a sweater and then the Irvine jacket which includes the 'Mae West', the inflatable life jacket named after the buxom Hollywood actress who was 48 in January 1942. On their feet, silk socks are worn under woollen stockings and the flying boots lined with lamb's wool. They will not forget their flying helmet with its oxygen mask and radio links, and they check their parachute bag is to hand.

Each crew member is given a bag of rations for the flight.

The contents will depend on what is available but ideally some sandwiches, biscuits, chocolate, an apple or orange, barley sugar, chewing gum and raisins. Some will keep the chocolate for later to impress a WAAF or one of the local 'popsies'. They also clutch a thermos flask each, filled to the brim with tea or cocoa. They probably won't touch it until they are well on their way home.

The nerves are suppressed. They are just anxious to get on with it. This is no time for 'LMF' which stood for 'Low Moral Fibre.' Airmen who cracked under the pressure of repeated night sorties into flak and fighters were not offered counselling. They were removed immediately from the squadron, charged with LMF, given menial jobs, demoted to the lowest rank in the RAF (AC2) and sometimes imprisoned.

One of the crew idly wondered if any of his chums had been out with a 'chop girl' the night before. This was the name given to an unfortunate woman whose first dates never returned from the next mission. Even the most beautiful woman would be avoided by a crew if she got that unlucky reputation. Superstition was rife. Some of the men stuffed a pair of their girlfriend's knickers or a silk stocking in their flying jacket as a lucky charm. Others insisted on urinating on the tail wheel of the bomber before they scrambled aboard, much to the chagrin of the chief engineering officer who persistently pointed out its corrosive effects.

The man who first flew the Wellington prototype got his nickname from this practice. Joseph 'Mutt' Summers used to shower the tail wheel or skid of any aircraft he was testing which his friends likened to a dog marking its territory. Summers, who played a pivotal part in the development of the bouncing bomb and is played by actor Patrick Barr in *The Dambusters* film, took the first Wellington aloft in June 1936 with Barnes Wallis on board.

The small lorry heads off round the perimeter track,

dropping off crews at their allocated aircraft. The silhouettes of the Wellingtons loom out of the dark winter sky. The ground crew bustle around, ensuring the crew hatch door under the nose is open and the ladder in place. The six crew disappear into the fuselage and go to their positions. The hatch is pulled shut and they pray that the next time it opens, it will be to let them drop back down onto the good earth of Oakington and not to plunge out in the night sky over the sea or enemy territory and hit the silk.

The six Wellingtons of 101 Squadron are divided into A and B flights for tonight's mission. In A flight are X9920 captained by Sgt Callender, R1801 and Sgt Dowling, and Z1110 under Sgt Chapman. B flight has R1780 captained by Sgt Lunt, Z1081 under Pilot Officer Clough and W5716 under Sgt Denning. Each bomber has six men on board. Two other Wellingtons are scheduled to undertake a couple of hours night flying training and another has been allocated to sea rescue duties for any aircraft that comes down 'in the drink' as it returns from Germany. These also wait as reserves in case one of the six goes unserviceable at the last minute.

Pilot Officer Colin Curtis is the second pilot in Z1110, working to the captain Sgt Peter Lewis Chapman. This 21 year old is from Ware in Hertfordshire. Chapman is the 'skipper' of the aircraft and responsible for its crew. His second pilot Colin, although commissioned as an officer in the RAFVR and a year older, defers to him. Rank does not indicate seniority or experience. Wellingtons are regularly captained by a Sergeant with an officer as his second pilot. The whole crew are in the Volunteer Reserve.

The navigator (called Observer in the early days of the war) and bomb aimer is Sgt Alan Herbert Hancox, at only 20 the youngest of the six. He is the son of Herbert and Maud Hancox of Southall in Middlesex. He unpacks his bag of protractors, dividers, coloured pencils and Very pistol cartridges. He will have his sextant to help him navigate by the stars if they are visible tonight. Spread out on his table in the aircraft are the 'flimsies' which have the type-written procedures to follow if they get lost or have to make emergency radio broadcasts. They are called 'flimsies' as they are made of rice paper and can be eaten to stop the enemy getting their hands on them.

The eldest on board is 27 year old Sgt Arthur Sidney Spackman, a wireless operator and air gunner and the son of Leonard and Maud Spackman of Forest Gate in east London. The two other air gunners are also 21. They are Sgt Francis Ernest Dunn, who could also double-up as a wireless operator, and Sgt Herbert William Mantle, son of Sydney and Ella Mantle of Sittingbourne in Kent. Mantle had given up his job with Bowaters, the paper and pulp company, to join the Royal Air Force.

The crew have all memorised where their instruments are and where to find the required handle, lever or switch. Lighting is kept to a minimum or completely dimmed so that they do not attract unwelcome attention in the night sky. The cockpit instruments emit a faint green glow.

The Wellington that they are to take to Germany had recently been on the books of 311 Squadron at RAF East Wretham north east of Thetford. The squadron personnel had been mostly Czechoslovak aircrew who had escaped from Europe after the fall of France and wanted to take the fight to the Germans from British soil. It had got its crews home from many missions over Germany. By the time 311 Squadron transferred to Coastal Command three months later, the Czechs had flown over 1000 sorties and dropped more than 1,300 tons of bombs.

Z1110 now carries the 101 Squadron identification letters SR next to the RAF roundel on the fuselage. Within the squadron, it has been allocated the letter 'A' for Able or Apple. It was last used on the 8th January for the raid on Wilhelmshaven.

—m—

For many Wellington crews, the first sense that strikes them when they climb aboard is the smell of dope, the plasticised lacquer that is applied to fabric-covered aircraft. It tightened the fabric stretched over the airframe and made it airtight and weatherproof. It is cramped with the crew having to clamber over the main spar of the wings. Once the two Bristol Pegasus engines are wound up, the noise is horrendous.

Two Wellingtons over East Anglia head off for Germany. From an original painting 'Moonlight over Norfolk' courtesy of Denis Pannett (see deadlines101.com)

The quiet calm of Oakington airfield is broken by the sound of these 12 engines spluttering into life. The pilots apply the brakes and push forward the throttles to check the engines are producing full power. Around each aircraft, the crew share some idle banter to dispel the apprehension of going to war. They are now anxious to be on their way. At the given signal, the first of the Wellingtons under Sgt Callender lurches forward and lumbers off its hardstanding onto the perimeter track. The ground crews salute or wave, giving a 'thumbs up.' A small group of WAAFs have come out to see them off.

The Wellingtons will take off at two minute intervals. Sgt Chapman follows the lead aircraft to the end of the runway which is now lit by 'goose-neck' flares which can be seen at ground level but are covered on top to stop them being visible to any enemy aircraft overhead. Lined up on runway 23 into the prevailing south westerly wind, Wellington Z1110 awaits the steady green light from the Perspex dome on the black and white chequer-board control caravan. It will take around 15 minutes to get the six Wellingtons away.

The official take-off time for Z1110 is given as 17.54. Chapman pushes forward the throttles and the engine roar increases as they reach full power for take-off. The propellers cut through the air only a couple of feet from his cockpit windows. The bombed-up 'Wimpy' accelerates slowly down the 6000 feet of runway. Just after the half way mark and nudging 80 miles an hour, Sgt Chapman pulls back on the control column and the bomber crawls into the air. Once safely airborne with the wheels up, he banks it round to the right and sets course. The front gunner can now take up his position as the bomber is airborne. At 7000 feet the Norfolk coast, somewhere near Cromer, slides away behind them. They pray that they will see it again hours later.

The six bombers are in two loose formations of three, visible to each other but not too close to avoid collisions. Each captain is responsible for getting his aircraft there and back regardless of the others heading for the same target.

Chapman continues to climb through 10,000 feet. He settles the Wellington at 13,000 feet, some 5000 feet below its official ceiling height. They are travelling at around 210 miles an hour.

The crew constantly worry about ice forming on the wings and control surfaces. They are breathing oxygen through their face masks, knowing that ice crystals could form in the tubes and block the air flow. Ice could also affect the guns and the engines. They have left a frozen Cambridgeshire and are heading for a frozen continent. Temperatures in north Holland that day had been minus nine degrees centigrade.

That winter was severe enough in the Frisian (or Wadden) Islands for the *Elfstedentocht* to take place only two days after Z1110 flew over the area. This was a 120 mile long ice skating tour between the 11 historic cities of the province. It still attracts thousands of skaters even though they only get 48 hours notice that the natural ice is thick enough (6 inches at least) all the way along the course. Sometimes the event can be held on consecutive years. Sometimes there was a gap of up to 20 years before it could be staged. The weather of January 1942 was one of those years when the ice was thick enough for the *Elfstedentocht* to go ahead, and despite the German occupation.

The gunners test their machine guns, creating for the first time that night the smell of cordite throughout the aircraft. The rear gunner checks the catch on the turret door which lies between him and his parachute. It is too bulky to wear at his war station. When he collected it, he had to endure the usual joke from the orderly yet again. 'If it doesn't work, bring it back and we'll give you another one.'

Colin, as he is not the pilot at the moment, checks the fuel flow to the engines for the Skipper then stands up in the astrodome, scanning the night sky for enemy fighters.

Chapman has engaged 'George' – the basic autopilot which still needs monitoring in case it wanders off course. Two hours into the flight, the Dutch coast is ahead with the odd light visible. Away to the south, German searchlights can be seen probing the sky, converging at around 15,000 feet.

Past the islands in the Wadden Sea off the Dutch coast toward Borkum, the Wellington turns south. The captain has 'desynchronised' the two engines, making them rev differently to defeat the sound locators on the German anti-aircraft guns which need a constant sound to work properly. He asks Colin to take over briefly as he needs to use the Elsan. He clambers down the fuselage, over the main spar and walks down the narrowing wooden floor to the gentleman's comfort room. There was little privacy on the chemical toilet which is set in a wooden platform on the left hand side of the aircraft. The rear gunner scans the night sky but if he cares to look back into the aircraft, he could catch his colleague with his trousers down.

Sgt Hancox leaves his navigator's desk and slides forward to the bomb-aimer position under the front gunner's feet. He is now in charge of where the aircraft goes as he lines it up for the attack. He calls 'Bombs Fused' and reports the bomb doors are open, creating more vibration. He is terse. 'Left, Left' he calls or a single 'Right' and the pilot responds. The word 'Left' is repeated to distinguish it from the solitary 'Right' above the cacophony of the aircraft noise and the anti-aircraft 'flak' exploding around them. This is the most dangerous part of the mission when, for several minutes, the aircraft must fly straight and level to ensure accuracy on the bomb-run and a steady photograph off the recently introduced night camera in the nose.

They are now really riding the fire storm. The 'flak' is incessant. The Wellington is shuddering. The noise is cacophonous.

Emden docks are in sight. Hancox calls 'Steady, Steady'

then 'Bombs Gone!' There is a flash of magnesium as the night camera freezes the moment and the bomb doors start to close. The Wellington pitches as the weight of the bomb load falls away. Chapman banks the bomber away and 'jinks' it to avoid the deadly lines of anti-aircraft 'flak' still streaming up at them. The compass rolls round to 300 degrees towards the north-west and Chapman levels out. A couple of the crew risk some rations, still anxiously scanning the night sky for predators determined to kill them. They are heading home for bacon and eggs again, a hot bath and hopefully a long sleep if the adrenalin will let go of them. They yearn for the first cigarette after landing.

In the darkness on the ground, there is a lot of activity at the German radar station called Tiger near West Tershelling village off the northern Dutch coast. In an underground bunker, a Jägerleitoffizier (German fighter controller) is monitoring the radar returns on the Freya system. This is an early warning radar developed by Germany and named after the Norse Goddess Freyja. It had first been used successfully against 22 Vickers Wellingtons on a daylight raid in December 1939 when it picked up the formation more than 110 kilometres away. The German military was impressed and ordered more radar units to be deployed, including one on Terschelling island.

Across the water on the Dutch mainland was the airfield at Leeuwarden which had opened just before the war. After the Germans invaded the Netherlands in 1940, they commandeered such airfields. Leeuwarden was now home to Luftwaffe Squadron 6 of the night fighter wing Nachtjagdgeschwader 2 (NJG 2). The Wellingtons and Hampdens heading from Emden are within range of the Terschelling radar and it picks them up. The fighter controller is in touch with a single German night fighter which had been allocated a sector off the coast not far from the base. It is the only German fighter in that area – a tactic which had been introduced by the Luftwaffe after numerous 'friendly fire' incidents.

Oberleutnant Ludwig Becker and his radar operator Oberfeldwebel Joseph Straub are in a Bf110 tonight. As 9pm approached, the radar operator on the ground and Straub in the back of the night fighter are now giving Becker a heading to intercept the first RAF Wellington as its makes its way home.

One of the Wellington crew thinks he caught a flash of something in the night sky. It looked like a twin-engined aircraft but was smaller and faster than a Wellington. Is the cold and noise and the tension making him imagine things? He radios the Skipper about his concern. The Captain hands over the flying to his second pilot and checks in again with all of his crew. He puts his head into the astrodome on top of the Wellington and scans the night sky. They had left the searchlights and the flak behind them but are the night fighters lurking out there?

A deadly line of tracer fire flashes across the darkness. The machine guns in the nose of the German fighter are clattering, ripping into one of the Wellingtons. Becker had been guided onto Z8370 from No. 12 Squadron which had taken off from Binbrook in Lincolnshire. The aircraft crashes on a beach on Terschelling at 9pm. Two of the crew are killed and the remaining four taken prisoner. Seven minutes later, another Wellington is attacked by Becker. Z1207 of No. 142 Squadron, which had taken off from RAF Waltham near Grimsby, crashes with the loss of all on board. He is creating havoc amongst the Wellingtons which had attacked Emden.

Becker was the first Luftwaffe pilot to shoot down an enemy aircraft using the Lichtenstein Air Intercept radar whose prototype had been installed on a Dornier Do215. He had also developed a tactic of approaching his targets from below where the rear gunners could not shoot at him and where he could fire his guns at the bomber's fuel tanks. Now, on the evening of 20th January 1942, he had claimed his ninth and tenth 'kills' and he was not finished yet.

Thirty minutes later, Becker opens fire on Wellington Z1110. He claims the 'kill' at 21.37. The bomber, with Chapman, Curtis, Hancox, Spackman, Dunn and Mantle inside, may have exploded, killing them all instantly. They were probably still climbing away from the target behind them. They may have had time to bale out if control had been lost or an engine was on fire but they did not. If they had gone low to shake off the attacking Becker and Straub, they may not have had time to use their parachutes.

The timings and stories from other survivors that night confirm that the Wellingtons were on their way back having successfully dropped their bombs. No one knows what happened to Colin's aircraft beyond Becker claiming that he shot it down. Nothing was ever found of the bomber. No bodies were ever washed up on Terschelling.

Was Becker's action helped by search lights and flak-ships, often converted barges equipped with anti-aircraft guns? Did Becker take out an engine and control wires, leaving the bomber uncontrollable? Were half the crew killed by the first wave of machine gunfire and the subsequent explosions around them? Were the cockpit instruments smashed, leaving the pilots disorientated? Did one of them try and put the Wellington into a spiralling dive to get away from Becker?

Were they badly injured or burnt in the attack, facing lost limbs and shot away faces as the bomber headed for the water? Did one or more get out but then drown in the cruel sea off the Dutch Friesian Islands? The official records state that the Wellington crashed in 'Northsea' and it is listed as 'FTR' – Failed To Return. The six men have forever been recorded in a stark dead line as 'MIA' – Missing In Action.

Chapter 13

The Royal Rota

A couple of months after starting at the *Lincolnshire Standard*, I was given a press release to follow up. It was about someone from the area who was the National Accounts Executive for a confectionary and cake-making company in the south of England. Its solemn headline announced: 'BOSTON MAN FOR PRINCESS ANNE'S WEDDING CAKE'. Surely just a picture story.

On a warm sunny June afternoon in 1977, the Princess had lunch at Waddington and watched a display by a Vulcan, then climbed aboard her sparkling scarlet helicopter for the short hop down to Boston. The Queen's Flight Wessex touched down on the playing field of Boston High School for Girls at 2.17pm (two minutes behind schedule) and HRH started an afternoon of walkabouts among her mother's subjects.

'Bells ring out a Boston welcome' and 'Princess walks the happiness trail' were just two of the gushing *Lincolnshire Standard* headlines that week as we reflected the visit of Princess Anne to open the new Pilgrim Hospital at Boston. Another one read 'Walkabout in park on happiness day'. The Queen's Silver Jubilee that year was already winding up the population into a frenetic monarchist mood, except for the Sex Pistols of course.

With our pink cardboard Royal Rota passes flapping

from our lapels, I joined my colleagues Pam Browne and Pat Ashberry trailing round after the Princess at the hospital and in the town centre. People were squealing, cheering, losing their minds and forgetting their names.

Along with the photographers, we pounced on people to whom the Princess had spoken. 'What did she say to you?… 'What do you think about meeting the Princess?'…'What did *you* say to her?' Some could not answer, others fell gibbering into the arms of friends or relatives. More than a handful forgot who they were and we had to ask their friends for their name. The Press Association paid me £4.70 for copy on 'Princess opens hospital.' The Happiness Trail indeed.

I found Sgt Terry Holmes from RAF Benson in Oxfordshire who organised five three-man teams to travel around the UK ahead of the arrival by a Queen's Flight helicopter. His team covered crash duties, crowd control, marking the landing site and maintaining the ground to air radio link with the Wessex crew. 'We always have to be prepared for emergencies, though in the eight years I've been doing the job I've never had one – and I wouldn't tell you if I had!' he smiled. 'Of course,' he added, 'In an emergency everybody gets the same treatment – Royalty are no different.' Yeah, right.

The Princess was accompanied by the Lord Lieutenant of Lincolnshire, Captain Sir Henry Nevile. Years later at BBC Radio Lincolnshire, I sent our new young female reporter to interview the good Captain about something in the news. He opened the front door of his country pile near Lincoln and looked at the BBC representative and said: 'My, you *are* a pretty little thing, aren't you?' Our reporter bit her lip but let rip with a fine apoplectic outburst on her return to the radio station. Nevile's quaint, old fashioned greeting was supposed to be a chivalrous compliment but of course came across as nothing of the sort in the early 1990s. The reporter went on to great things with Sky News.

The Labour MP Willie Hamilton, who represented Scottish seats in Fife for many years, is best remembered for his stridently anti-royalist views, which he set out in detail in his book *My Queen and I*. He had irreverent names for most of the Royal family, including calling Princess Margaret a 'floozy', although he did admire the Queen Mother. Princess Margaret was the Honorary Commandant of RAF Coningsby and, by coincidence, Willie Hamilton retired to a town not far from the base.

We discovered this controversial figure had, for his twilight years, chosen the genteel splendour of Woodhall Spa, famous for its golf course and the Petwood Hotel which had served as the Officer's Mess for the Dambusters squadron for the last 18 months of the war. However he became somewhat coy in his retirement and I do not recall him ever being persuaded to comment on Royal issues for Radio Lincolnshire. So we never got our opening line: 'A Lincolnshire man has dismissed today's Royal visit as…'

Benson village was the home of a pioneering meteorologist William Henry Dines who started his weather watching in 1915. Despite the fogs that roll into the area off the River Thames, the RAF built an airfield at Benson just before the war and it remains open today as one of the RAF's main helicopter bases. At BBC Radio Oxford around 1980, we dialled up the Benson met office and its forecasters like Harry Petitt two or three times a day to get a 'live' run through of the forecast for the South Midlands. Fog aside, Benson also records some of the lowest temperatures in Britain (minus 18c in January 2010 for example). It has its own micro-climate due to its location by the Thames and the local soil full of gravel and sand which allows the ground to cool rapidly at night.

I spent an afternoon in an RAF Wessex helicopter from Benson in 1981, although it was in considerably less sparkling condition than the sprightly Queen's Flight variant across the airfield. The Wessex Training Flight had just moved into Benson to leave more room at RAF Odiham for the arrival of the new big Chinooks. Wessex pilots spent eight weeks on the course learning how to 'fight' with their machine rather than just fly it.

Part of the training involved picking up and dropping off troops, thus giving the crews the opportunity to learn how the Wessex flew differently when it was empty down the back compared with having a dozen heavily armed and fully kitted troops on board. For my trip, I was in the second of two Wessex 'helos' which were off to RAF Halton near Aylesbury where volunteers had been assembled to play pretend soldiers for the afternoon. In fact most of them *had* volunteered. The chance to fly around in helicopters was a welcome change for the technical training cadets and the off-duty nurses from the RAF hospital there.

A picture of me interviewing one of the pilots appeared in the service newspaper *RAF News*. With my Uher (German-made) reel-to-reel tape recorder hanging at my side, the article described me as 'an intrepid young reporter' (we were always intrepid or roving) and headlined it all 'Radio Oxford visits Benson'. My overriding concern during the four hours or so was hanging on to that Uher in flight. The big side door of the Wessex was open and as the aircraft banked round the grass airfield at Halton and lurched in to pick up or deplane the troops – either on the ground or in the hover by rope – the Uher acquired a mind of its own, not least when I tried to shout commentary into the lip-microphone attached to it.

The flight crew always needed to know exactly how many

troops were due to board their aircraft so that they could calculate such things as take-off weight. On one exercise, one of the crew checked with a very pompous Army officer about the number of men about to scramble on board and was told there were 12. However, the helicopter crewman counted 14 waiting for the signal and checked again. 'Exactly what I said. 12 *men*, plus my sergeant and me.'

In the cockpit of an Andover, the twin-engined transport that the Queen's Flight operated from Benson in the 1970s and 1980s, a Royal consort was in the right hand seat. The captain asked him if his Royal spouse, who was back in the cabin, would be interested in coming up front to the flight deck. 'Oh no, don't worry. Frankly if it doesn't fart or neigh, she is not really interested' came the reply. The same Queen's Flight captain was in his hotel room during a Royal visit abroad when his room phone rang. 'Is my bloody husband there?' demanded a female voice with a somewhat familiar regal lilt.

Most RAF bases had some Royal connection which meant a 'state visit' at some time or other, requiring an awful lot of work, drill practice, rebuilding, change of routine and a check that plenty of the correct tipple (usually gin) was on hand in the Officer's Mess. The RAF declined to comment that it had sprayed the grass green for one Royal visit. However in the hot dry summer of 1976 (the year that Dennis Howell was appointed as Minister for Drought) the grass around the Officers' Mess did look suspiciously lush compared to the brown arid scorched earth elsewhere around Lincolnshire.

Ahead of a Queen visit to the RAF College at Cranwell, someone decided that one corner of a barrack block that the Monarch was due to pass was unsightly so a false corner was built, blocking the doors to two cadet rooms. It meant that the two occupants had to scramble in and out of their windows until the visit was all over. And the media always spared a thought – if not a penny for them – for the hapless female police or WRAF officer who had to guard the washroom allocated to the Royal visitor, ensuring no one else went near it.

The Royal Rota was a centrally organised pool system to enable relevant media to cover Royal engagements. As soon as it was announced that one of the Windsors was coming to your patch, you submitted an application for a place in the pool which would be ahead of or trailing behind the regal visitor. The national newspaper reporters were always bolder than the locals, shouting at Prince Charles: 'Are you enjoying your visit, Sir?' As if he would turn round and say it was a bloody nightmare and everything smelt of fresh paint.

Following the Queen around the sprawling Army base at Bicester in Oxfordshire at the end of the 1970s, I ended up on the media bus sitting next to the photographer who took the famous shot of Her Majesty's Secretary of State for Defence apparently fast asleep at the Queen's Silver Jubilee Review of the Royal Air Force at Finningley in 1977. Fred Mulley was sitting next to the Queen, eyes closed and head tipped towards her and resting in his left palm, apparently at peace with the world. The MoD said that he had momentarily closed his eyes but the photographer was adamant he was out for the count, confirmed by video now on line.

Having a small sleep during an exercise was referred to in the RAF as having 'a Fred Mulley' after that photo went round the world. The magazine *Private Eye* mischievously suggested that Mulley was guilty of treason as he had slept with the Queen. The Defence Secretary, like many before and after him, clearly had little interest in military aircraft because what was going on above him was enough to convince any enthusiast that they had died and gone to heaven. Vulcans flanked by Canberras, Nimrods with Phantoms and Buccaneers, Harriers and Jaguars, Victors with Lightnings and Phantoms on their wings and 22 Jet Provosts in a '25' formation. And they made a bit of noise, you know.

—ᴡ—

Princess Diana was the Honorary Air Commodore for RAF Wittering near Stamford between 1985 and 1996. For the first six months of 1996, her Media Advisor was Jane Atkinson who was born in the Lincolnshire market town of Sleaford. Not long after Jane resigned, I persuaded her to do a sort of *Desert Island Discs* programme with me for Radio Lincolnshire. We talked about her whole life but obviously it was the Royal connection which provided the peg for the programme. She was discreet about her time working for the Princess but gave an intriguing insight into how her own life had changed in those six months.

Jane was one of several head-hunted candidates who were interviewed just after the Princess of Wales had done the famous *Panorama* interview with Martin Bashir. They were not told initially who was the 'client' but eventually Jane met the Princess for a 'quite formal' final interview. As soon as she was appointed, the media firestorm started for her and her phone did not stop ringing. Her own career and experience was picked over and she was 'door-stepped' outside her own home.

At times she was paid just to say 'No comment' such as when the media got obsessed about whether or not the Princess had cellulite issues. The daily phone calls from journalists to Jane varied between a minimum of 30 to a maximum of 100.

When she went to a friend's wedding, she switched off her phone for a couple of hours. When she switched it on again, there were about 30 voicemail messages from the media to wade through.

She said she found Princess Diana 'quite charming' but six months in the hothouse of the media's relentless interest and pursuit of her was enough. She also found that her own PR company was being neglected as her time was fully taken up with Royalty. Rumours abounded that she was off, with *The Sun* newspaper saying she was about to be axed. On the day it was announced she was leaving, there were 20 reporters at her front door and she had to be smuggled back into her own home 'unceremoniously' through the garage. Just over a year later, the Princess of Wales was fatally injured in the road accident in Paris.

A friend, the singer Lois Lane, was also born in Sleaford and agreed to talk about her life and pick some music for another radio programme with me. Born Lois Wilkinson, she formed The Caravelles with Andrea Simpson and they had a hit single in 1963 called 'You don't have to be a baby to cry'. The Americans were particularly keen on them, with that single making number three in the US charts and a follow-up called 'Have you ever been lonely?' making the Top 20. The Caravelles were on the same bill when The Beatles performed their first ever concert in the United States at the Washington Coliseum in February 1964. The two girls shared the same dressing room (although not at the same time) as Ringo and Paul. Lois later went solo and carved out a successful career as a jazz singer, regularly appearing at the famous Ronnie Scott's jazz club in London, on television shows such as the BBC's 'That's Life' and with the Barron Knights comedy group.

Given time, Jennifer Saunders may have got the call. 'Edina Monsoon' was born in Sleaford as well, sweetie. Her father was an RAF pilot who rose to the rank of Air Marshal.

—ɯ—

Eric Spencer fell asleep with the RAF in 1977 as well as Fred Mulley. Eric was one of the two staff photographers at the *Lincolnshire Standard* in Boston. Eric and I joined the RAF parachute display team The Falcons in their C-130 Hercules for a couple of jumps over Lincolnshire on the weekend of the Queen's Silver Jubilee. There was an air show on at Coningsby and we joined the Falcons there, introduced first to their leader at the time Simon Bales, one of those surnames that resonates with the holder's day to day work.

The Hercules took off and the team jumped out over Coningsby through a break in the cloud at 2,500 feet. Conditions were really not very good and the 'Herkybird' had to make three run-ins before the team was cleared to jump. On the flight deck for the low pass along the crowd line, I failed to remember it concluded with a steep climb, grabbing the nearest metal support as my knees buckled. We landed to pick up the team for their second jump over Central Park in Boston. The drop zone team were already hurtling off to Boston in their Land Rover to set up the markers in the park.

On the flight deck, the crew took in Boston, again from only 2,500 feet. Boston Stump in the rain was the only threat. 'Where's that steeple? I see it – don't lose it,' said the co-pilot, wearing a Silver Jubilee hat under his head-set. Someone else said: 'That steeple looks fairly well away from the DZ zone, well it's....... '. They have studied maps and aerial photos of the area but the Stump of St Botolphs was now facing them directly – for years a visual reference point for pilots but also a potential hazard on the rain-lashed flatlands of south Lincolnshire.

For the second time within a couple of hours, The Falcons took the leap and all landed safely in Central Park. Our Hercules did another low pass in salute – this time over the centre of Boston ('Hmm, may be a few complaints about that one' muttered someone). We pulled up and headed for Cranwell to hold, awaiting clearance to recover back at Coningsby in between the air display slots. At that point, I see Eric Spencer, who ran the Air Training Corps in Skegness, sat down the back, eyes closed and asleep and oblivious to tremendous noise of the four engines. Job done.

Who else passed through Boston in the Queen's Silver Jubilee year of 1977? Ted Heath was the chief guest at the annual dinner dance of the Boston Conservative Club. I reported insightfully that his speech was amusing and undramatic and that, according to some present, he was 'not as tall as he looked on television.' Tom Baker, the current Doctor Who, came to sign copies of his book for hordes of humanoids in a local superstore, as did Arthur Askey. The BBC *Nationwide* presenter Frank Bough (famous then only for his cardigans and unflappable presentation) accepted an invitation to speak to Boston Ladies' Lunch Club, and Manchester United stars Gordon Hill and Steve Coppell helped support a local sports centre.

A teenager called Sharon Whitelam was crowned as Boston's Jubilee Queen in a glittery night at the Boston Gliderdrome, a venue that had seen Jimi Hendrix (25 March 1967), Otis Redding, Elton John, Stevie Wonder, The Kinks, Marc Bolan and T-Rex over the years but on that night settled for Mr Kenneth Ball and his Jazzmen.

While all this was going on, Bert would have been lurking if he was not in prison. Bert was a familiar figure at Boston magistrates court where he regularly appeared to face a number of minor offences over the years. He often slept rough or got lodgings from some sympathetic local or a charity.

Bert would often try and get into prison for Christmas by stealing something like a bottle of milk in full view of a uniformed representative of the Lincolnshire Constabulary, only to be hugely disappointed when the magistrates adjourned sentence until *after* Christmas 'for reports'. For Bert, prison at Christmas meant good food, the festive telly and a warm bed.

On one occasion, some local teenagers tried to cash a cheque in a Market Place bank but the cashier refused, saying the cheque was not signed. The youngsters came out of the bank to see 'Uncle Bertie' loitering without much intent and got him to sign it. They went back into the bank and proffered the cheque again, only for the cashier to call a constable who charged Bert with fraud.

Standing beside some scrap metal, Bert was asked by a passer-by if the metal was his and he said it was. The man offered to buy it and Bert settled for ten pounds and wandered off. As the new owner was loading it onto his pick-up truck, the actual owner appeared, demanding to know why he was stealing his scrap. He replied he had just bought it from the owner. 'But *I* am the owner!,' said the owner. A few days later, there was the familiar call in Boston magistrates court. Finding him guilty, the Chairman of the Bench nevertheless did wonder aloud about the sanity of anyone who would enter into any business arrangement with the defendant.

'Some folks' lives roll easy,' sang Paul Simon at the time. 'Some folks' lives never roll at all.' Whatever Bert's horoscope might have said, things rarely rolled well for him. One week our newspaper's astrologer failed to post the weekly horoscope column to us. The subs made the call, asking what they should do. 'Oh, just use an old one from a month ago,' came the unforeseen reply.

Chapter 14

Pushing the Envelope

It all began at Farnborough in Hampshire. It was where Samuel Franklin Cody, a Wild West showman and pioneer of manned flight, became the first man to fly an aeroplane in Britain in 1908. Only 54 years later and eight years after I was born, it was where I was transfixed by a cacophonous stream take off by The Blue Diamonds and The Tigers. It was my first connection to the RAF wings on the photo of my uncle on my father's desk.

The sixteen blue Hunters were exciting enough but the nine Lightnings of 74 Squadron (The Tigers) stole the show. As each pilot lifted off Runway 24, they tucked up their undercarriage and roared off at low level towards the Laffan's Plain end of the airfield. Then they pulled back on the 'stick' and went vertical, two blazing fires spewing out the back.

My mother's brother was in the Army and, unsurprisingly, his tours of duty included a few years at Aldershot as well as Korea, Malaya and Germany. Aldershot was called 'The Home of the British Army' and my uncle and his family lived in Army married quarters opposite the big green expanse of Queen's Parade. We went to stay with them a couple of times a year, marvelling at some of the toys and furniture brought back to the UK from West Germany. A scooter bike was one such oddity – a bike that could be pedalled but also had a flat base so it could be used as a scooter.

Queen's Parade was just to the south-east across the A325 and not far to the north-west was the world famous Farnborough, home of British aviation since 1905. In 1962 with me aged eight, our two families went to the Farnborough air show. It was a day out with the promise of picnics and Vimto and ice cream and no doubt minor squabbling between siblings and cousins. It turned out to be one of the more significant days of my life although I hardly realised it at the time.

The experimental delta shaped HP115 appeared suddenly from behind the crowd and made me jump. Looking back at the list of other appearances at the 1962 show emphasises what a golden era it was for British aviation. The Fleet Air Arm displayed Scimitars, Sea Vixens and Buccaneers. The Hawker P1127 (the prototype of the Harrier jump jet) made its debut, as did the VC10 and the T188 research aircraft. To relive those glories we have to rely on grainy video film shot at those 1950s and 1960s Farnboroughs when photographers were allowed to stand right beside the runway and all wore suits and trilbys.

Two years later, we were back for Farnborough week. On the day before the public display, we were at the south western end of the runway over the famous Eelmoor Bridge which is still standing fifty years later. The Red Pelicans (Jet Provosts of the Central Flying School) and The Yellowjacks, flying yellow Gnat trainers from Valley in Anglesey, swept over us. The Yellowjacks were initially called The Daffodils but the name was deemed somewhat flowery for a bunch of fast jet fliers. In fact the name Yellowjacks and the colour scheme were both disliked by the top brass. The jets were painted red and renamed in tribute to an earlier team.

The fore-runners of today's Red Arrows, the Black Arrows were a display team of Hunter pilots from 111 Squadron.

They established a world record over Farnborough in 1958 as the biggest formation of aircraft ever to complete a loop. Borrowing more Hunters and pilots from other squadrons, Squadron Leader Roger Topp led 22 Hunters into a formation loop. No other display team in the world has tried to top it and probably never will.

The man who succeeded Roger Topp as the boss of Treble One Squadron was Peter Latham, who left the RAF as an Air Vice Marshal. I met him at the International Air Tattoo at Greenham Common where, in a wide ranging conversation, he told me how he got in to a Farnborough show when he was not working at it. Dramatically arriving on a motorbike at one of the back gates, he shouted his name at the sentry and barked: 'Any messages for me?' The surprised guard stammered: ' Er, no sir, I don't think so....' at which the young officer bellowed over the bike noise 'Ok! Thank you!', opened the throttle and was away and in without pass or payment.

The Fleet Air Arm used to put on exciting and memorable shows at Farnborough. There was 'Simon's Circus' – a team of six Sea Vixens named after the boss Lieutenant Commander Simon Idiens. Formations of Buccaneers and helicopters mounted mock attacks. One year the Scimitar team split into two and actually landed simultaneously from both ends of the runway, folding their wings up to give each other more room as they crossed in the middle. It was an extraordinary manoeuvre and would never be countenanced at air shows today, rather like the supersonic bangs which still make news when a military pilot gets permission to get somewhere quickly or accidently 'overcooks' it.

Farnborough was exciting if you loved aeroplanes. Away from the air show, I glimpsed strange new shapes or abandoned experimental relics through the trees and behind the high wires. The orange nose of a trials Beverley transport, the tail of a Hunter or the remains of a Whirlwind helicopter fascinated me.

Even the names of aircraft manufacturers in the early 1960s had a magical ring to them. Saunders-Roe, Armstrong-Whitworth, Handley Page, English Electric, De Havilland, Folland, Supermarine and Avro are all long gone now, with just Hawker Siddeley surviving in somewhat less glamorous voltage distribution.

Across the north-east side of the airfield were some hangars which were given the name 'The Black Sheds'. No air show commentary at Farnborough was complete without phrases like 'Now away to your right and from over the Black Sheds comes Beamont in the P1', or else ' Now look away to your left towards the Laffan's Plain end and you can see the Westland combine running in.'

'Beamont in the P1' was English Electric test pilot Roland Beamont flying the prototype of the Lightning supersonic interceptor. Years later, Beamont told me how he flew the P1 some 40,000 feet above the Farnborough air show a month after its first flight in August 1954 but they had not clocked up enough hours for it to be demonstrated in public. Although the P1 had made 14 flights, it had not accrued the total of ten hours needed before any new aircraft could be displayed in public. The display authorities were still understandably nervous about new aeroplanes in front of the British public after the terrible tragedy at the 1952 show.

The DH110 was the prototype of the Sea Vixen, the twin-boom tailed fighter that eventually was ordered for the Fleet Air Arm. Test pilots like John Derry in the DH110 were on the cutting edge of supersonic flight research and breaking 'the sound barrier', complete with huge bangs, had gripped the public. The David Lean film *The Sound Barrier* was released in 1952 and thrust the lives of real test pilots into the public arena, even if those in the industry snorted at some of the liberties taken with the aeronautical science.

At Farnborough in 1952, John Derry broke the sound barrier over the airfield in the DH110 but, as he swung round and headed towards the crowd, his aircraft broke up. Chilling film exists of the two engines hurtling forward into the public area. Derry and his colleague Tony Richards died as well as 29 people on the ground.

I was in a queue driving out of the Farnborough show in 2000 when news of another devastating aviation tragedy started to come through on the radio. An Air France Concorde had crashed on take-off at Charles de Gaulle airport north of Paris. It looked like all 100 passengers and the nine crew had died. Every time I see the pictures or the film of the doomed Concorde with flames coming out of one of its port engines, I remember exactly where I was – at Farnborough, the home of British aviation.

When RAF Binbrook was closed in 1987 and the Lightning phased out of service, I seized the opportunity to talk to its test pilot and get an interview for BBC Radio Lincolnshire. Through the media team at British Aerospace at Warton in Lancashire, I got the address of Roland Beamont and wrote to him at his home in a village near Salisbury, asking if he would be willing to do a radio interview. He replied by return of post. 'Yes of course I'll be happy to help see the good old Lightning off into a well-earned retirement.'

Roland Beamont spoke passionately about the Lightning as the finest aeroplane that he ever flew – and spoke politely but disparagingly about politicians who effectively wrecked the British aircraft industry. He did all the initial testing on the TSR2 before it was scrapped by the Labour government in 1965. A few years earlier, Duncan Sandys was the Minister of Defence who proposed that the days of the manned fighter were over and that the RAF should be chasing up missile technology. It was a short-lived policy but nearly threatened the future of the Lightning. Beamont was proud that the Lightning had survived 30 years since Sandys' outburst.

On 4th August 1954 and three months after I was born, Roland Beamont eased the P1 (the name given to the Lightning prototype) off the runway at Boscombe Down in Wiltshire and took it up to 14,000 feet. At this point, the radio failed so he could not talk to the Tower or get radar directions back to base which was now shrouded in mist and rain. 'It certainly tested my airmanship,' he told me. 'Back on the ground after a successful maiden flight, the chaps self-consciously muttered 'Good Show' or something like that!'

Roland Beamont never had to actually use the 'bang seat' to eject from any aircraft that he was test-flying. However there were plenty of incidents, including a terrifying moment when he ended up flying just below the speed of sound in an open cockpit. The two-seater trainer version of the Lightning – commonly called the T-Bird – had numerous issues with the cockpit canopy during the development work.

On one flight, Beamont was travelling just below the speed of sound when the canopy was ripped off and headed off to the Irish Sea below. 'There was an enormous bang followed by a tremendous roar like a continuous explosion. My eyes hurt so much that I had to close them. My helmet and face mask were dragged off me and I was being exposed to the blast round the windscreen which was still intact'. He had to hunker down behind that windscreen and bring the speed of the jet right down before limping back to English Electric's airfield at Warton in Lancashire. Despite modifications, a few weeks later the same thing happened to one of the other test pilots who *was* travelling at supersonic speed at the time.

The morning of the first flight by the TSR2 was quite foggy and nothing was expected to get off the ground at Boscombe Down before 11am. Roland Beamont climbed into the cockpit to run through some checks and unwittingly pressed the two buttons that operated the fire extinguishers. 'There was a snap and a hiss – and the engines were flooded with foam. The engineers had to clean it all out and the flight was postponed until the following day. They were very reserved about it all,' he said.

The day after the TSR2 made its first flight off the long runway at Boscombe Down in 1964, the *Daily Mail* ran a big story and photograph. 'Britain's supersonic atom-strike bomber, the TSR2, made its maiden flight yesterday. At the controls 44 year old test pilot Mr Roland Beamont radioed back: 'She's a natural – a beautiful aircraft.' The flight lasted 14 minutes and the undercarriage was not retracted. The story ended: 'The bomber, which has been beset by political rows, will now start a severe air-testing programme designed to give an initial 50 to the RAF. It is almost certain that, if the aircraft proves a success, defence chiefs will press for the order to be doubled.' In fact only one prototype actually flew and the project was scrapped seven months after that first flight.

Roland Beamont also flew the Canberra for the first time and recalled delivering the first operational aircraft to 101 Squadron at Binbrook in January 1951. After a short display, he landed the Canberra and taxied in. The station commander immediately asked to be taken up so that he could fly it – a sort of 'Can I have a go, mister?' With this elderly Group Captain at the controls of this brand new aircraft, Roland Beamont had to stand beside him in the well of bomber making sure the right buttons and levers were pushed. He described it as 'hilarious'.

Roland Prosper Beamont was born just a year after Colin Curtis. He had his first flight when he was seven years old – a quick up and down in an Avro 504k bi-plane. Rejected by Cranwell, he took civil flying lessons at White Waltham airfield from where I experienced my first aerobatics. During the Second World War, he took part in the Battle of Britain and was later shot down and captured. At one point he faced a court martial for flying a WAAF to a party on his lap in his single seat Hurricane. The charge was dropped because they needed him in the air. He then went on to become one of Britain's greatest test pilots, flying machines that were in the vanguard of British aviation technology. He died in November 2001 at the age of 81.

I found him a modest and inspirational man to interview. I sent him a copy of my 30 minute documentary which I called 'Life with the Lightning'. Beamont liked the documentary, writing: 'I think you have put the Lightning piece together very well (and professionally!), and the personal side seems to flow along quite well too. For once, I don't have any corrections or misgivings about anything I said! It is easy to respond in interview to a good interviewer!' His first letter was signed Roland Beamont. This last one was signed 'Bee' Beamont, which was what his friends and colleagues called him. It was a privilege to meet him.

Fighter pilots can really 'push the envelope' over the vast deserts north of Las Vegas. The RAF is one of more than 30 air arms which send aircraft and crews to Nevada to participate in the 'Red Flag' exercises. These replicate as near as possible what it would be like to fly in combat for real, including at very low level and at supersonic speeds. In October 1992, it was the turn of the Tornados of 5 Squadron at Coningsby.

On the television, George Bush (senior), Bill Clinton and independent Ross Perot campaigned for the votes of Americans a month ahead of the presidential election which gave the Democrats victory. Neon signs on the Vegas strip proclaimed shows by Paul Anka and Terry Presley, said to be a cousin of the King. In the hotel lift I asked two little old ladies if they were winning at the tables and the machines. 'We're losing all the time – period.'

The view from the 24th floor of Circus Circus, a 'Big Top' themed hotel with 2,800 rooms, offered a sea of flashing lights. On one side, the glitter gulch of downtown 'Lost Wages'. On the other, away on the horizon marked by the last rays of the desert sunset, you could just make out the winking red lights of Nellis Air Force Base eight miles up Interstate 15.

Nellis was dubbed 'The Home of the Fighter Pilot'. It was aviation heaven with relentless activity by all sorts of aeroplanes and helicopters, not just fighters. It was arrivals and rehearsals days at the Fairford air tattoo bundled up with those mass take-offs from Waddington during days of the ACMI range off the Lincolnshire coast. And then some more. Hell, even The USAF's aerobatic team The Thunderbirds was based further down the ramp.

In the Red Flag exercises, the Tornado F-3s acted as defenders for the bombers. They faced threats from the ground such as a lock-on from an anti-aircraft missile system but the real challenge came in the air. Some of the best fighter pilots in the USAF flying F-16s forced the Tornados into dogfights. The clipped tones of the controllers, watching it all unfold on the big computer screens on the ground, informed the luckless crew by call-sign and emphatically stated: 'You're dead'.

'The Vietnam War demonstrated that new pilots with no combat experience were extremely vulnerable on their first missions, as they were during the Battle of Britain. Red

Flag aims to make things as realistic as possible so that new boys don't die so often,' explained the deadpan Colonel Bill Sweatkey.

Before we left the base each day, the setting sun bathed everything in pink as B-52s, F-16s and C-130s wheeled in against the 'Sin City' skyline to set down on the long runways at Nellis. Then we abandoned the taxi-way lights for the spotlights and fountains of Vegas. In the evenings, Her Majesty's Media covering Red Flag roamed the gambling casinos, strolled the 'Strip', baulked at the bulky buffets and doled out too many dollars at the Crazy Horse Too Club.

North of Nellis lay the myth-laden secret testing ranges of Area 51 and 'Dreamland'. The Red Flag ranges covered an area bigger than Scotland. There could be up to 50 aircraft in the air at any one time. If a pilot taking part in Red Flag accidently overflew any of the secret areas, he could be arrested when he landed and sent home.

Each day, unmarked white Boeing 737s left McCarran Airport and headed north, taking workers on the 'Janet' flights to the secret research bases at Groom Lake and Tonopah. 'Janet' was the call-sign for these flights operated by a contractor on behalf of the USAF. You did not drive or take the commuter train if you worked in Area 51.

The vast desert north of Nellis was where 'stealth' technology was tested and where rumour and speculation rose and fell to match strange noises in the night and strange shapes in the sky. At that time in 1992, all the conspiracy and secrecy stories surrounded 'Aurora', believed to be the United States' latest military so-called 'black' project that flew higher and faster than anything else ever invented. There was also something called Astra – Advanced Stealth Reconnaissance Aircraft.

'The seismic people out here, they say the sonic booms have different characteristics than previous booms. There's something different flying around here. Not just Aurora but maybe another as well, helping stealth fighters to find their target. So we have possibly two aircraft that we don't know about.' So said Frank B. Mormillo, an aviation journalist and photographer whose distinctive by-line graced many aviation publications on my shelves and who introduced himself to me on the Nellis flightline.

People camped out in the Nevada desert for days trying to photograph and record something unusual. It was all early *X Files*. Rumours around Aurora were rife in the UK as well. Did this secret machine use the remote Machrihanish airfield on the Mull of Kintyre as a staging post? It had a long runway and remote hangars and was on the edge of the Atlantic. Was one involved in a mystery crash at Boscombe Down research airfield in Wiltshire in September 1994? I have no idea.

There were red lines painted on the Nellis ramp to mark out the restricted areas. There were no barriers, just the red lines. You should not overstep them or you would be in trouble, even for a minor infringement. I asked one USAF officer what would actually happen. 'Well,' he intoned slowly behind shades,'Shooting is the last resort.'

Chapter 15

Postcards of Scarborough

After getting the aeroplane bug as an eight year old at Farnborough in 1962, I tried to persuade my parents to take me to or past any airfield. Holiday journeys to Cornwall were examined in an old yellow AA book in which I had ringed places with airfields. Yeovilton and the Fleet Air Arm museum was a good stopping place to break the A303 journey to Cornwall. If we were going to be in Penzance for two weeks holiday, the Royal Naval Air Station at Culdrose, which actually had a car park for people to stop and watch their Navy helicopters at work, was on the 'definite' list of places to visit as well as the beaches of Praa Sands and Sennon Cove.

A trip up north to the grandparents in Sunderland would take us up the A1 so that would be Dishforth, Leeming and Catterick with a ring round them in the AA book. A day trip to the Northumberland coast or Rothbury would highlight RAF Acklington, now a prison. South down the A1 brought a glimpse of Cottesmore, the runway lights at Wittering and the fervent wish that a Phantom would crawl out of Alconbury as we pootled past in the Vauxhall Victor or the Fiat 124.

For a few years, Dad was Vicar at Westcliff-on-Sea near

Southend. The memories include the famous long pier and the Guinness clock on the sea front, along with the bulbous-nosed Carvairs that droned in and out of Southend airport. The huge door at the front could swing open to enable up to five cars to drive up the ramp and into the fuselage for the hop across the Channel. It was a glamorous alternative to the car ferries out of Dover and Folkestone.

A holiday at Dunwich on the Suffolk coast took us tantalisingly close to the American air base at Woodbridge. We once stopped for a picnic lunch in some woods and we could hear the constant roar of jets but my parents did not know exactly where this airfield was. If only they had driven further up the B1084 and turned right, we could have had our sandwich spread and dandelion and burdock at the end of Woodbridge runway watching F-101 Voodoos in the rain. Voodoos Vicar, for God's sake!

Woodbridge was at the centre of one of the great UFO mysteries of the United Kingdom. In late December 1980, strange lights were seen in Rendlesham Forest off the eastern end of Woodbridge's runway. There were claims that a UFO had actually landed in the forest. It all spawned conspiracy theories and allegations of government cover-ups. A senior USAF officer at Woodbridge believed he saw something extra-terrestrial that night. Spoilsports say it was effects created by the Orford Ness lighthouse a short distance away.

Just up the road from Woodbridge was its 'twin base' of Bentwaters. In the now dated BBC Radio comedy *The Men from the Ministry,* the misogynist old goat Sir Gregory Pitkin persistently pursued one of the girls from the typing pool called Daphne Bentwater (without an 's'). It is not a surname you come across much. I wonder if the inspiration came from Suffolk......

Sometimes when I said I lived in Filey, just south of Scarborough on the North Yorkshire coast, people would say: 'Ah, the golf balls! ' In fact these were on Fylingdales Moor between Whitby and Pickering. Despite early complaints, many came to regard these three 'golf balls', housing the ballistic missile warning radars, as iconic architecture and were sorry to see them go, replaced by a single concrete block. They sat alone, strange, sinister and mysterious. They were an incongruous and intriguing sight, glimpsed fleetingly down the valleys or through breaks in the low clouds on the moors until you were upon them on the A169. The station's motto is 'Vigilamus', translated as 'We are watching'. Apart from any missiles heading our way, the radars also track some 30,000 pieces of space debris and now have a direct line to the team in touch with the International Space Station.

Did anyone working at Fylingdales on the night of 8th September 1970 see or hear anything strange out over the North Sea? Did an unexplained 'unidentified flying object' sweep out of the night sky and abduct the American pilot of a Lightning from Binbrook? Some people think so and have fuelled conspiracy theories for years that the story behind the mysterious disappearance of 28 year old Major William Schaffner has been covered up and that documents relating to the incident have been shredded.

Major Schaffner, on an exchange posting from the USAF, took off from Binbrook on a routine interception exercise, chasing an RAF Shackleton maritime reconnaissance aircraft over the North Sea. Others say the American was 'scrambled' to intercept a UFO which was being tracked by RAF radar stations down the East coast. Whatever happened, the Lightning crashed into the sea and the body of Major Schaffner was never found.

The Shackleton was overhead quickly and, with the help of flares, the crew saw the pilot get out of the cockpit before the jet sank under the waves. There was no sign of him or his dinghy when the rescue helicopter arrived at the scene five miles off Flamborough Head just south of Scarborough.

One of the salvage vessel crew told my father, then Vicar of Filey, that when they raised the Lightning three months later, it was hardly damaged. The cockpit was closed and the ejector seat was still intact but there was no body inside. There are still those who claim that the Lightning had an altercation with a UFO and the pilot was abducted. The official line, outlined in documents finally seen by a BBC *Look North* investigation team after 30 years of secrecy and accepted by the family, is that the Major lost control at low level in the dark and the Lightning crashed into the sea. The ejection seat did not fire and he got out the aircraft before it sank. However he never made his dinghy and drowned. The force of the sea closed the Lightning cockpit canopy again.

Another Lightning flight that ended in tragedy off the Yorkshire coast occurred in August 1983. The aircraft was flying from its base at Binbrook to Middleton St George, which was now Teesside Airport, for an air show the following day. The pilot, who was the very experienced official display pilot for that year, was asked if he could make a couple of flypasts in support of an RAF recruiting event on the North Bay at Scarborough.

The official report stated that, if possible, he said he would do two turns over the sea before heading off to Teesside. After one flypast, he turned in towards the beach but appeared to stall as he pulled a tight turn to avoid getting too close to the prominent headland that separates the two bays at Scarborough. The report says the aircraft was actually over the road at the base of the cliff at one point. The Lightning crashed into the sea before the pilot could eject. Eye witnesses believed he stayed with it to ensure it did not head for the crowded beach and promenade.

The inquest was held a year later, not long after I had become News Editor at BBC Radio Lincolnshire. The widow of the pilot turned up unexpectedly at Radio Lincolnshire reception, accompanied by an RAF officer, to complain about the media coverage and asking to speak to the person in charge of news. The point at issue was the suggestion during the inquest that the display was 'unauthorised' and which was duly reported by all the media, not just the BBC.

The tension in our meeting evaporated considerably when I said that I had actually met her husband – Flt Lt Mike Thompson – and talked to him about his display only a month before he died. I was working with the commentary team at the International Air Tattoo at Greenham Common where his display routine that year was described by many as one of the most impressive Lightning solo shows for many years. Against some strong international competition, he won the Solo Jet Aerobatic Trophy at the show.

A month later he died just north of Paradise, the road on the cliff top behind Scarborough castle, which was name-dropped in Michael Chapman's desolate song 'Postcards of Scarborough'. A short distance to the south, Colin Curtis had spent six weeks early in 1941 as part of his initial RAF training at the Grand Hotel. My parents lived in retirement just off Scarborough's North Bay and I was reminded of the tragedy every time I walked that promenade. Mike Thompson's body was recovered from the North Sea and he is buried in the churchyard at Binbrook.

On one of the mid-week trade days at the 2004 Farnborough Air Show, the crowd was looking forward to a couple of flypasts by a USAF B-52 Stratofortress bomber. As the time for its slot approached, we could see it away to the north-east, no doubt awaiting clearance from Air Traffic Control. The display commentator indeed confirmed that next on the programme was the B-52 'which some of you may be able to see away over the Black Sheds.' However the bomber was not getting any closer and then appeared to be heading off straight and level in a north westerly direction.

The B-52 made an exciting and dramatic flypast over Blackbushe airfield, to the consternation of everyone at Farnborough and the surprise and either delight or horror of people at Blackbushe. This small airfield is some five miles to the north west of Farnborough and the bomber crew had obviously mistaken it for the home of British aviation. After their unexpected flypast they didn't hang around and continued heading west. They were lucky that there was nothing in Blackbushe circuit at the time. Farnborough later issued a straight-faced statement: 'We can confirm that the Boeing B52H Stratofortress did not arrive at the airfield.'

Something similar happened at the RAF Battle of Britain air display at Abingdon in September 1979. The flying programme included a display by a Danish duo, a Draken and an F-100 Super Sabre. They were holding somewhere out to the west although we could not see them – but they never turned up. Later I discovered that the control tower at Abingdon cleared the pilots to do their display, got the acknowledgement and then watched as the pair of jets headed west away from the base. Apparently they started their exciting routine over a baffled Brize Norton, nearly 20 miles west of Abingdon.

The B-52 flypast was probably the most exciting thing that had happened at Blackbushe since 250,000 people, including me, descended on the airfield in 1978 for a concert featuring Bob Dylan, Eric Clapton, Joan Armatrading and local boy Graham Parker and his band the Rumour. The Blackbushe concert was added to a string of London dates due to the demand to see Dylan that year.

Three years later, both Bob Dylan and Paul Simon reached their respective 40th birthdays. They never knew but they each got a 40th birthday tribute programme on Radio Oxford after the station manager Ted Gorton, another aviation enthusiast whose son was particularly enthused by Phantoms, boldly agreed to my suggestion. My hour long programmes went out on two Bank Holiday Mondays in 1981.

If you look at the back of Bob Dylan's very first LP released in 1962, you will find a review of his performances at Gerde's Folk City in New York. It was written by Robert Shelton, music critic of *The New York Times* and encapsulated this new singer so well that it helped to launch Dylan's career and get him a recording contract with CBS. He later wrote a book about Dylan called 'No Direction Home' which was published in 1986.

Nearly 20 years after that first *New York Times* review, Robert Shelton was working in London and living in Mount Gardens in Sydenham. I sent him a cassette tape of my Dylan programme and got a long letter back. He liked what I had done and suggested catching up in London to dwell on Dylan over a drink. I regret it didn't happen. He moved to Brighton the following year and we lost touch. He died in 1995. I still treasure his letter, glued to the inner sleeve of Dylan's debut vinyl album.

—ᨈ—

As the sun set, there was a familiar growling sound getting louder and louder. The huge crowd was growing more expectant and the anticipation was now at its height after a long day in the summer sun. Suddenly two Spitfires roared in low over the crowd and pulled up over the stage. The Spitfires were gone as quickly as they had appeared and the main feature was about to begin. Not the Red Arrows or the Lancaster but the Pink Floyd. This was the Knebworth Festival in July 1975 and the headliners had booked the Spitfires as a dramatic opening for their set. Earlier we had watched the Steve Miller Band, Captain Beefheart, Roy Harper, Linda Lewis and Monty Python's Graham Chapman.

The idea was for the Spitfires to arrive and pull up into the vertical as the Pink Floyd struck their first chord on 'Raving and Drooling' (which later became 'Sheep' on their *Animals* album). Permission for the flypast was secured and an Air Traffic Controller at nearby Luton airport agreed to be the liaison figure between the pilots and the concert organisers. The Spitfires were kept in the 'hold' for ten minutes while a minor technical issue on the stage was sorted. Then the two pilots were asked to arrive in exactly ten minutes which they duly did. It nearly came off. The Floyd hit their first chord 90 seconds later.

A year later we were back at Knebworth for another rock extravaganza, featuring Lynryd Skynyrd, 10cc and topped this time by the Rolling Stones popular musical combo. Despite coming on stage very late, the headliners played one of their longest concerts, remaining upright for three hours. The bass player was born William Perks but took the surname of a friend he met while doing his National Service. Bill Wyman did two years in the RAF from 1955. We made no attempt to get out of Knebworth Park that night, sleeping in the cars until woken by some bellowing berk who was wandering around still trying to find *his* car and his mate. Hot dogs were 15 pence and a chicken curry was 55 pence.

Film of Lynryd Skynrd playing their epic song 'Freebird'

at Knebworth later became an internet and music video hit. I must be on it somewhere as the cameras panned round the huge audience. Just over a year later, three members of the band were killed in an air crash. After a concert in South Carolina, the band boarded a chartered Convair CV300 to fly to the next concert in Louisiana. A faulty engine meant the aircraft ran low on fuel and, as they diverted to the nearest airfield, the fuel ran out completely and the pilots attempted an emergency landing before crashing into a forest. Six people were killed including the lead singer and two other band members. The accident happened three days after their latest album called *Street Survivors* was released. The cover showed the band engulfed in flames and was quickly pulled.

One summer evening in 1980 I lifted off the runway at RAF Abingdon in a little two-seat Bulldog trainer. I was in the lead aircraft of a diamond formation which staged a flypast over Abingdon to mark the Freedom of the town being given to the RAF station back in 1953. My task was to do a report on my flight and mix the inserts into some commentary by Ron Tandy, another reporter positioned in Abingdon town centre who had described the march past and recorded some links to introduce my bits in the air. I was allowed to have my Uher tape recorder on my knees in the right hand seat and did my descriptions using a lip-microphone like those used by sports commentators.

I recorded some of the briefing on the ground ('diversion airfields are Brize and Lyneham – Benson is out with an unserviceable radar') then we went out to climb into the Bulldog. No ejection seat here. If there is a problem, pull the canopy back, step out onto the wing and hurl yourself into the void with your hand firmly on the D-ring of the ripcord.

We apparently appeared over Abingdon town centre bang on time, followed a short time later by a more impressive and considerably noisier single Jaguar aircraft. Back over Abingdon airfield, the formation broke individually in a hard left turn and landed after about 40 minutes in the air.

To my dismay, you could barely hear me on the tape and there was no way it was fit for broadcast. Despite shouting into my lip microphone (lip-mic), the noise of the Bulldog engine in front of me was just too loud. The recording was useless – or was it? When I got back to the station, there was no one else around as the late news producer was in the Dewdrop pub next door taking the traditional break in his shift. I wrote down what I could remember that I said in the air and what I could make out on the tape. This included a 'Whoa-hey – I was not expecting that' as the force of gravity hit me as my pilot banked hard left to lead the four aircraft in for a stream landing.

Sitting at the radio studio desk, I played the tape of the Bulldog engine loudly in my headphones and began shouting into the microphone as if as I was back in the air over Abingdon again. After a couple of attempts, I got it right and had something useable. And nobody had seen this Partridgian madman shouting to himself in the studio. 'How did it go? Will it make a decent piece?' asked the producer on his return. 'Yes sure, good job I took the lip-mic though!'

Chapter 16

Time of No Reply 1942

The raid on Emden was the only one launched by Bomber Command on the night of 20th January 1942. Of the 25 aircraft involved, 18 crews claim to have attacked the primary target. Three attacked other targets at Oldenburg, Norden and an unidentified one south east of Emden. Four made no attack. Twenty three tons of high explosive and 1000 incendiaries were dropped. There was good visibility and no cloud over Emden but slight ground haze was encountered. Bursts of flak were seen across Alter Binnenhafen which was just north of the docks and some was reported just south of the town.

The dockyard at Emden was one of the recurring targets for Bomber Command in the winter of 1941/1942. Another raid would have come as no surprise to the Germans. On the night of 15th November 1941, 49 RAF aircraft were in the Emden overhead but cloud cover meant no one knew how effective they had been. Four Wellingtons were lost that night.

On the night of 26th November, 100 bombers were sent to Emden – 80 Wellingtons and 20 Hampdens. Only 55 actually dropped their weapons and once again there was no report of whether the raid was a success or a failure. Two Wellingtons and a Hampden were lost. Good results were reported when 50 aircraft returned to Emden on 30th November although one Wellington and one Whitley failed to return. After a Christmas break, 40 bombers went back again on the night of 28 December. Five days before Colin got his one way ticket to Emden, 50 aircraft launched yet another attack, reporting many fires. One Wellington and one Whitley were lost.

The four members of the Binbrook crew who survived and were taken prisoner said later they were attacked 'returning' from the raid on Emden docks. Z8370 had taken off at 18.34 and Becker attacked it at 2100 – two and a half hours later. The first burst of machine gun fire ripped through the tail turret, killing 26 year old rear gunner Sgt Bill Rutherford. The second burst hit the forward gun turret and the astrodome, wounding Flt Sgt George Groves in the legs and feet and killing the second pilot, 20 year old Sgt Edmund John Roberts Fowler.

The pilot, Flight Lieutenant Bill Thallon, told George Groves to bale out. The engines were still working but the aircraft was becoming uncontrollable. Groves crawled back from the front gun turret and opened the hatch near the pilot. 'There was nothing to see but the ominous blackness of the North Sea. True I was badly shot up but I was only twenty years old and not quite ready for a death by drowning. I asked the pilot if he could make it to the island ahead,' said George Groves, quoted years later in an on-line account of that terrible night faced by the 12 Squadron crew.

Three of them – Groves, Ross and Walker – did 'hit the silk' and landed on the dry land of Terschelling island. The pilot thought the second pilot was still alive and said he could not abandon him. Much later, they learnt that Bill Thallon had successfully crash-landed the Wellington on a beach on the north side of the island where it became a much photographed wreck. Fowler was indeed dead and he and Rutherford were buried on Terschelling a few days later. The three who had baled out, along with Bill Thallon, were taken prisoner early next morning. Due to the ice and snow in the tidal zones, they could not be moved off Terschelling by boat immediately. Groves, who was injured, was picked up by a small Luftwaffe aircraft, probably a Fieseler Fi 156 Storch, and flown to hospital. All four remained prisoners until the end of the war.

William Herbert Thallon stayed in the RAF after the end of the conflict. For a couple of years in the early 1950s, he commanded 617 Squadron (The Dambusters) which was then flying the new Canberra. He left the RAF as a Wing Commander and had a second career as a stockbroker before retiring to his native Northern Ireland. He died in September 1996.

The second Wellington that Becker shot down seven minutes later was seen to crash into the sea. No one survived. At least two of the bodies were recovered and buried locally. Belonging to 142 Squadron, Z1207 had taken off from Waltham at 19.21 and was claimed at 21.07, presumably still on its way to the target. Its captain was Pilot Officer John Scott of the Royal Canadian Air Force. The other crew members were Sgt Kenneth Archibald Parslow, Sgt Gwladgwyn John Sharpe, Sgt Michael Thomas O'Brien and Sgt Albert William Kerrisk (Royal New Zealand Air Force).

The five Hampdens that were tasked to join the attack on Emden docks belonged to 49 Squadron, then based at RAF Scampton near Lincoln. It is believed the Hampdens took off around 1700, almost an hour before Colin's Wellington. Two of them failed to attack any target due to icing problems and the failure of the aircraft heating system. Two of the other Hampdens reportedly bombed the primary target but no signals were heard from the fifth aircraft.

This Hampden (AT148 S-Sugar) was shot down by another German night fighter pilot, Obfw Paul Gildner also of NJG2. The location was 7 kilometres south west of the Dutch town of Groningen, indicating that the Hampden crew were taking a different route home to the Wellingtons. The five men on board all died and were buried nearby at Noorddijk cemetery in Groningen. The pilot was Flying Officer Alex Harvey and the rest of the crew were Sergeants W.A Gray, J.W.Hallam and R.M Knapman.

—m—

The three Wellingtons shot down by Ludwig Becker that night brought his Wing's tally to 100. Born in Dortmund in 1911, Becker had joined the Luftwaffe volunteers in 1934 and was a test pilot at the start of the war. His first confirmed 'kill' was a Wellington in October 1940. Six months after shooting down Colin's Wellington in January 1942, he was awarded the Ritterkreuz – a Knight's Cross of the Iron Cross and one of the highest awards that a German soldier could attain. By the end of the year, he had shot down 40 Allied aircraft at night and had been promoted.

On Wednesday 21st January 1942, the daily *Wehrmachtbericht* (German Armed Forces radio report) reported on the British attacks: 'In the last night the enemy dropped bombs with weak forces in the northwest German coastal region. There was some damage to houses. Four of the attacking British bombers were shot down. Here First Lieutenant Becker achieved his ninth, tenth and eleventh night fighter victory.'

The following day, Becker was given a silver cigarette case by the owner of the Heinkel aircraft company, Ernst Heinkel. Although Becker was not flying a Heinkel, the businessman was impressed by the pilot's achievements sufficiently enough to make the presentation. The inscription in German read translated as: 'In memory of the 3 kills over Holland in the night of the 20th of January 1942'. It took me until February 2017 to learn that Colin's death had been celebrated by a silver cigarette case.

Becker was called 'The Night Fighting Professor' and was regarded as an inspiring fatherly figure by the crews around him. He was thirty years old when he shot down those three Wellingtons on the night of the 20th January 1942. Just over a year later, Becker and Straub suffered the same fate as Colin and his crew after being moved from night operations to fighting in daylight.

Twelve Bf110s took off from Leeuwarden at 11.35am on 26 February 1943. Becker, who had now shot down 44 enemy aircraft and had just been informed of the award of the Oak Leaves to his Knight's Cross, was taking part in his very first daytime sortie. Their target was a large formation of United States Army Air Force B-17 Flying Fortresses and B-24 Liberators on their way to bomb Wilhelmshaven. Becker and Straub, without the cover of darkness, fell victim to the machine guns of the American bombers and their aircraft was seen to crash into the sea off Schiermonnikoog, an island to the east of Terschelling. Like Colin and his crew, their bodies were never found.

Five of the six Wellingtons that took off for the raid on Emden got back to Oakington. The weary crews, exhausted by noise, cold and 'flak', clambered out of their claustrophobic bombers. They breathed in the fresh cold night air of Cambridgeshire and inhaled deeply on their first cigarette since take-off. They headed off for their debriefing and a hot drink. Out on the airfield, a handful of ground crew waited in the dark for the sound of more Pegasus engines that would tell them that Z1110 was coming home.

The other 101 Squadron crews had no news of their colleagues. No one had seen the Wellington in flames or in trouble. No one had picked up a radio message. They hoped that it had limped home to another UK airfield, or that the crew, having gone 'down in the drink', were all in a dinghy somewhere. Had they even been taken prisoner after crash landing or parachuting down into Holland or Germany?

Many feared straightaway that all six had 'got the chop'. Colin and his colleagues had 'gone for a Burton' (a common wartime phrase for dying and possibly arising from the ale of the same name). They had just 'bought it'. Conversation moved on quickly. It was accepted by all aircrew that you just avoided discussing death as much as possible.

After landing back at Leeuwarden, Becker and Straub logged their three victims with the duty intelligence officer. Some of the pilots hung around in the bar of the 'Offizierkasino' (Officers' Mess), raising glasses to mark the 100th Allied aircraft shot down by the wing. Becker, serious about his flying and his role, did not hang around long and was probably now fast asleep in his quarters.

There was another cold dawn at Oakington on Wednesday 21 January. The hard-standing where the six men of Z1110 had climbed into their Wellington the night before remained deserted. There was still snow on the ground – there would be for another two months. No other station or unit had reported a lone Wellington making an unexpected appearance, including the emergency airfields with their coastal locations and extra wide runways at Woodbridge, Manston and Carnaby. No one at Scampton, Binbrook or Waltham who had been on the Emden missions had any news. Silence. The squadron commander and the adjutant knew there was no alternative but to inform the families immediately.

Few people had telephones in 1942 and the quickest way of communicating was by telegram. The adjutant contacted the General Post Office in Cambridge and dictated 48 words.

'PRIORITY MRS L E CURTIS CHERRY HOLME LONDON RD WYBERTON BOSTON LINCS = REGRET TO INFORM YOU THAT YOUR SON P/O COLIN HUBERT CURTIS IS REPORTED MISSING FROM AIR OPERATIONS JAN 20 TH 1942 STOP LETTER FOLLOWS STOP ANY FURTHER INFORMATION RECEIVED WILL BE IMMEDIATELY COMMUNICATED TO YOU AEROS BOURNE'

The blunt telegram delivered to Colin's
mother the day after his disappearance

Bourn (without an 'e') was the satellite airfield for Oakington and 101 Squadron would move there shortly afterwards on February 11th. The telegram was dictated to a clerk in the GPO in Boston. A 'Boy Messenger' and his bicycle was summoned. The RAF would pick up the bill. Nine words cost six pennies and then it was a penny for each additional word including the address. The telegram was put in a small brown envelope with the word PRIORITY in red on a blue background down one side of the front. It measured some 7 inches by 5 inches.

In modern times, the family at home dread the sight of two RAF officers, one of them often the padre, arriving at the door with grim faces, bearing news of a casualty in some foreign field or desert. In 1942, the dreadfully regular bad news was delivered by the telegram boys who were nicknamed 'Angels of Death'. Hearts sank and stomachs churned as mothers watched a young boy in his GPO uniform cycle down a street. Whose garden path would he turn in to today? Whose door would he stop at?

—m—

The telegram details were received at Boston GPO at lunchtime on the Wednesday. The boy delivered it to Colin's mother a short time later. In the quiet of a winter afternoon, she contemplated the worst scenario and wept. She gazed at the staccato dead lines in the telegram – and then at the painted portrait of her husband and Colin's father above the piano in the front room. The stern-looking side profile of the recently deceased Harold Eaton Curtis had hints of the facial features of her three sons but all she could see was Colin.

On the mantelpiece above the fire was the picture in a frame of her son. The photograph was taken only weeks earlier when Colin was awarded his wings and commissioned as an officer into the Royal Air Force Volunteer Reserve. He brought the photograph home just before he reported to 101 Squadron at Oakington. Lillian wanted to drop the telegram on the fire but instead placed it on the table. She opened the drawer where she kept the Christmas card sent by Colin a month earlier. Outside snow flurries from a grey, leaden Lincolnshire sky swirled against the window.

Somewhere in the house, the oak-cased grandfather clock made by Washingboroughs of Bristol struck the hour. Lillian rose and went into the hall, momentarily contemplating a halt to the relentless swing of the pendulum and its two weights. Time had stopped for her but she withdrew her hand from the 100 year timepiece and returned to her chair. Colin's sisters and brothers were at work and she would wait there until they returned before wordlessly passing them the telegram.

Not far away, another telegram was delivered to a house in Sutton St James where Colin's fiancée Doris May Fines lived with her parents. A day later, a friend of Colin drove up from Oakington to talk to Doris but there was little more to add. A month later, this friend was shot down as well. Doris went to Oakington herself to talk to the squadron boss.

Six days later, the local paper carried the news. 'The thoughts of their many friends will be with the mother and family and fiancée of Pilot Officer Colin Hubert Curtis who is reported missing since Tuesday on an operational flight.'

It hit both families very hard. Did they listen on the radio to Lord Haw Haw, the wartime traitor William Joyce who broadcast Nazi propaganda at the British? Starting each broadcast with an upper-class accent announcement of "Jairmany calling, Jairmany calling", Joyce occasionally released the names of airmen who had been captured. There would be no mention of anyone on Z1110.

Whenever someone went missing on operations, the Air Ministry sent the family a small leaflet. First published in 1940, it was entitled 'Memorandum on the steps taken to trace missing personnel'. It outlined how the International Red Cross in Geneva was informed of all names and, through the International Convention of 1929, it had access to special information as 'each belligerent power is bound to set up an official bureau to give information about prisoners of war.'

Relatives were assured that, without any application on their part, every endeavour was made to trace missing personnel. If it was confirmed that someone was indeed a prisoner, a further leaflet was sent telling relatives how to correspond with him or her and how to send parcels. It also reminded relatives that the German radio broadcasts were solely to make people listen to German propaganda and that the lists of prisoner names were inaccurate and unreliable. The BBC sent a full transcript of every Haw Haw broadcast to the RAF, Army and Navy for analysis.

Doris' father Charles had served in the Light Horse Artillery in the Great War and had nearly died when a piece of shrapnel went through his neck. He had warmed to his daughter's fiancé and took the loss badly. Charles had a farm at Sutton St James which was not far from Kings Lynn. When German bombers attacked the docks there, he would go outside and loose off a few shotgun cartridges. He knew it was a futile effort but it made him feel better. Both families realised as the days turned into weeks with no news that Colin was never coming back. A new branch of the family trees never got a chance to flourish.

Doris joined the women's branch of the Army known as the ATS (Auxiliary Territorial Service) and trained as nurse. She kept the engagement ring that Colin had given her. Eventually, in 1954, she married Roddy Rawson who had served with distinction with *The Desert Rats* (7th Armoured Division) in North Africa and Italy, including at the Battle of Monte Cassino as the Allies fought to take Rome. The couple went on to have three sons. Roddy died in 2005. Doris lived for another 10 years, dying in February 2016 at the age of 94.

A few weeks after Colin was reported missing, Bomber Command introduced a radio navigation system codenamed Gee to help crews plot their positions more accurately. Before then, the navigators looked for land marks on the ground and used the stars. At the same time, the Avro Lancaster began to replace the older smaller aircraft like the Wellington on the nightly raids to Germany.

In February, Air Marshal Arthur Harris was put in charge of Bomber Command and changed the policy on bombing Germany to include non-military targets. In the light of The Blitz air raids across Britain over the past two years, Harris said: 'The Nazis entered this war under the rather childish delusion that they were going to bomb everybody else, and nobody was going to bomb them. At Rotterdam, London, Warsaw and half a hundred other places, they put that rather naïve theory into operation. They sowed the wind, and now, they are going to reap the whirlwind.' The whirlwind quote came originally form the Book of Hosea in the Hebrew Bible.

Colin's principal at Borough Road College in west London sent out a newsletter to former students in January 1942. Mr E.R.Hamilton wrote: 'You may be an airman, a soldier or a sailor. Wherever and whichever you are please take this letter as conveying cordial good wishes for your well-being in 1942…... Warmest wishes for your personal happiness and welfare in 1942 and for a speedy, overwhelmingly victorious end to the war.' As it was prompted by the New Year deadline, Colin may have seen it before his warmest wishes and welfare ran out.

In May 1951, a Memorial Room was opened at Borough Road College to commemorate former students who had lost their lives in the war. The Roll of Honour had 21 names including C.H.Curtis.

After the telegram, a letter to Colin's mother arrived two days later from the Air Ministry confirming that he was 'MIA'. Wing Commander Nicholls, the boss of 101 Squadron, also sent a personal letter, saying he was 'deeply grieved' that Colin was missing. 'During the short period he was with this Squadron he proved to be a very popular member and his courage and devotion to duty were at all times of a very high order and he is a great loss to the Squadron.'

One of his former head teachers at Moulton Grammar School, a Mr M.B. Westmoreland, wrote to Lillian on the 1st February, also 'grieved' to learn that he was missing and hoping that news might yet come through that he was a prisoner of war. 'We all realised that he had an unusual amount of grit and perseverance; and with it all he was very gentle, patient and in every way gentlemanly. How unlike the vision he had of his future was the career that this sad war caused him to choose. And his choice in this respect, we know, was largely guided by his deep sense of duty.'

Six weeks later, another letter arrived. This one was from the office of the Director of Personal Services at the Air Ministry. The writer had been 'directed to inform you that no news has been received of your son.' Occasionally a personal letter, which crews were not supposed to take with them on operations, or a laundry label from their home base was found and offered a clue. Not this time. Nothing further had been heard of the Wellington or any member of the crew. The Air Ministry added 'an expression of the Department's sincere sympathy with you in your great anxiety.'

A further letter from the same office on 29th May confirmed that all efforts to trace Pilot Officer C.H.Curtis 'have proved unavailing'. It went on: 'In view of this lapse of time, it is felt that there can now be little hope of his being alive, but action to presume that he has lost his life will not be taken until at least six months from the date on which he was reported missing.'

The letter proposing to take action to presume his death for official purposes was posted to his mother on 9th July. This letter asked her 'that you will be good enough formally to confirm that you have received no further evidence or news regarding him.' The Air Ministry confirmed in the first week of August that Colin's death 'has now been presumed, for official purposes, to have occurred on the 20th January 1942.'

—⟶⟵—

Gladys Eva may have been one of the last people to follow the Wellington bomber of Colin Curtis and his crew. In May 1941, she was posted to RAF Watnall near Nottingham, home to the control and administration centre for Fighter Command's number 12 Group covering the Midlands, Norfolk, Lincolnshire and North Wales. The young WAAF plotters not only monitored the incoming German aircraft but also the outbound and inbound flights of the RAF bombers. For her, it was the 'saddest part of the war', as she watched RAF aircraft limp back toward the English coast, badly damaged and with injured crew on board. There were many instances when a returning bomber was lost to the plotters who knew it had finally plunged into the sea.

Gladys was one of the first women to 'go underground' in the bunker at RAF Bentley Priory in north London just before the Battle of Britain. Aged just 20, she worked in the Filter Room at Fighter Command headquarters, plotting German aircraft as they headed over the sea towards Britain. A bronze statue modelled on her can be found in the Bentley Priory Museum. I interviewed her in 2015 on behalf of the Royal Air Force Association.

During her time off, Gladys went home to her parents in Wimbledon or up to the West End. One evening in March 1941, she and a friend were near the Café de Paris off Piccadilly when it was bombed, killing more than 30 people including swing band leader Ken 'Snakehips' Johnson. Gladys returned to her car to find it unscathed but with a bomb crater on either side. She has many memories of travelling back to work on the London Underground in the evenings and seeing station platforms filling up with families taking shelter ahead of the German bombing.

Not long before Gladys left Bentley Priory, she remembers plotting three aircraft over the Thames Estuary. The three suddenly became two – and she discovered later that the missing aircraft was being flown by Amy Johnson, whose body was never found. The record-breaking pilot was flying an Airspeed Oxford for the Air Transport Auxiliary at the time.

Gladys left Bentley Priory in May 1941 as a Flight Sergeant and was posted to Watnall. A couple of weeks beforehand, Colin Curtis arrived at No 20 Elementary Flying Training School to learn how to fly in a Tiger Moth before being sent to Canada for more advanced training. Gladys was still working at Watnall in January 1942 when Colin's Wellington disappeared into the North Sea.

Sometime during that month, Lillian Curtis bought £1000 and a further £800 of War Bonds. These bonds were initially set up during the First World War to help finance the war effort. You lent the government your own money and, by 1939, the Government was paying you 3.5 per cent interest on it. It is not clear whether she bought the bonds before or after Colin disappeared.

The Worcester accounts office of the Air Ministry began to wrap up Colin's finances from his time in the RAF. In November 1942, Lillian was told that a payable order would be made to the estate of her deceased son to the sum of £25 and 9 shillings and three pence. £14.10s was for his pay between the 1st and the 20th January and there was a further £13 described as 'post casualty pay' up to 17th February. His last mess bill from RAF Oakington – just over three pounds – was taken off the pay that was due. His mother noted there was £27.17s in his bank account in March 1942.

Lillian not only had to come to terms with losing one son but then spend the rest of the war worrying about her other two. Hugh joined the Army and served in India and Burma as part of the logistics teams that got food and equipment to the front line. Wilfrid (my father), who had been working in an insurance office and at a solicitors, was called up later in 1942 and embarked for North Africa with the Royal Army Service Corps some 12 months after Colin was killed.

Because of his love of motorbikes, Wilfrid immediately volunteered to be an Army despatch rider. He got his wish and served in North Africa and Italy. As he went off to war, his mother gave him a copy of the *Book of Common Prayer* and wrote two verses inside the cover.

'When life slips a sorrow, Into joy's bright square. Just remember that in suffering, A drift of Heaven is there.

For misery and loneliness, are not moments spent in vain. They're the little empty fields of life, Where joys are sown again'.

In Africa a year after Colin disappeared, Wilfrid prayed that there might be a flicker of hope and wrote in his diary: 'One year since Colin flew out from England and failed to return. May God keep him and his colleagues safe and well and may they be taken safely back to England in God's own good time'.

Years after Colin's death, his mother confided in Wilfrid that she had dreamt about Colin on the night he disappeared. She said he was coming towards her across the lawn of the family home and said he had died. The following night she dreamt of him again. He was coming across the same lawn and said he was all right. Alive? Or at peace?

Certainly by nightfall on the 21st January 1942, his lifeless body was somewhere in the North Sea. There was no search and rescue mission for the crew of Z1110 as no one knew where and how they had disappeared. Colin was 22 – the average age of those 55,573 men killed in Bomber Command across the war.

Chapter 17

Much Finding on the Marsh

The first *Airfix* kit that I was given to stick together was a Wellington in memory of Colin Curtis. Rushing at it with scant respect for the instructions, I stuck one engine on in the wrong place, giving it a permanent lop-sided look and serious aero-dynamic complications.

Outside on sunny or wet days, I had my airfield chalked out on the concrete back yard where numerous *Airfix* kits in various states of repair would be lined up and flown round the yard and garden by me making growling noises. This airfield changed its name according to what I picked up about my new interest. Sometimes it was RAF Enfield Down after I had read about Boscombe Down. Another Wiltshire airfield, Hullavington, spawned the much ridiculed and very brief appellation of RAF Boxbavington.

For a week, it may have been called Much-Binding-in-the-Marsh after hearing about the radio comedy set initially on a fictional RAF base of the same name. Both Kenneth Horne and Richard 'Stinker' Murdoch were in the RAF during the war. Horne joined the RAF Volunteer Reserve and, as an acting Pilot Officer, was posted to a barrage balloon squadron. Murdoch worked with radio star Arthur Askey where he got the nickname 'Stinker' due to his posh education at Charterhouse. He joined up in 1941 as a junior intelligence officer with Bomber Command. Both Murdoch and Horne ended up sharing an office at the Air Ministry and started writing comedy together. They worked together on *Much-Binding-in-the-Marsh* for ten years from 1944. Murdoch went onto to further success in *The Men from the Ministry*, while Horne's later achievements included fronting the iconic radio comedies *Beyond Our Ken* and *Round The Horne*, laden with its ground-breaking double-entendres.

Whatever name I gave my *Airfix* airfield, it always had a clothes line stretched over it. My mother would thus hang out the washing on warm sunny days when my airfield was at its busiest. Washing day was usually Mondays when a NOTAM (Notice to Airmen) would have to be issued warning of random laundry in the overhead and the left and right hand circuits. She did have to ask permission to cross the runway which I would routinely refuse until I had safely recovered a Javelin or a Scimitar to the airfield. I was a model child – well, I had a lot of models.

Having seen a Land Rover being used as a bird scarer at one airfield, a similar scenario was devised for my establishment. This involved a *Corgi Toys* Land Rover being driven down the runway with one hand while the other hand fired a cap gun. You could buy rolls of caps and feed them into a metal gun. They were much used in the traditional Cowboys and Indians conflicts of school children at the time who were brought up on *The Virginian*, *Rawhide*, and *The Lone Ranger*, who always left a silver bullet behind after saving a town or a damsel in distress.

Occasionally I would subject the family to an airshow and got my Dad to type up my flying display. The highlight was undoubtedly 'A Canberra PR7 on reconnaissance is attacked by a Scimitar and then rescued by a Lightning.' Air Force and Naval rivalry was alive and well in Airfixland in 1964.

The Boulton Paul Defiant was lost en route to the show and eventually found in a nettlebed during some extreme gardening a year later. My 'Yellowjacks' aerobatic team only had two Gnats as I only had two hands.

An old school friend of my father came to visit us one day with his wife and, through an unfortunate coincidence on their part, found themselves as spectators at one of my *Airfix* aeronautical extravaganzas. This was rather exciting for ten year old me as this man had been a real pilot in the RAF, having flown Canberras with 149 Squadron in the mid-1950s. The friend was now on his last tour and was Officer Commanding RAF Wainfleet. This was a weapons range on The Wash where British, American and other NATO air forces came to practice. At night the skies lit up for miles around with flares and flashes and the sounds of bangs and thumps.

We were invited to visit one afternoon and watch the activity from the control tower. A Canberra came through to practice what was called 'toss-bombing', formally known Low Altitude Bombing System in which the aircraft came in low and pulled up as it released its bomb. A couple of Hunters paid a visit but that was all. Three aircraft in two hours – that's a result for photographers who spend half their life waiting at the end of a runway for something, anything, to happen. As a bonus, I came away with a 149 Squadron tie and lapel badge – a flash of lightning in a horseshoe more commonly called 'The Flash in the Pan'.

The squadron was one of the first in the RAF to be equipped with the Wellington in the months before war was declared. A former 149 Squadron Vickers Wellington is one of only two surviving examples of the type. N2980 suffered engine failure on a training flight in December 1940 and ditched into Loch Ness. The rear gunner was killed when his parachute failed to open but the rest of the crew escaped. The bomber was found in 1976 by a group of Americans who were searching for the

Loch Ness Monster. It was salvaged some ten years later and is now in the Brooklands Museum in Surrey on the site where more than 2,500 Wellingtons were built. The other example is with the RAF Museum. The Loch Ness Monster remains elusive.

—ᜠ—

Since the war, aircraft noise continued to be the background soundtrack to life in south Lincolnshire. Military jets followed routes round Boston and Spalding as they wheeled in to line up over the marshes for the Wainfleet and Holbeach ranges. Huge bird colonies and basking seals were found alongside the military. Students of history hoped that the constant bombing of The Wash would one day throw up the Crown Jewels supposedly lost there by King John in 1216.

In the early summer of 1975, a local clergyman was out bird watching on the marshes near Boston where the River Witham runs into The Wash. He reported seeing a bomb sticking out of the mud but could not get near it. This was not totally surprising as the location was under the flight path into the Wainfleet range targets. The bomb with two clear fins appeared to be rocking in the tide which was on the turn. The Harbourmaster at Boston and the local police were alerted and tried to work out exactly where it was on the marshes. However the tide was coming in fast and there was no chance of safely getting out there again before sunset.

The following day was very hot, sunny and humid. Police in boots assembled by a pub called The Plummers Hotel on Freiston Shore down near the marshes. The media had been tipped off too and, on behalf of the *Lincolnshire Standard* and local television, Bob Whitaker and I went to the scene to ascertain the threat to public safety and to shipping coming in and out of Boston docks. I made sure I had plenty of two pence pieces to enable me to phone in a report from The Plummers public phone.

Sweating policemen returned to base camp at The Plummers with no sign of the wretched bomb. The world's media waited with bated breath, sipping pints outside the pub. Every so often, a police radio crackled into life and the unenthusiastic voice of a young constable, one of several out on the marsh negotiating the slippery banks and judging which mud would suck you in or provide a fleeting stepping point, assured those back on shore that there was no sign of the bloody thing. 'Keep at it lads – and smear a bit of mud on your face. The press are here.'

The sergeant in charge raised his binoculars again and scanned the marshes. They would have to find it. Hundreds of people went walking on the marshes each weekend, especially in summer. Still fresh in the mind was an incident at Lutton Marsh when two practice bombs 'fell off' a jet heading into the Holbeach range. They narrowly missed some houses before creating two new holes in the ground. The heat haze on the horizon shimmered in the high noon, obscuring the thin line of the Norfolk coast that could be seen across The Wash on a clear day. A bomb disposal team from RAF Wittering near Stamford had been alerted.

I found a few locals and asked for their take on the bomb mystery. I called the Editor who said there were probably better things for me to do than sit outside the pub with a beer and wait for something to come up or blow up. The headline was likely to be 'Bomb Scare on Marsh' or mischievously 'Vicar's Bomb Agony'. It was high summer and a thin news week. The bomb story would be front-page news what ever happened and would probably be illustrated with a couple of photographs. One of these would undoubtedly be of a police officer looking through binoculars or pointing out to sea.

Suddenly the police radio burst into life again. One of the

constabulary, who had been joined by the man of the cloth, was pointing to something with two fin-type things rocking in the water. The police team edged closer. Finally the news came through. 'We've got it. It's safe.' That was quick, we all thought.

It had not taken the marsh team very long to identify a bag of fertiliser. Lying in the back of a police van, the sack with two 'ears' (where it had been tied at the top) did not look remotely like a bomb with fins. Police said it had probably been left there by a local fisherman with no malevolent intent. It had stuck upright in the mud and swayed gently with the tide. I had my front page story and Bob got a photograph of a sack of fertiliser.

Two Boston fishermen found themselves in the middle of a rescue drama as they headed home to the docks with their catch of mussels on one winter's evening in 1975. The Bagley brothers – Steven and Roy – were on their boat the 'Boy Alan' when an American F-111E bomber came to grief above them. The swing-wing aircraft was on a run into the Wainfleet range about four o'clock on a November afternoon.

'It exploded only about 200 feet above us,' 18 year old Steven told me later that evening. 'There was a terrific bang and the whole boat shook. It certainly made us jump. But the wreckage fell into the sea about 150 yards away.' His 27 year old brother Roy turned their boat around to head for where they saw a parachute come down. Another local fisherman George Lineham actually reached the crew first and pulled them out the water before transferring them to the Bagley's boat.

The two on board the F-111, which belonged to the 20th Tactical Fighter Wing at the American base at Upper Heyford in Oxfordshire, escaped serious injury. An RAF rescue helicopter later lifted them off the Bagley's boat and flew them to Boston's Pilgrim Hospital for a check-up. The inquiry revealed that the aircraft had suffered a bird strike, probably a duck. It hit the right hand side of the windshield, causing a 'catastrophic failure' of the windshield and the canopy. The Weapons System Operator in the right hand seat initiated the ejection which involved the whole cockpit in a capsule-like device.

A year earlier, the Bagley brothers were out working in the Wash when another military jet came down as it headed for the Wainfleet range. Roy Bagley saw 'a big mushroom of flame' but this time he was two miles from the scene rather than underneath it.

Coverage of the Buccaneer crash which cost the life of the pilot in November 1974

They joined other boats in the search for the two man crew of a Royal Navy Buccaneer after it crashed around five o'clock on 11th November in 1974. The jet's observer was found alive soon after the crash but the pilot was killed. The accident happened on a Monday evening and I was asked to pull together the many aspects of the incident before deadline time on Wednesday afternoon.

Both crew members, who were serving with 809 Naval Air Squadron which was then ashore at RAF Honington in Suffolk, ejected as the Buccaneer hit the ground. The crew of the Boston dredger *Jean Ingelow* saw 'a brilliant flash but no bang' and headed for where the parachutes came down. They picked up a flashing white light which they believed was one of the crew in the water. As they approached, the boat got grounded on the ebbing tide. Another shallower vessel, the *Arthur Lealand* got closer and confirmed it was one of the crew.

The man they had found was the back seat observer who was badly injured and having trouble freeing himself from his parachute straps. In a moment of real heroism, 21 year old Michael Green jumped into the sea off the *Jean Ingelow* and swam 100 yards through the icy, murky Wash water to reach him. The skipper of the nearby *Arthur Lealand*, 24 year old John Holland, joined Michael Green in the water to help free the Navy airman and get him safely onto a boat.

The parachute straps then got entangled round the propeller of the *Arthur Lealand* which meant it had to be rescued by a tug which had also joined the search for the pilot. The crew of the stranded *Jean Ingelow* left their dredger to search on foot – in the dark – and they found the pilot nearly two hours later and half a mile from the crash scene. His body was retrieved by an RAF rescue helicopter from Coltishall. Across several stories on the front page that week, I unpicked the chain of events from the Buccaneer's take-off from Honington carrying 'live' practice ammunition to the tragic conclusion as the jet started its sixth run-in to the targets. Amid the sadness at the loss of life, there was admiration for the nautical men of Boston who risked their own lives to go and help.

Four months later, I reported on the inquest on the pilot,

28 year old Lt Stephen Kershaw. It heard that the observer escaped with his life because the impact of the crash fired both ejection seats – something described as most unusual. He said everything had appeared normal and then there was a bang. The pilot died from asphyxia due to drowning associated with multiple injuries. Michael Green later received a gallantry medal from the Queen for his courage.

—ᴍ—

Derek Macintosh Bates served in Bomber Command during the Second World War. He was a pilot on the Handley Page Halifax but he also became a bomb disposal specialist. After the war, he set up his own demolition business and over the years brought down 500 chimney stacks across the country as well as removing tree stumps and blasting through rock to help make way for the M6. He was also a stunt motor bike rider and eventually a raconteur and comedian.

Derek went by the nickname of 'Blaster Bates'. He came to Boston a couple of times and I went to talk to him and do a review for the paper. He had built up a formidable reputation as an after-dinner speaker, especially for all-male gatherings like Lions Clubs and Rotary. Some said he only felt comfortable performing in front of male-only audiences because of the language that he used. Certainly the two events that I saw him at were all-male. Strangely one of the venues was Kitwood *Girls* School but long after the young ladies had all gone home. Compared to today, the language was pretty tame but you always got 'a rollicking good evening'. He was the same convivial company at the bar in the interval as he was on stage.

One of his stories concerned the oil tanker *The Torrey Canyon* which ran aground between Cornwall and the Isles of Scilly in March 1967. First the authorities put a foam rubber collar round it to try and contain the oil but the sea wrecked it in no time. The tanker split in two and nearly 120,000 tonnes of crude oil spilled out, much of it coming ashore all along the south west coastline, causing considerable damage. Eight days after the tanker got stranded on the rocks, the Royal Navy and the RAF were ordered in to shift it and also set fire to the remaining oil.

Eight Buccaneers from Lossiemouth were sent to drop 42 one thousand pound bombs on the Torrey Canyon. Then the RAF sent Hawker Hunters from Chivenor to drop aviation fuel on the oil to try and set it alight. The mountainous seas extinguished the fires and the tanker stayed stubbornly on its rocks. More attacks by Buccaneers and Hunters were required, along with a fresh mission by Navy Sea Vixens before the tanker finally sank.

When the combined might of the RAF and the Fleet Air Arm initially failed to shift it, one of the national newspapers asked 'Blaster Bates' what he would do. 'You have to vaporise oil before you can burn it. Do that and get some thermite and magnesium on the decks, light it and whoomph! Not only do you burn the oil, it smashes the boat up and shifts the rock it's bloody sitting on!'

He was also invited onto local television to talk about it and met a Fleet Air Arm Commander in the hospitality room before the show. In his usual blunt style, 'Blaster Bates' chided the Navy for failing to hit the target properly. 'There's one thing about it, in the next war I am going to stand slap bang in the target area. After all it was stuck on a bloody rock and it wasn't even firing back, you know.'

'Blaster Bates' said that when he did jobs for the military, he always knew if it had an element of danger because they sent a car for him. If it all went wrong, they did not want his car left in the car park and people asking whatever happened to 'that poor bugger'. When he was blowing up tree stumps at a crematorium, he said the workers warmed up his meat pie lunch for him in the crem furnace.

Late one Saturday night he was called out to remove two white sticks of mining dynamite which had been found in someone's coal shed. After he picked one stick up, it did not feel quite right. He then heard a dog bark in the house and realised that at 11pm on a rainy Saturday night, he was standing in a stranger's coal shed in the dark, a long way from home, with two long white dog turds in his hand. 'And you don't know what to do with them really.'

'Blaster' died aged 83 in 2006 and is buried at St Mary's Church in Sandbach in Cheshire.

I wonder what Jean Ingelow would have thought about having a dredger named after her? She was born in Boston and achieved fame as a poet in the nineteenth century. Her first (anonymous) volume was called 'A Rhyming Chronicle of Incidents and Feelings' and was published when she was 30. It was described as 'charming' by Lord Tennyson, also Lincolnshire-born, and they later became friends.

One of her best known poems was called 'The High Tide on the Coast of Lincolnshire' about a terrible storm that lashed the coast in 1571. 'Men say it was a stolen tyde – the Lord had sent it. He knows all,' she wrote, adding later in her epic: 'It swept with thunderous noises loud, Shap'd like a curling snow-white cloud, Or like a demon in a shroud.' She died in 1897 at the age of 70. I found out about her from a dredger.

Most of the stories we covered in local papers was a 'scoop'. Nobody else had it because no one else was there or because nobody had told anybody else. Or maybe it was not that interesting. The same stories come around years later. The council scrapping lunchtime lollipop patrols, massive rent increases for pub landlords, local MP in another anti-Common Market rant, nurses at a local hospital march in protest at low pay, hospital beds crisis with 5000 on waiting list, elderly widows terrorised by teenagers, a restaurant fined after a council health check, the new Mayor appointed, a day with the female lorry driver which was deemed unusual at the time, St John Ambulance on hand at a local cinema as people faint watching the controversial new film 'The Exorcist'...

The board game maker Waddingtons was best known for *Monopoly* but it also had a game based on newspapers called *Scoop*. Significantly in view of my subsequent career, I enjoyed playing this game as a youngster more than any of the others like *Risk* or *Cluedo*. You had to fill up your front page which involved dialling the Editor on a cardboard phone. You were given a three digit number to dial and awaited the random verdict from the phone. Your story could be given three stars, deemed worthy of a special edition, syndicated around all papers, scrapped (or 'spiked') or lambasted by the lawyers as libellous. The worst outcome of the 'call' was that your story was rubbish and that the Editor wanted to see you.

One report of a crime story worried me and came to mind every time I answered the Vicarage phone at home. It told how a millionaire playboy was murdered by telephone in his Mayfair flat. A pin point blob of blood on his right ear revealed to Scotland Yard a fantastic story of how the playboy answered his telephone and as he placed the receiver to his ear, he got a sting of death from a microscopic needle point firmly affixed to the earpiece and smeared with delayed action poison. He was found dead on his sofa at 11pm by ' a woman friend whose name the police refuse to divulge.'

Other stories included a robot bricklayer which could

build a house in two hours, an aircraft that was powered from an 'atomic ground station', the discovery of a panacea to cure all diseases in the world, and a television set that could pick up the past, allowing you to tune into to any period in history and see delayed 'TV pick-ups' of actual incidents of those times (an early if extravagant version of on-demand viewing). The apparatus would operate on the theory that everything that has happened on Earth since time began still remained in space in the form of recurring light-waves into which you could tune.

These stories were a treasure trove for April Fool jokes and possibly the templates for headlines in the *Sunday Sport* newspaper which specialised in stories such as 'World War 2 bomber found on Moon' or a man divorcing his wife to marry a cabbage. In the era of 'fake news' and constant clickbait, they would surely now be treated as 'alternative facts'.

Chapter 18

Glamour Profession

Speedway riders go round an oval track at high speed and have no brakes on their machines. There was still a track and a team at Boston when I first started at BBC Radio Lincolnshire and we had a freelance who filed a report over the phone after every home meeting. However he failed to tell us that he had been banned from the Wyberton Chain Bridge stadium after falling out with the team owner. The Sunday night reports kept coming, always there on the newsroom voicemail machine for the early team on Monday. So it was somewhat embarrassing to find out weeks later that he was banned. He never told us, continuing to file reports each week. He was effectively 'Our man in the raincoat standing on the railway embankment outside the stadium with a pair of binoculars.'

My Dad loved speedway. He grew up with motorbikes and even after he became an Anglican clergyman, he kept a motorbike and used it on his parish rounds. After a couple of top speedway riders took their own lives, Dad offered his services to the authorities as a sympathetic 'speedway chaplain' with an understanding of the bike world who was a phone call away if anybody wanted to talk.

Several took him up on the offer, including Erik Gundersen of Denmark whose career as one of the greatest riders of all time was ended by a crash in 1989. Gundersen nearly lost his life as a result of the accident but he recovered to raise money for the hospital that saved him and go on to manage the national team. He was happy to record a message of thanks for my Dad which I played at his retirement party. Speedway was very popular but never got the television coverage that reflected the crowds at meetings. Dad took me to the World Final at Wembley in 1981. More than 92,000 people witnessed the Californian Bruce Penhall clinch victory over two other Danish riders Ole Olsen and Tommy Knudsen. It was a far cry from the motorbike scrambling races I used to watch as a youngster on the black and white television on Saturday afternoons when Arthur Lampkin dominated the endlessly muddy race tracks.

Jim Montgomery made history for Sunderland football club thanks to his mesmerising double save in the FA Cup Final in 1973. Second division Sunderland beat top club Leeds United with a goal by Ian Porterfield but it was Monty's saves that kept them in the game and ultimately ensured they won it. I witnessed an even better save from him a week earlier when Sunderland were at Hull City's Boothferry Park in the league, with Hull featuring their striking twin strikers Chris Chilton and Ken Wagstaff ('Waggy').

Dad became a Sunderland fan after meeting my Sunderland-born mother. Like his bee in the bonnet about the lack of speedway coverage on BBC television, he felt that Jim Montgomery should have been the number one goalkeeper for England. He wrote to a national newspaper to make his point and they published it with a photo of the keeper. 'Monty' was someone else who agreed to record a short tribute for Dad on his retirement as Vicar of Filey and he also made an offer for both my parents to watch a match from his VIP box at Roker Park, something they were unable to take up due to Dad's health.

In my Oxford days, I would sometimes get a guest seat in the Oxford United press box for home matches. As the Radio Oxford sports reporter Nick Harris kept listeners up to date across the game on a Saturday afternoon, that local freelance and mischievous wag Colin Fenton would occasionally be heard in the background helpfully and confusingly enunciating in a ponderous tone: 'Come on the Varsity.'

Des Portas covered Boston United for BBC Radio Lincolnshire. Boston's press box was behind one of the goals at their York Street ground which made unpicking what had gone on at the other end very difficult, particularly during a winter evening match under floodlights. Sometimes fans and the media would have to shout at the players on the pitch 'Who got that goal?' I was working one evening when Des rang in to record his 45 second match report on Boston Utd's mid-week game. After he finished, I asked him where he was because it did not sound as though he was still at the ground. Indeed he was ringing from home. 'Once more from the top then, Des, but this time can we lose the bloody budgie in the background.'

In November 1973 I was given a seat on the team coach to accompany Boston United on the trail of FA Cup glory. After a goalless draw at home to Hayes on the Saturday, the replay was set for the following Wednesday afternoon (not evening) down at Hayes. More than 40 years on, I remember hearing Ritchie Havens singing 'What you gonna do about me?' on the crackly radio on the coach . The weather was cold with a frozen pitch and light dusting of snow. It was the first football match that I had ever reported on.

Boston United went through to meet another glamour club, Hitchin Town, in the second round by winning the replay 2-1 after extra time. Boston United's player/coach was Howard Wilkinson, who went on to manage Notts County, Sheffield Wednesday, Leeds United and Sunderland. He also had a spell as caretaker manager of England.

Back in Boston, cup fever was at a high pitch as the *Lincolnshire Standard* switchboard was swamped by people ringing up to find out the Hayes result. Did I mention this was years before mobile phones and Five Live and talkSPORT and rolling news? (You did). The sports editor wrote in the paper: 'So intense was the pressure on our telephones that our reporter at Hayes was unable to get a call into us – and we were unable to get one out to Hayes. So please fans, while we are happy to help on such occasions, give us the breathing space to find out the news for you.'

'Our reporter!' He did not even put my name against the match report. The dynamic reporter who had rode the team bus, shivered in the press box by a frozen pitch and then shovelled his own coins into a public call box (press button A) to try and file the report that everyone was waiting for. He could at least have put 'by Mike Curtis' at the top of the match report.

When I did finally get my first ever newspaper by-line shortly afterwards, my surname was broken in half. It was a story about a blind man who weaved baskets and the panel beside the story said 'Mike Cur' on one line and then '-tis went to see him' on the next two. I must let it go and move on.

Only two months after their triumph over Hayes and Hitchin, Boston United nearly pulled off a giant-killing act against First Division Derby County. They were drawn against the top flight club in the Third Round of the FA Cup in January 1974. About 4000 fans in 70 coaches and a special train made the pilgrimage from south Lincolnshire to support The Pilgrims. The result was 0-0 but the non-league side nearly nicked it. I was standing behind the goal to witness a perfect cross from Howard Wilkinson which was met with a diving header by Alan Tewley. It beat the goal-keeper, hit the inside of the post and rolled towards the goal line only to be held up by a lump of mud on the quagmire of the Baseball Ground. That was the season when a groundsman had to come on during a match and find and repaint the penalty spot, such was the state of the pitch.

Three months earlier, Brian Clough and Peter Taylor had been sacked by the chairman and Dave Mackay was installed as the manager. Derby came to Boston's York Street ground for the replay and halted the Pilgrim's Progress, winning somewhat convincingly 6-1. The locals still enjoyed shouting 'rubbish' at Derby's international players like Archie Gemmill, Alan Hinton, Roy McFarland, Kevin Hector and Colin Todd.

—ᴍ—

Boston United had reached the final of the FA Trophy and the team was off to Wembley to play Wealdstone. Twelve thousand supporters followed them to the national stadium along with BBC Radio Lincolnshire, mounting a significant outside broadcast to reflect the big day out. Our Lincoln City reporter came with us to Wembley to help with the coverage, leaving the Bradford v Lincoln match at Valley Parade in the hands of a local Yorkshire freelance. He was asked to file a report at half time and at fulltime on Bradford's last game of the season which was an occasion of celebration. The Bantams had won the Third Division while Lincoln finished mid-table. The date was Saturday 11th May 1985.

I was the on-site producer at Wembley. Our sports editor at the time, John Inverdale, was doing the match commentary and we had two or three other colleagues in the tunnel and with the Boston fans. Shortly before half time, the newsreader back in Lincoln rang me to tell John not to hand over to the freelance at Bradford for the Lincoln City update as he had just left the press box due to 'a small fire in the stand.'

As the second half got under way at Wembley, I got another call on the landline from our Lincoln newsroom. The situation at Bradford was now looking serious and the match had been abandoned. In the main BBC newsroom at Television Centre a few miles from Wembley, the on-duty journalists were watching the *Yorkshire Television* 'live feed' from Bradford, showing a stand engulfed in flames and people spilling onto the pitch with their hair on fire.

We carried on with the Wembley commentary, now aware that something had happened at Bradford but we still did not know the extent of what was unfolding. I got another call to say that some bodies had been seen laid outside the ground at Valley Parade. The Wembley game came to an end with Boston losing 2-1 to Wealdstone. A fan slipped onto the centre circle and lay on his back, eyes closed, and savoured his Wembley moment. We wrapped up the post-match interviews and headed for the A1, desperately trying to tune into radio bulletins to find out what had actually happened at Bradford. One of the bulletins that we caught took our breath away. More than 50 people were now feared dead.

We drove straight to the Radio Lincolnshire newsroom to help the couple of journalists that were trying to make sense of the tragedy. One had gone to Sincil Bank (Lincoln's ground) to meet Lincoln supporters returning from Bradford. We did some extra news bulletins that evening and we were back again early on the Sunday morning. 56 people died and more than 260 were injured. Two of those who lost their lives were Lincoln City fans – Jim West and Bill Stacey.

The day had started in high spirits as we headed off to

Wembley with Boston United. Although Boston lost narrowly, 12,000 followers had a great day out until they, like us in the media, began to hear how another fun football occasion had ended in utter horror. Fans had gone to watch a football match and died. Those who got out the ground had to find a public phone box or beg a nearby householder to use their phone to call home. While such a story was breaking and developing, journalists went into a kind of 'autopilot'. When you finally got that moment to stop and reflect, you realised the enormity of what had transpired and what you had packaged up and passed on to people desperate for information.

A couple of weeks later, the Lincoln City manager Colin Murphy took the team away to Majorca for a break to help get over what they had witnessed at the Bradford match. On their return to Leeds/Bradford airport, their British Airtours TriStar overshot the runway and ploughed into a field. The aircraft was evacuated with only minor injuries sustained by the 14 crew and 398 passengers. One of the other passengers on the TriStar was Tony Delahunty, the commercial radio football commentator whose graphic description as the fire in the Bradford stand took hold was heard around the world.

The father of Colin Curtis was briefly a professional footballer. In fact, it seems to have been an extremely brief career. Aged 19, Harold Eaton Curtis turned out just once for Lincoln City (nickname The Imps) in 1885. The away game at Grimsby Town is marked in the Lincoln City archives as both his debut and his last match. It was the third round of the FA Cup and Lincoln lost one-nil. He later played as an amateur for Gainsborough Trinity who were in Division Two of the National Football League. Many years later his great grandson Mark (my younger son) would be a mascot at a Lincoln City match and go on to work for West Ham and as a first team analyst at Arsenal.

Colin Murphy had two periods as manager of The Imps and got them promotion each time he was in charge – up to the Third Division in the 1980-81 season and later pulling them out of non-league football back into the Fourth division in 1987-88.

Colin is fondly remembered by football fans for his programme notes which were surreal and astonishing in their use of the English language. When I was an instructor at the BBC local radio training unit, I sometimes used his mystical musings from Lincoln as a training exercise. 'You work for a local radio station, the manager has not got the time to do the usual pre-match interview but he has faxed over his programme notes and said feel free to use those in the sports bulletins. You have 15 minutes to write them up for broadcast – then we will discuss.' Everyone had a different interpretation.

He used to say that his 'Murph's Messages' might be difficult to understand but he did not think they were unintelligible. 'It just depends in what light people read them. If you get people thinking a bit, you might educate them a bit,' he said. He was nominated for awards for his programme notes and took it all in good humour.

An example of 'Murph's Message' from a Lincoln City programme. 'As I explained last year, fate is a strange thing but the repetition of fate, whilst being even stranger than fate itself, could well be a lot stranger to one's coronary circumstances if we are to leave the outcome until the last game of the season again. Maybe some things cannot be better stage-managed but to manage the stage a second year running is riding the wall of death which, incidentally, seems to have disappeared from our entertainment.'

He won an award with this one: 'We cannot fall into the trap of committing practical haplography. It is also a dangerous feeling to consider that where we are in the League is of an acceptable standard because standard is relevant to the standards we have set which thereby may well indicate that we have not aspired to the standard which we set ourselves. It is also a dangerous feeling to concede we must be the harbingers and nothing else than this can be acceptable.'

I hope that I have avoided any examples of haplography in writing this memoir. It was a word that I had never heard of until used by the manager of Lincoln City Football Club. I had to look up its definition and so I learnt something new. Thank you, Colin.

Chapter 19

Sparrow and Stump

Boston Stump got me banned by a television company and reprimanded by my employers after my first fateful cock-up in my early journalistic career. The pressure of deadlines and a youthful gamble conspired to land me in hot and holy water with a threat of legal action by the Church of England and months of mirth afterwards.

The parish church of St Botolph's in Boston has been a famous landmark since the tower was added to the original building in the 14th century. It is 272 and a half feet high, which is slightly above the 250 feet low flying minima for military fixed wing aircraft in the UK. In stories about low flying complaints by the military in Lincolnshire, I would sometime add the line that the limit was almost as high as Boston Stump to give people some idea of what 250 feet was like. If the Tornado (bit longer than a London bus) was perceived to be lower than the top of The Stump, then maybe the pilot had got his altimeter settings up the QNH.

The Vicar of Boston, one Canon Trevor Collins, launched a new initiative to encourage the wider community to come through the doors of the parish church and he spoke to a senior editor on the newspaper about his plans. Bob Whitaker got wind of the story and shot off some 'general views' (again) of the famous Stump and sent them over to *About Anglia* at Norwich. As with all of his films, he had to drive along the A17 to Sutton Bridge to physically handover the video cassette to a motorbike despatch rider who would take it on to Norwich.

I knew nothing about this latest development in the story of the Stump until one of the editors at Norwich rang me as I was about to leave work. He said they had no words to go with Bob's film. Could I help? There was about an hour to go before the start of the programme.

I found the carbon copy of the story on the spike on the editor's desk. In those days, you typed your story on the cut-offs of the big rolls that the newspaper was printed on, making a copy at the same time with a bit of carbon paper. The top copy went off to the sub-editors to be pulled apart and prepared for publication while the carbon copy was 'filed' on the lethal metal spike on your desk for future reference.

Being a regular supplier of copy to go with Bob's films, I said to leave it with me. It would be another £2.50 at the end of the month to supplement my meagre newspaper salary. I rang the editor on his home number but no reply. So I tried the Vicar as well but again no reply. Have I mentioned this was years before mobile phones? (Many, many times) With less than 20 minutes to go, *About Anglia* rang again. They only wanted a couple of paragraphs to cover a few seconds of film showing The Stump.

With nowhere to go, I re-fashioned the carbon copy using the words and details already there and filed it across to Norwich. The vicar of Boston was planning social events like dinner dances to bring new people into his church to hear The Word of God and learn more about the Christian message in south Lincolnshire. Did Christ not turn water into wine at a wedding and feed 5000 with some loaves and fishes? What's not to like?

The phone on the wall at the hospital radio studios rang. The caller identified himself as the Canon of Boston who immediately fired off a broadside. He reloaded and fired again. His evening vespers had been disturbed by a stream of parishioners ringing to ask what in God's name he was thinking of, staging 'dinner dances' in the parish church? You know what they are associated with, don't you? Men dancing with other men's wives and no doubt coveting their asses. Alcohol – and not the Communion wine. Loud music not associated with being a Pilgrim or being the Lord of the Dance. Revealing tops and short skirts instead of cassocks and surplices. Boston was on its way to become Babylon.

Canon Collins had not seen the item on the television but it looked as though most of his congregation had done so and were now in Anglican angst. Collins had rung *About Anglia* who kindly said they got the story from me. He in turn ruthlessly tracked me down to the hospital radio studio. He was indeed looking at ways to entice more into his church and had spoken to one of our senior newspaper people about the story. But the editor had rung him back to check what he had written which is when the cleric said 'no, no, no' to the reference to 'dinner dances'. The top copy was to be corrected for the paper but the carbon copy remained unchanged and in the form that I found it. Sod it again.

The Canon was now talking to one of his church wardens, who was a solicitor, about legal action against me for damaging his reputation in the eyes of his flock. He signed off in a fury and I was left staring at the phone handset and wondering what Act of God was about to envelop me. All journalists get legal threats during their careers but they seldom go anywhere. However the first one – and delivered personally by a particularly peeved parson of all people – was a salutary and chastening experience. This was the Vicar's son and grandson of a long serving south Lincolnshire vicar to be sued by the

Vicar of Boston. I checked the Seven Deadly Sins – at least a scribe's screw-up was not among them.

The editor at *About Anglia* rang the next day and commiserated but confirmed that they were going to put out a correction in the programme that night. Their line was that 'the information was provided by a freelance, not by one of our team.' I was only trying to help them as they put the pressure on for copy but, on that morning, that counted for little. The senior board had decided to ban me from supplying copy to them for three months. I was also summoned to Lincoln to the headquarters of the *Lincolnshire Standard Group* to be roundly chastised for nicking the editor's original story without his permission and for upsetting a senior clergyman in the south Lincolnshire patch. The relationship between The Church and The Fourth Estate had always been fractious over the centuries and my contribution was not helpful.

Having exploded and fired off a fusillade, the Canon calmed down and there was no legal action. His congregation was assured that Satan and his Bacchanalian friends had not descended upon The Stump and the story faded away. I was actually eased back into favour at *About Anglia* within three months as Bob urged them to reinstate me to supply fast and, er, accurate copy for them from that area. Except of course the story did not die among friends and journalists. Every night out in a restaurant or a gathering in the folk club or pubs of Boston involving me would feature the question: 'Where shall we go next?'….Or 'Where shall we finish the evening?' The answer was always the same. 'Why of course, The Stump!' or 'Stump A Go Go!' or 'The Canon's Calypso!' For months and months.

Respect for the clerical collar got us those childhood visits to Binbrook, Strubby, Manby and Middleton St George in the mid-1960s. My Dad was held in high esteem in all the parishes that he was entrusted with, protesting in vain at free entrance to all sorts of establishment or the donation of a fresh salmon from a Filey fisherman. Returning to his car with a pile of parcels up to his chin, he found a traffic warden about to slap a ticket on his windscreen. As he tried to explain overstaying his time, he started to remove the parcels and put them in the car. As the parcels came down, the clerical collar came up. 'That's ok, Padre. I'll let you off this time,' said a clearly discombobulated parking enforcement officer, probably anxious about his place in Purgatory.

On his parish rounds, Dad called on a cafe owner with me in tow. Seated at one of the tables was a rowdy group of what were then known as rockers, callow youths all brylcreemed and winklepickered. On seeing the vicar, they all shut up and mumbled as quiet as church mice. When he went out, they burst out laughing and started up again. So he put his head back round the door and asked them if the BSA 650 motorbike outside belonged to one of them. A ten minute conversation round the bike followed with no mention of God, salvation, sin or sub-culture. Just bikes.

When she was about five, my sister Alison playfully put a brown paper bag on my Dad's head. The doorbell rang and, behold, there was an itinerant man of the road on the doorstep enquiring about the opportunities for any ecclesiastical largesse. As the 'tramp' looked up, he stared north of the dog collar and lowered his eyes and indeed his head. Clutching his newly acquired cash, he proceeded back down the drive, walking backwards and bowing constantly. Mystified, my Dad waved and closed the door and then caught himself in the hall mirror. The paper bag was still resting lightly on his head and must have convinced the visitor that he was indeed dealing with some higher being.

—m—

'Two JPs through the Gap.' The leader of Sparrow formation radioed in to the area radar at Waddington to clear us through the air corridor separating Waddington and Cranwell from Coningsby. With Lincolnshire being an area of intense aerial activity with a number of active military airfields, the controllers had their work cut out. A short time earlier, it had been the Mark One Eyeballs of the JP pilots as two American A-10 Thunderbolt aircraft streaked over us right to left near the Belmont television transmitter. 'Tally right, one o' clock. A-10s,' snapped the lead pilot.

I was in the right hand seat of a Jet Provost T5A (XW431) belonging to the Low Level and Air Defence Training Squadron of No. 6 Flying Training School at RAF Finningley in South Yorkshire. The squadron boss, Squadron Leader Mike Jukes, was my pilot although today (6th March 1990) he was the number two in the formation, call sign 'Sparrow'. I was on board at his invitation to gather material for a radio documentary on why the RAF still needed to fly low and what lengths it went to stop upsetting people and animals on the ground. I introduced it with the hit single 'Low Rider' by the American funk band War.

Whenever you went fast jet flying with the RAF, they gave you a medical. The Finningley medic said she would have to take my word that I had never suffered from a collapsed lung or a burst eardrum. She pronounced me 'fit to fly' and praised my 'squeaky clean' eardrums. It was then onto helmet fitting and a lecture on the ejection seat. You had two options of black and yellow handles to pull on the Jet Provost seat – one between your legs and the other over your head. The new jets such as the Tornado and the Hawk only had one between your legs. 'If nothing happens when you pull it, it's just not your day,' said the ejection expert who had survived a 'bang-out' from a Canberra more than ten years earlier.

'If I say eject, just go!' said Mike Jukes as the Jet Provosts lined up on Finningley's long runway 20 which had been built for Vulcans. He was stylish enough not to offer the standard additional line: 'If you say Pardon, you'll be talking to yourself.'

A radio check between the two JPs and a hard bank to the left and we were heading to the east past Gainsborough for the first part of the exercise. The two aircraft would split up occasionally and rendez-vous further down the track at exactly the same time and speed, puddle-jumping along at 250 feet and 300 knots over the Lincolnshire Wolds. Then it was through 'The Gap' and up to around 10,000 feet over Spalding for some higher level interception training resulting in a 'splash' (kill) after some low yo-yos and some high yo-yos that left me feeling distinctively so-so.

At the top of a loop, I suffered a 'white-out' – some way towards a black-out but you remember everything if somewhat in a blur. I was conscious of what seemed like a white milky liquid starting to cover my eyes and I could see nothing but whiteness. As we came out of the loop, the whiteness rolled back and normal vision gradually returned but I felt somewhat unsettled. I clutched a sick-bag but did not need it. Mike called up the other aircraft for a moment's 'straight and level' to let me settle down.

After one more interception exercise, we headed for home. The Finningley circuit was busy and windy, with the control caravan at the end of the runway constantly calling out the wind speeds. On the final approach, we heard '28 from the right'. Mike muttered that the JP limit was 30 knots. 'Thirty from the right,' sang the controller then almost immediately dropped below 20 as the gusts came and went. We kissed the surface and rolled out without incident.

Every RAF pilot had a callsign usually assigned by their

colleagues. Mike Jukes was known as 'Tommy' after The Who's rock opera, having seen the band's show-stopping performance at the 1970 Isle of Wight Festival. He was most associated with Phantoms but his last posting before leaving the RAF was a more sedate return to Cranwell, flying the Dominie navigation trainer (a military version of an executive jet). After years trussed up in Jet Provosts, Hawks and Phantoms, he said it took him a few trips to get used to someone putting their head in the cockpit not long after take-off and asking if he would like a coffee.

—∽—

I first saw The Who a few months after the Isle of Wight Festival when, on a cold December evening, they came to The Futurist Theatre on the sea front at Scarborough. It was a big leap from Woodstock or East Afton Down but it was the first really big-name rock band that I had seen 'live'. I was tucked away 'in the Gods' way up at the back but still closer to the stage than most people would have been at those two famous festivals.

My mum and elder sister came to pick me up and appeared at an open door near the stage. Some of the exits had been opened for those who wanted to miss the rush but I was determined to stay to the end. Thus my Mum and 13 year old Alison peered in to the theatre and were told by a security guard that they could move into the front row as the band was nearly finished for the night.

This experience left a lasting impression on the wife of the Vicar of Filey. The Who were coming to the thunderous climax of their show with Pete Townshend's windmilling arm thrashing through the chords, Roger Daltrey swinging his microphone wider and faster and Keith Moon enveloped in a blizzard of drumsticks. And it was certainly the loudest noise that Mrs Curtis had heard since German bombs fell on Sunderland before she was evacuated.

Scarborough band The Mandrakes were the support act for The Who when they played Bridlington Spa in 1966 just a week before England won the World Cup. The lead singer in the Mandrakes was a local lad called Allen Palmer who worked as a lithographer on the *Scarborough Evening News*. He later became world famous using his first forename Robert. Other Scarborough bands included 'Grandads Don't Indicate' and 'The Scurvy Reptiles', the latter featuring my younger brother Chris channelling Joe Strummer of The Clash.

Someone at Radio Cornwall had been in a band called 'The Reginald Simpson Trio' which had seven members and no one called Reginald Simpson.

I have been listening to the American rock band The Doors since 1967. Although they only did six studio albums before the lead singer Jim Morrison died in Paris in 1971, the music has stayed with me down the years. With *Morrison Hotel* running blues out of the car stereo, the Stow-on the World Fosse Way to Fairford becomes the Santa Monica Freeway.

Due to an on-going pocket money shortfall in my 13th year, I borrowed their first album to record on quarter inch tape and played it through my old reel-to-reel Grundig tape recorder. You cleaned the playback and record 'head' with a bit of surgical spirit on a cotton bud. Little did I know then how tape reels and recording would come to play such a big part of my life some ten years later when I joined the BBC.

Not long before I left Radio Lincolnshire for the BBC Asian Network in 1998, a news release arrived about a book festival in Lincoln highlighting autobiographies. The honorary patron was revealed to be John Densmore who had been the drummer with The Doors. I checked the date – still a month or so before April the First. I looked away out of the window before returning my gaze to the piece of paper in my hand. The name John Densmore was still there. He had written a book about his time with the band called *Riders on the Storm* but how on earth was he linked to little old Lincoln's modest book festival?

'I was sitting in my office, facing the blank page of my second book, noting that for me writing an autobiography was easier than fiction because I knew the story, when this fax came through, filling another blank page,' he was thus quoted in the publicity for the festival. 'The fax didn't help fill up my novel but it did divert me from the void for a moment. And a sweet moment it was!' Steady on! The invitation to be honorary patron of a book festival in Lincoln had arrived from Lincolnshire County Council.

The organiser had been in Los Angeles recently and was struck by how often he had heard The Doors on the radio and how the band seemed to epitomize LA for him. Being a bit of a fan and having read Densmore's book, he thought 'Why not?' I asked if he had a contact and he gave me the number of the drummer's agent. At 5pm UK time, I rang it at 9am LA West Coast time and it was answered almost straightaway.

The number he gave me was in fact for John Densmore himself, not his agent. '*This IS John Densmore,*' drawled the LA voice down the phone. 'Hell's Teeth!' as *Likely Lad* Terry Collier was wont to say. Gathering my composure, I explained who I was and asked if he would be prepared to do an interview over the phone about his support for this book festival. Indeed he would but could I give him 15 minutes as he had to do the school run? Oh, they grow up so fast. The Doors, teenage musical heroes from the dark side and leading lights of the social and sexual revolution of the late 1960s, are now immersed in all those domestic diversions of the mere mortal man.

John did not know a great deal about the festival but thought it was 'cool' for a council to stage such an event. He talked about his writing experience and encouraging others to write, including me. Needless to say we moved on to The Doors and his sometimes rocky relationship with the controversial and unpredictable lead singer. During the course of the 15 minute conversation, I had to confess that I had been a fan since the beginning and even had a Butts Band LP, a short-lived project that he and guitarist Robbie Krieger got involved with after Morrison's death and after The Doors called it a day. He said he enjoyed the interview and added: 'Thanks for being a fan!'

Listening to The Doors in my 13th year opened up new and exciting avenues of culture that I would spend years exploring. Reading articles about and around the band gave me in-roads into the writings of William Blake, Aldous Huxley and the great French authors like Zola, Flaubert and Camus. Some of Morrison's lyrics were very much of their time and the lizard and the leather malarkey wore very thin very quickly, as it did with Jim Morrison himself. Beyond the alcohol and excess, he was an erudite and well-read young man. Backed by guitarist Robby Krieger, keyboard player Ray Manzarek and the tight blues and jazz-influenced drumming from John Densmore, the overall sound has remained fresh to my ageing ears.

In July 1971, Jim Morrison followed Brian Jones, Jimi Hendrix and Janis Joplin into what became known as The 27 Club. He was buried in the Père Lachaise cemetery in Paris alongside Balzac, Molière, Edith Piaf, Oscar Wilde, Delacroix, Proust and Chopin. Some insist that, like Elvis, he is still alive somewhere. There was no media maelstrom around his passing.

Not long after talking to John Densmore, I met a family from Sicily who were staying with some friends in Lincoln. In the course of a wide-ranging conversation, their 15 year old daughter was asked what sort of music she liked (a Sicilian teenager in 1998). She said that her favourite band was probably one that we had never heard of. They were called The Doors.

My Finningley flight had been in a Jet Provost with the serial number XW431. Five years later it was decommissioned from the RAF and sold to a private owner. On Christmas Eve 1998, the aircraft crashed into the sea off the Essex coast after the pilot lost control and it went into a spin. He successfully ejected but died after landing in the cold sea. The rescue helicopter from RAF Wattisham found his body just after 9.30am on Christmas morning.

My first Jet Provost flight was in 1984 when the Central Flying School, the world's oldest military flying establishment, moved from RAF Leeming in North Yorkshire to Scampton. I was offered a seat in one of the Jet Provosts that was part of a formation overflying bases in Yorkshire and Lincolnshire in what was called a 'Farewell-Hello' salute. Allan Burney, the then editor of *Aircraft Illustrated* magazine, was also offered a place and we were told to report to Scampton for the coach north to Leeming the night before.

The formation was led by nine piston-engined Bulldog trainers, taking off from Leeming at 10am. Some minutes later, the 'Vintage Pair' of the Meteor and the Vampire, plus the spare Meteor, got airborne, followed by 16 Jet Provosts in 'box four' formations to create a large diamond in the sky. As I was strapped into the right hand seat of my JP I was praying that the aircraft was working properly. If it went unserviceable, my pilot would race to a spare but the rule was that the passenger would stay put. I would have to make my way back to Lincolnshire by road or train.

The JP *was* behaving and we rose off runway 34 and took our place in the middle of what was called 'Pelican' formation, named after the bird on the crest of the CFS. The 28 aircraft headed for the RAF bases at Linton-on-Ouse, Church Fenton, Finningley, Scampton, and Waddington. Transit height was 1,500 feet, coming down to 500 feet when overflying each base.

Above us a Hawk two-seat trainer circled round and darted forward. This was 'the whipper-in' or 'the whip' with someone on board telling the pilots if one of them was out of formation and thus making things look uneven from the ground. The Hawk also stayed in touch with each radar controller as the formation progressed from Yorkshire to Lincolnshire, obtaining the en-route clearances. 'Pelican' formation would only be flown VMC (visual meteorological conditions). In other words, it would not risk 28 aircraft in close formation in cloud.

After a flypast over the centre of Lincoln, the formation gradually broke up to recover to Scampton. There was a small crowd to greet us and I anticipated nonchalantly waving a white gloved hand at it as we taxied past. However I struggled to insert the ejection seat safety pins into their correct sockets and by the time my head came up from inside the cockpit, the moment had passed. Never compromise safety for vanity.

Chapter 20

Wear and Tears 1940-1953

The sound of the air raid siren at the end of every episode of *Dad's Army* chillingly resonated down the years through my Mum's life. She was nine when she first heard that wail roll round the night sky of Wearside. Her elder brother Frank became a bomb disposal expert with the Army – the sort of chap to be called out to defuse a device (or a bag of fertiliser) washed up in The Wash.

As the threat of German bombs falling on Wearside intensified, Sheila and Frank were evacuated from their home in Hastings Street in Sunderland and sent to the Yorkshire Dales. The winter months of early 1940 were long and hard. There were many days in the Dales without school because the snow was so deep. The RAF dropped hay to the scattered farms to feed the sheep and cattle. The ice on Semerwater was so thick that the Army could drive a 15 hundred weight truck on it, sometimes towing local youngsters on their skates.

There was an option for evacuees and the elderly to be sent to relatives in Canada but the parents of Sheila and Frank declined. One of Sheila's school friends *was* sent to Canada and embarked on the *SS City of Benares* in Liverpool in September 1940. He was one of 77 evacuees who died when the *Benares* was torpedoed by a U-boat 250 miles south-west of Rockall.

There were 407 people on board and 260 were lost. Most of the survivors were picked up from lifeboats by a warship 24 hours later.

'Despite the stories of the way some evacuees were treated, I looked back on it with great pleasure,' said Frank years later. 'Some people did not take kindly to this influx of townies from Sunderland but most of the locals were marvellous. Both my sister and I stayed in contact with the people we lived with until they died.'

Later in 1940, Frank reached school leaving age and returned to Sunderland. The phoney war was over and the serious bombing started around the shipbuilding yards on the Tyne and the Wear. 16 year old Frank joined the Auxiliary Fire Service, first as a messenger, then as a junior fireman and despatch rider.

'I was frightened by what I saw as a result of the bombing. The modern word would be traumatised. One evening I heard a German plane and then there was an enormous flash which blew me backwards. A whole street was devastated. There was a horrible smell of smoke and dust. There were gas leaks. I could hear people crying and shouting. I tried to lift a large piece of wood to help an old woman who was trapped. I swore at a chap who was trying to help because I thought he was making matters worse. I then realised I had sworn at my father, who served as a medic in the trenches of the Great War. He was in charge of the First Aid party.

'Further down the street, there was another wrecked building. Lying in the debris of what looked like a bedroom was a woman who had been split open down the length of her. Can you imagine it? In the light of the torches and the flames, I could see this. I turned away and I was sick and crying and shaking. An old copper came and put his arm round me and said 'Steady on, lad. Go and take a walk along the road.' That was me finished for the day. I wandered around in a daze. It really was horrific and haunts me forever. God, it was a terrible sight.'

—⟋⟍—

The iconic store of Binns in Fawcett Street was hit and set on fire. They pumped water out of the Wear but the fire raged all night. The gutted store was not rebuilt until after the war, finally reopening in 1953. Fires lit up the shipyards and the town night after night. Some bombs plopped harmlessly into the river. A corrugated tin roof at Hendon Dock took three days to burn out. It was red hot and the water bounced off it with an angry hissing sound. A warehouse full of butter and sugar was hit one night and the burning combination poured into the gutters.

'I was terrified at times. I was also elated to be involved. There was no time to think about it. I hated the Germans for what they had done to my life and my town but I could not personalise it to the man in the plane.'

For the next three years, the teenage Frank worked with the fire service. It was exciting at times, riding on the fire engines, ringing the bells as they rushed through the streets. There was no call-up for Frank. He won a scholarship to Sunderland Technical College to study marine engineering and an apprenticeship at one of Sunderland's big ship builders, John Dickinson and Son.

Dickinsons had suffered during the Depression but its facilities and workforce were back in demand for the war effort. The company repaired damaged ships including those from the Dutch navy who could not return to their occupied country. The workers were a combination of the very young and the old men who had come out of retirement to help. Men aged between 18 and 50 were away with the Forces. There was a brief strike which dragged in apprentices for the first time, in contravention of their contract. Frank benefitted with a doubling of his pay to £2.10 a week.

While working at the shipyard, Frank was also in the local Army Training Corps. He reported for training every Wednesday afternoon and on Saturdays to be shouted at by a Sergeant in his father's old regiment, the Durham Light Infantry. They were later subsumed into the Home Guard sometime after the original 'Dad's Army' was established in 1940.

Frank had no memories of VE Day in May 1945 other than he went for a bike ride in the country. The men were still away on the battlefields of the world. He had a day off but there were no street parties or 'nonsense like that.' He qualified as a junior draftsman in 1946 and got a new job at the Aberdeen shipbuilders of Hall, Russell and Company. Before he could take it up, he was called up for national service as an RAF driver.

He made it clear in his first RAF interview that he wanted to be in the Army – specifically the Royal Electrical and Mechanical Engineers. The RAF Sergeant took him down the corridor to the Army office and said: 'He wants to join your lot – God knows why.' With his marine engineering background and the qualifications that he had already acquired, he joined the Royal Engineers and was earmarked for a commission.

Frank passed the officer's selection course at Malta Barracks at Aldershot, the garrison town that he would return to with his family and a short distance from the airfield at Farnborough. Now a Second Lieutenant, he was given no choice in his first posting. He was sent to No. 7 Bomb Disposal Squadron at Bristol. It seemed no one volunteered for bomb disposal work but were assigned to it at random.

—m—

His first bomb proved troublesome. One of the many dropped on Avonmouth near Bristol two or three years earlier, it had failed to explode and had sunk 18 feet into the ground. The team dug down to create a shaft lined with timber. However at 14 feet, the earth changed to running sand and silt, requiring sheets of steel piling to keep the shaft secure.

With a pump constantly working to drain water out of the hole, the bomb slipped down another two feet. Frank could feel it in the slime but it was still slipping away from him. It took the team another year to finally retrieve it after pumping concrete underneath it to stop it sinking further into the earth.

A transfer back to the north-east, where his fiancée Mavis was waiting for him, was granted and Frank became an acting Captain with No. 20 Bomb Disposal Squadron. In 1949 at the age of 25, he had responsibility for clearing unexploded bombs across all of Northern England and Scotland. To the envy of more senior ranks, he was allocated a staff car because of the huge number of miles that he was clocking up.

One call was to a dredger in the Victoria Dock at Hull. An unexploded Type C parachute mine had been inadvertently hooked by the dredger crew and was now sitting in the bucket. It could have caused considerable devastation if it had gone off. It took two days for Frank and a Navy team to make it safe and put it on a lorry. They took it to a range near Otterburn in Northumberland where it was exploded, leaving a crater 20 feet across and 12 feet deep.

Hundreds of thousands of bombs and mines were dropped on the UK during the Second World War and many did not explode. Just because there was a crater and considerable damage did not mean the bomb had actually gone off. Some 50,000 unexploded bombs were made safe during the war by bomb disposal teams. Around 750 members of those teams lost their lives.

In the years immediately after the war, the country was

littered with what were called UXBs. They could be buried up to 60 feet from the surface. Seventy years later, German bombs are still being found, usually by people working for building companies. An estimated 15,000 items ranging from unexploded bombs to small mortar rounds and grenades were removed from UK construction sites between 2006 and 2008 alone, according to the Construction Industry Research and Information Association.

One of the great characters in the television series 'MASH' was called Frank. Major Frank Burns, played by the actor Larry Linville, lusted after Major Margaret 'Hot Lips' Houlihan (Loretta Swit) who led him on and knocked him back mercilessly. Frank Burns was second in command of the 4077th Mobile Army Surgical Hospital with American troops in Korea. He was also the butt of most of the jokes. He aspired to greater rank and crawled to those above him. Called in to the office of Lieutenant Colonel Henry Blake, the boss offers him a cigarette and asks 'Smoke, Frank?' Burns replies: 'If you want me to, Sir.'

For my generation, 'MASH' (the book, the film and the 256 television episodes) was the entry point for finding out about the Korean War which became known as 'The Forgotten War'. The storylines and rapid-fire wit were regarded as metaphors for what was going on in the Vietnam War which was still in progress when the film came out and the television shows began. The real Korean War began in June 1950 when the North Korean army poured over the 38th parallel that served as the border with the pro-Western South Korea.

Frank Smith did not think much of 'MASH' and he did not talk much about his experiences in Korea. In his time on the peninsula, he sustained terrible injuries and was lucky to stay alive. His problems did not come from combat but from an unusual form of 'friendly fire' courtesy of his American counterparts. The story did not emerge until his grandson Paul unearthed some recordings Frank had made for the Imperial War Museum.

—⁓—

To get a full-time commission, acting Captain Frank Smith needed broader experience. He knew a great deal about bomb disposal but had spent little or no time with frontline units. In December 1952, they sent him to Korea where the war had been waging for more than two years. He embarked on a troopship in Liverpool and arrived in Pusan (Busan) on the other side of the world 30 days later.

The world maps on the office door or the classroom wall came to life for him. There were still vast swathes of pink on these maps, signalling the British Empire. 'We stopped in Gibraltar where the Union Jack was flying. Then still-British Malta and down the Suez Canal to Steamer Point at Aden where the Union Jack was flying. On to Ceylon (now Sri Lanka) and Singapore and Hong Kong – still the Union Jack,' he said years later. In fact Frank did not see much of Malta. He succumbed to appendicitis and had the irritating organ whipped out by the troopship's medical team en route.

Reporting to the 28th Field Regiment in Korea, he found himself drawn back into bomb disposal as that expertise was thin on the ground. He was introduced to the boss of the U.S Army's 24th Explosive Ordnance Disposal Control Detachment who offered to get him involved in what his unit was doing and invited him to join their missions. He learnt about Russian and Chinese-made weapons that the North Koreans were using and pulled together some examples to be shipped back to the UK for analysis.

Packing them carefully, Frank flew across to Japan in a transport aircraft of the Royal Australian Air Force. He returned to his contacts at the British Commonwealth Engineer Unit in the rapidly recovering Hiroshima and began work on preparing the shipment. It was at this point that he realized the Americans had left a detonator in one of the devices, despite assuring him that they had all been made safe.

'While I was handling this damn thing, the detonator exploded. It blew the ends of my fingers off. Peppered my face. That's how I hurt myself. I had carried this blessed thing on a RAAF aircraft. Whether it was the heat from my hand, whether it was the heat and cold it was subject to lying in a field in a Korea, whether I squeezed it or knocked it, I don't know. All I know is that it went off in my hand.'

Frank was taken to the British Commonwealth Military Hospital at Kure to the south-east of Hiroshima. 'They did a bloody marvelous job on me. Colonel Wright, the surgeon, sewed my hands up. I had skin grafts on my fingers. My eyes were treated by an ophthalmist called Ken Milne. He took fragments of the detonator out of my eye and sewed up my eyeball. Just think about it. He put three stitches in my eyeball. Can you imagine it? Brilliant! You hear today about the marvels of surgery but here he was in a military hospital in Japan in 1953. Incredible!'

Three days after all the surgery, Frank came round from the general anaesthetic but he could not see anything or feel anything. He had to be fed by a nurse who had been brought up on a sheep farm in Australia. They talked a lot but he never actually saw her. Two weeks later, the bandages were removed from his eyes and the stitches taken out. He remembers first seeing the light of a window across the ward and the red cape of a Nursing Sister called Marie McDonald.

After three weeks in hospital, Frank was sent to Miya Jima in Hiroshima Bay for recovery and rehabilitation. Wearing special gloves to cover his damaged hands and an eye patch over one eye, the piratical-looking Captain Smith took to the waves in one of the sailing dinghies that were provided for the resting troops. A storm blew up and he struggled to get back to the shore, finally being rescued in the dark by the crew of a local fishing boat.

The saltwater had opened the wounds on his hands and the skin grafts were coming away. So it was back to the hospital at Kure to be patched up again by a surgeon with sympathy in short supply after hearing about his patient's nautical expedition. Frank was sent back to his unit and not long afterwards was up on the front line in Korea. There was not much action as the war had reached a stalemate, with most of the exchanges being described as nighttime skirmishes.

One of his last tasks in Korea was serving as a Liaison Officer back with the 28th Field Regiment. When the war ended, he was assigned to help one of the Armistice Commissions which had the task of drawing up the new border between North and South Korea. The agreement was that each side would pull back one kilometre from the agreed line, thus leaving a two kilometre gap which would be a demilitarized zone.

With a party of sappers doing the hard work, the Commission decided where the border line should run and marked it by getting stakes driven into the ground and fixing white tape to them. When the group came to a minefield, Frank suggested conceding it all to the North and thus let it be their problem. The Swedish Army Colonel from the neutral Commission insisted they followed the line and the white tape duly went through the middle of the minefield – after the lucky sappers had cleared a way through it. 'If we deviate from it by one millimetre, it could lead to an incident in the future,' said the Swede.

Frank conceded he was right but grumbled about the lives

of British troops being risked to draw a straight line. If his suggestion had been taken up, the border separating North and South Korea would have been that little bit different. A British Bomb Disposal man selflessly tried to donate rather than detonate a whole minefield to the Democratic People's Republic of Korea, now the world's most militarized nation. Nice try, Frank.

Frank Smith left the Army as a Major and embarked on a second career with the Civil Service. He and Mavis had three children, two of whom pre-deceased Frank before he died in April 2013 at the age of 88. His ashes lie in Sunderland cemetery, alongside those of his wife and his mother and the graves of his father and grandparents.

My maternal grandfather and the father of bomb disposer Frank was called Robert Francis Smith. He was the son of another Robert Francis Smith who, in 1903, was a Committee member of the evocatively named 'Monkwearmouth Poor Bairns' Fund'. Young Frank joined the 2/2nd Northumberland Field Ambulance of the Royal Army Medical Corps Territorials in Gateshead in January 1915. After training, they embarked for France in April attached to the Durham Light Infantry. Frank worked as a medic in the trenches at Ypres, the Somme, Arras and Passchendaele.

He never talked about what he went through. He was taken prisoner on 27th May 1918 (six months before the war ended) at a place called Corbeny, south east of Laon in northern France. The Germans were launching what proved to be their last attack towards Paris and got within 40 miles of the French capital. Frank and five colleagues got separated from other British troops and, not long after 1am, were staring down the barrels of ten German machine guns.

Corporal Robert Smith, with his medic's armband, before embarking for the battlefields of Europe 1915

More than a month later, news got through to his parents that he was a prisoner. The card from the Red Cross said his name had come through on a list of prisoners of war at a 'Camp Unknown'. Someone had hand-written above his name 'He is well' but there was no more information.

The Germans got him to move ammunition around at their railhead at Amifontaine. He was held captive in a pigsty and fed on potato peelings and cabbage leaves. When British aircraft bombed the railhead, the British prisoners suffered further casualties. His best friend was badly injured and subsequently died. Despite being a Medical Corps orderly, my grandfather was not allowed to treat his best mate. Years later, he returned to see if his friend had been given a proper burial in a Commonwealth War Graves cemetery. He had.

Corporal Robert Smith's fiancée Emma Florence Craig did not recognise him when she went to collect him from Sunderland railway station after the de-mob in 1919. Having been gassed, taken prisoner and fed badly, he was given six months to live. Emma said she would marry him immediately and look after him. Having survived the Somme and witnessed indescribable deaths and injuries, he lived until he was 87 and fathered Frank and my mother Sheila. He was a commercial traveller working for the Spillers Milling Group for 46 years before retiring in 1959.

Robert Smith was taken prisoner just two months after the Royal Air Force was formed. He was born at the dawn of aviation, just before the Wright Brothers made the first powered flight in 1903. A generation before, flight meant little more than falconry. By the time he died, it was F-16 Fighting Falcons.

In his lifetime, he saw global air travel for the masses become unremarkable and watched men walking on the Moon. He lived through two World Wars and the Cold War. He tried to keep up and then gave up with the pace of change in culture, science, and technology. He benefitted from the huge leap in provision of healthcare and medicine. He continued to suffer terrible nightmares from his times in the trenches but never ever talked about his war experiences to anyone except his wife.

Emma died in 1984 aged 88 but never passed on the horrors that she heard from him. She succumbed to dementia in her later years, and moved into a nursing home in Sunderland where, one night, the ceiling of her room fell in on her. She 'escaped' once with her little brown suitcase which contained a bottle of brandy. When she was found, she ended up swearing at the police and trying to fight them. One constable told my parents that she had created more mayhem than a bunch of football supporters after a Tyne-Wear derby.

Chapter 21

Reds in the Med

'Come in, come in, sit down, sit down,' said Mr Magic. 'Red Arrows – Viva! Viva!'…..A group of journalists with their RAF minder had stumbled on a restaurant called the Maos Tavern which also appeared to be called The Red Arrows Tavern. We said we were with the Reds at Akrotiri and could we have a look at his estimable eaterie? He waved us in enthusiastically.

We all wanted to inject some local colour into our television, radio and newspaper coverage of the month or so that the Red Arrows spent in the Cypriot sun to perfect their displays for the coming season. The Reds had the weekend off so the journalists were off the leash, leaving the Akrotiri dispersal to immerse themselves in Greek-Cypriot culture. Coming across a place called The Red Arrows Tavern at Ipsonas near Limassol was an unexpected blessing for our merry bunch.

In the morning we had found some locals flying their radio-controlled models and, thank you God, one of those models just happened to be a Red Arrows Hawk. While some Cypriots resented the British military presence on their island, many others were won over by the presence of the Red Arrows every spring. The team would usually do three training sorties a day in the Akrotiri Sovereign Base Area and the Hawks and their smoke could be seen for miles around. This model flier and his friends had an ambition to fly several radio-controlled Hawks in formation. Good luck with that, Sir!

The self-styled Mr Magic waved us to some tables and, without us ordering anything, food started to arrive along with bottles of Keo beer and Othello red wine. It was late Saturday afternoon. The restaurant started to fill up and the atmosphere became extremely convivial. We thought no more about looking at menus. The food that was arriving was very good and we had plenty of Cypriot pounds in our pockets to pay for it.

The restaurant was now heaving with people, especially local families with young children. At one point, our new friend took to the stage and, with a small band behind him, launched off into some ballads and folk songs with lots of clapping. At the end of one song, he addressed the crowded restaurant in Cypriot Greek which indeed was all Greek to us. The one word that we did understand was when he waved his arm with a flourish and pointed at our table and shouted 'Peelots!'

'Bloody hell, he thinks *we* are the actual Red Arrows pilots,' said one of our number. Small children with wide eyes appeared beside our table and everyone seemed to be applauding. We smiled somewhat thinly as we muttered to each other about how we were going to extricate ourselves from this misunderstanding. I have never produced my BBC identity card so fast in my life. Mr Magic was not fazed. 'BBC – Viva , Viva!' At least he knew that I was not a Red Arrows pilot. The others could sort themselves out.

The magnificent evening ended with him refusing to charge us, despite our protestations and thrusting wads of cash at him. Waving to all as we made our exit, we agreed in the mini-bus on the way back to our accommodation at Episkopi that we would pool our Red Arrows news releases and photographs and return to the tavern the following morning. We would hand them over and see if he was up for photographs and interviews. If he decided in the cold light of dawn that he had been hoodwinked and turned nasty, we would pay for the Saturday night and head for the hills.

So on the Sunday lunchtime, we tentatively returned to Mr Magic's emporium. He was very pleased to see us again and posed for photographs and brief faltering interviews in English for television and radio. He then insisted that we all stay for lunch as the locals were enjoying a village festival with stalls and dancing. We accepted but repeatedly insisted he must charge us this time. 'Yes, yes of course,' he said. He did not. We had arrived about 12 noon and finally left about 5pm. As a bonus half way through the afternoon, one of the Red Arrows pilots rolled up on a motor scooter as he toured the area. We fell upon him and pointed out his photos in the brochure to Mr Magic. 'He is a *real* pilot,' we enthused, ensuring lots of photographs were taken of the pair together.

The courses kept coming and the locals came to talk to us. Mr Magic's father told me he drank a bottle of brandy a day and was feeling fine at 70 years old. We ended up pushing cash at some of the staff as tips as Mr Magic resolutely refused to give us a bill. Quite extraordinary generosity from a madly hospitable man.

'We'd like to make an early start,' said Carole, the public relations lady. 'Fine! Tell us what time and we shall be ready,' said the press pack as one. The night was warm, the hour late, the day long and the tavern at Pissouri was friendly and relaxing with lights on the ships and boats twinkling out on the dark Mediterranean. 'Alarm at 5.30am, breakfast at 6 and transport leaves at 6.30 – ok?' The small party representing Her

Majesty's Media flinched slightly. This was almost 'crack of sparrow fart' or 'O Christ hundred hours' in military parlance. The whole trip to Cyprus had started in the early hours with a dawn chorus of alarms in the Gateway Hotel at Brize to catch the VC10 out east.

Early starts were part of the working life in radio. Full nightfly shifts were very rare on local radio stations except for elections coverage and major incidents. Instead the breakfast team would set their alarms for 4am or earlier and make the gesture of going to bed earlier than everyone else in the household. For me, the setting of the alarm would often trigger a night of disturbed sleep, opening half an eye towards the bedside clock invariably an hour at a time before finally sliding off into a deep sleep just before the alarm burst into life. I was lucky though. The longest continuous stretch of early shifts that I undertook was only six weeks when standing in as presenter on Radio Oxford's breakfast programme 'Oxford AM'. Some people do it for years.

In the early days before all things digital, one of the first jobs of the day for the Station Assistant (SA) on a local radio station was to check that the clocks were accurate. You did this by ringing the talking clock. This had been introduced in 1936 and was obtained in major UK cities by dialling the letters TIM (also the numbers 846) on a telephone. The talking clock was thus often referred to as 'TIM'.

On his first morning, a new SA on one radio station was asked by his producer to 'Ring TIM and check the time on the studio clocks'. The radio station boss just happened to be called Tim. When his bedside phone rang in the darkness way before the dawn, he anticipated a big news story or something serious involving his radio station. 'Hello, is that Tim? It's the early SA. What's the time?'

—✺—

Having spent ten minutes wrestling with the bedside alarm clock in Room 1 of Block 354 at the Officer's Mess at Episkopi army base, I dropped off. Almost immediately it seems, there was a hammering on the door. A Cypriot gentleman swept into my room, head swathed in a scarf and a woolly hat and clutching a teapot. Batman. 'Morning Sir! Tea Sir?' He had beaten the alarm by five minutes. It seems the military abroad in 1992 still had their batmen or 'battys' and were not going to let the journalists miss their transport.

It was a 20 minute drive to RAF Akrotiri. The Hawks loomed into view, neatly lined up on Alpha dispersal. Sitting on tatty blue chairs outside an even tattier hut that was their flightline base, the tanned and sun-shaded pilots listened to the 'Boss' who ran through the briefing for the first sortie. The sun forced its way through the high thin cloud and the birds sang. A C-130 Hercules lumbered off Akrotiri's Runway 28, heading for the UK.

The pilots were relaxed and friendly with the journalists but you never really got 'in' with them. Each pilot usually only did three years with the team unless selected as Red 1 (the team leader) who would return for another three year tour a few years later. A 2014 television documentary on the Reds was called 'Inside the Bubble', emphasising that the Reds and their support team are a tight-knit bunch despite the turnover. In Cyprus the pressure was on to get the Public Display Authority signed off for the summer, something that the three FNGs were particularly aware of. (FNGs – 'Flipping New Guys' it says here….)

You have to be more than a good pilot to join the Reds. You have to be a team player and comfortable with being in the public eye for three years or more. The questions at the shows come thick and fast. 'Is it dangerous? How far apart do you fly? Are you going to be scrapped as part of defence cuts? Can you open our garden fete? How much will it cost me to fly with you? Are you better than the French and the Italians then? Are you married?'

I have a copy of the Red Arrows brochure for 1968, which was the 50th anniversary of the founding of the Royal Air Force. I even got an autograph in it but not from any of the pilots. That honour fell to the 'mange' (team manager) at the time, Flight Lieutenant Lewis Willcox, who was on the crowd line at some point in the huge display at RAF Abingdon on the 15th June that year. The team leader was the renowned Ray Hanna, a founder member of the Reds, and the Station Commander at Abingdon was Group Captain Norman Hoad, who became one of the UK's leading aviation artists.

When I was at BBC Radio Oxford, the Red Arrows were based at RAF Kemble in Gloucestershire. The team had also spent time at two other Gloucestershire airfields – Fairford and Little Rissington. So I was pushing my luck when, as a Radio Oxford reporter, I asked my editor if I could go to Kemble and cover the media event marking the change of the Red Arrows aircraft from the Gnat to the Hawk. One of my arguments was that there was no BBC Radio Gloucestershire (that would not open for another eight years) and that my report could go on the BBC circuits for all local radio stations to pick up and run.

Squadron Leader Brian Hoskins had the task of guiding them through the significant changes presented by their new mount for the 1980 season. Squadron Leader Richard Thomas was one of the pilots who got a rare *four* year first tour with the team to help provide some continuity across the change-over. 'I remember picking up the Hawks from the (long gone) BAE airfield at Bitteswell – it was very exciting', Richard told me years later. 'The Hawk was a beautiful aircraft to fly but I had a lasting love affair with the Gnat. It was tighter and slower which allowed us closer to the crowd than the Hawk. The top of the loop had to be higher with the Hawk as well.'

The weather on the day of the Kemble media event was awful with rain lashing across the Cotswolds. Plans for a display by the new Hawks were abandoned and so there were no jet sound effects to embellish my report. The team had been due to run through its full routine from 11.33am to 12 noon before the pilots would be available for interviews and photographs. It was nevertheless exhilarating to be there on an historic day for the team which is still using the Hawk nearly 40 years on.

My elder sister Alison was getting married at our father's church at Filey on the Yorkshire coast on Saturday 27 July 1980. That day was later named as Lifeboat Day in Filey – an event usually held in August. One of the attractions, apart from the RAF rescue helicopter from Leconfield, was to be a display by the Red Arrows over Filey Bay. We discovered that the Reds display coincided exactly with the wedding ceremony inside St Oswald's church. What a dilemma! Do I sneak out of my sister's wedding service to watch the Reds? I was an usher so would be checking for late arrivals.

'Cupid aims his bow – but Arrows get in the way' was the imaginative headline in the *Northern Echo* on the day before the wedding, accompanied by a photograph of the bride-to-be. The story read that 'A group of noisy jet setters have forced a young couple to alter the time of their wedding.'

The Reds were due to display over Filey Bay at 1.30pm and would be using the church, which stood out on the cliffs to the north of the town, as a visual reference point. The time of the wedding was brought forward so that the happy couple and their guests would emerge from the church at the same time as the Reds arrived. Perfect planning.

The Law of Sod ensured that the weather in Filey on that day was not good. A sea fret – a thick fog that regularly rolls onto the Yorkshire coast off the North Sea – settled over the town. We caught one glimpse of the Red Arrows through the clag as they made one circle of Filey Bay before abandoning the idea and heading off to Plymouth. Smoke off, gone.

The Red Arrows introduced their 'Apollo' formation in 1970 as a tribute to the space programme that put the first man on the Moon the year before. Flt Lt Dickie Duckett, who was in his second season with the Reds and later returned as leader, recalled years later: 'On the night of the Moon landing, the team was in Strasbourg and had been out to dinner. On our way back, we stopped to watch some of it on the pavement in front of a television sales shop that had left a few sets on!' It is a great image. The Red Arrows watching the first moon landing in the shop window of a Strasbourg version of Radio Rentals.

The Eagle landed mid-evening UK time and the two astronauts took that 'One small step for Man, One giant leap for Mankind' some six hours later. I stayed up all night to watch it and fell asleep just before Neil Armstrong's foot and leg finally and gingerly slipped into that grainy camera view. The world witnessed the first landing on the Moon (20 July) and the Woodstock Festival (15-18 August) less than a month later. At the same time the USA was drafting young men only three years older than me to send them off to fight in Vietnam.

Only seven months earlier, the crew of Apollo 8 were the first to see the far side of the Moon. On Christmas Eve 1968, they went into the first lunar orbit and took the first photograph of an 'Earthrise'. Borman, Lovell and Anders read from *Genesis* and wished a Merry Christmas to the millions listening 'on the Good Earth', adding on Christmas morning 'Please be informed there is a Santa Claus'. Proof indeed that the Moon landings were not elaborate hoaxes filmed in the Nevada desert.

That period was a strange and exciting time to be a teenager and, as my curiosity about all such things grew, perhaps the seeds were sown then for a lifetime in journalism.

Back at Akrotiri, we had been driven from the Reds dispersal to a vantage point near the runway not far from the Wessex helicopters of 84 Squadron. The Reds were preparing for the second sortie of the day. Suddenly a big 4x4 vehicle appeared and out stepped a large guy in a baseball cap, jeans and trainers.

'Morning Gentlemen. Sure appreciate it if you could put your cameras away. Our bird is coming in.' His *bird* was coming in? Our RAF escort officer nodded compliance and explained. This casually dressed chap was CIA and his *bird* was a Lockheed U-2 spy plane which had probably been on a mission over Lebanon. We duly downed cameras and recorders until the U-2 had glided past us on Akrotiri's runway and trundled out of sight. The following day, the same U-2 was in the circuit for more than 30 minutes and was snapped and filmed by Her Majesty's Media with no CIA in sight.

Trips with the military always threw up problems and issues and, if you had some understanding of military procedures and mind-set, you could roll with it although you would never be 'inside the bubble'. Some journalists and photographers got over-excitable at minor mishaps or when what was promised on the schedule did not or could not materialise. After one Cyprus trip, I got a letter from one of the RAF escort officers thanking me for my co-operation 'over all things trivial' and 'your helpful attitude throughout the visit.' Expect the SNAFU and look forward to the first stiffener in the Mess.

The RAF and the Reds got a lot of positive publicity out of me over the years without me hopefully ever compromising my journalistic integrity. Where your contacts and knowledge of the RAF really came to the fore was when something went wrong. There were several accidents involving the Reds while I was news editor at Radio Lincolnshire. However the one that came closest to testing my admiration for the team was when two of them collided and crashed not far from my home and family.

Chapter 22

Settle in the Straps

Another routine practice, working up the three FNGs. Seven of the nine jets are running up their engines for this sortie in the Scampton air space. There is a slight delay as Red 2 has problems with the air-brake under the fuselage which initially fails to extend. However after more checks in which the mechanism works as it should, the aircraft head off to the runway. Everything proceeds uneventfully with Red 2 deploying his airbrake several times.

As the formation rolls out from a right hand turn in a slight climb, the leader calls for airbrakes in preparation for a manoeuvre back over Scampton's runway. Red 2 selects his airbrake but it fails again as it had done on the ground. As a result, he begins to move forward under the lead aircraft. Red 2 calls for the leader to roll out of the formation but, before he can, the two jets touch. Both pilots eject as the others break formation and scatter.

One of the Hawks comes down in a field but the other clips a house in Monce Close in the village of Welton a couple of miles east of RAF Scampton. An old man is having a bath upstairs in the house that was hit. The village primary school is a few hundred yards away. My house is at the opposite end of the village.

When the first reports of the crash come into the BBC Radio Lincolnshire newsroom, they speak of one of the Red Arrows 'crashing onto Welton'. As colleagues start to ring the emergency services and get the radio car ready, I ring home. My wife Val and two toddler sons are fine. They had heard a big bang but had not actually seen anything. We later estimated that the collision may well have happened near our house. No one on the ground is hurt. The new team leader and Red 2 ejected safely but spend some time in hospital, one of them coincidently in the next bed to someone I knew. Some serious luck was with Welton and the Reds on that day, 16th November 1987.

Nearly a year later, the official report on the Welton crash was published. One of my contacts within the RAF media team tipped me off that the report had been placed in the House of Commons library. Early evening, she agreed to fax over a copy of it as it was now in the public domain. As nobody else in the media had it, I decided to spike it until the next morning rather than lose the exclusive to the regional evening bulletins.

However I did phone the team manager of the Reds for a comment but he was not aware that the report had been released. Nobody had told them. I said he could come and take a copy if he wished. Henry came down the A15 from Scampton within 30 minutes, grateful for the BBC's 'heads-up' on the official findings.

The inquiry determined that the accident was caused by the failure to maintain safe separation between the lead and the number 2 aircraft. Well, yes. The airbrake failure was cited as a 'contributory cause' although its failure to actually work at the required time appeared to have been at the crux of the collision. It added that 'Hawk airbrake selector switch maintenance had been reviewed and a redesign of the associated circuitry was being investigated'. It also stated that minor claims had been settled with interim payments made on those still to be finalised. In other words the old man whose bathroom suddenly acquired new views and ventilation rightly got his roof repaired courtesy of the MOD.

The Red Arrows do not do dangerous things but they do master difficult things. Flying nine jets in close formation at 400mph is not without its risks but, as one of their leaders told me, it was safer than driving on the motorway. In the Reds, you knew what the people around you would do next. On the M1, you could never tell.

I was being viewed very suspiciously by the groundcrew of 29 Squadron at RAF Coningsby. Oh God, not another civilian media man cadging a ride in one of our Tornado F3 interceptors. Yes, I had asked again. Any chance of a trip in a Tornado to illustrate on the radio what you get up to at Coningsby and why you make all that noise? Flt Lt Angus Elliott drew the short straw and, on a sunny morning in June 1992, we strapped into our Tornado inside one of the hardened shelters on the south side of Coningsby air base. As we taxied out, I was reminded to remove the last ejection safety pin and stow it in the appointed place. 'If we do have to bang out, I'll see you on the ground,' he said cheerily.

He also said: 'Whatever you do, tell me if you don't feel too good and make sure you have the sickbag ready.' I discovered that the squadron had flown a Radio 1 disc jockey only a couple of weeks earlier. The pilot had asked this character if he was ok and he said 'Yes, fine.' In fact he had thrown up all over the rear cockpit. The groundcrew had to clear it up and were very unhappy. It was still fresh in their minds and indeed up their noses when I bowled up.

'Two burners, looking good,' said Angus as the Tornado

surged down Runway 25. Once we were airborne and the undercarriage was tucked up, we launched into an afterburner vertical climb. It was surely the most exhilarating experience of my life. 15,000 feet in under 30 seconds. As the Tornado rolled off the top, the ribbons of taxiways and the runway from whence we had come slipped into view above me. I remembered those Lightnings at Farnborough in 1962 as they went vertical and now I had just done it myself.

With barely time to catch my breath, we were heading east for the coast. I looked at the on-board cassette recorder to check the tape was going round and recording all conversations. It had stopped. This machine was used on most flights to catch all exchanges between the two crew and between them and the radar controllers. It had chosen this flight with me on board to go unserviceable and get snagged. There was nothing for it but to settle in the straps, enjoy the ride and savour the experience.

Now we were over the North Sea and up to 35,000 feet. I was again asked to help keep an eye open for other aircraft. Radar controllers would warn pilots of other aircraft in their vicinity but sometimes the information was brief. 'Contact in your ten o'clock. Left to right. No height.' I spotted an American A-10 way above us to the left as we pulled into a climb but my pilot had already clocked it. If we had been on an interception exercise, the crew would get short bursts of information. 'One stranger, 10 miles and closing, slightly right, travelling south.'

The Mark One Eyeball was still an important asset for fast jet pilots and navigators. Later that year (1992), there was an incident involving a famous horse jockey rather than a disc jockey. As some Tornados emerged from cloud after taking off from Waddington, they had to scatter as a light aircraft hove into view. The Piper Seneca was tipped over by the Tornado jet wash before the pilot regained control. After a brief emergency diversion into Waddington, he continued on the flight, taking top flat jockey Lester Piggott to a race meeting in York. Piggott later gave an interview telling how he was thrown around in the aircraft, mumbling 'Flipping heck, what was that?' (or something similar). It was a close call.

Angus found some clear airspace and pulled up for a loop. The gravity pushed me into the seat and my anti-g suit inflated to counteract it and keep my blood in the right parts of my body. A barrel roll followed, rolling up and gently over and then a basic roll, fast and furious as the horizon revolved around me. My system needed a moment to settle down and Angus held the 'Tonka' straight and level. I burped into my face mask and everything seemed to clear. A minute or so later my equilibrium returned along with the grin.

No opportunity for me to fly the Tornado as this back seat had no joystick. However there was the chance to go supersonic. Turning the Tornado east and some 30 miles from the coast, Angus opened the throttles and the needle on the airspeed indicator eased past MACH 1. The second run was a 'supersonic slam acceleration' at low level. In the aircraft I barely noticed – the only indication being on the dials. Outside the sonic boom rolled round the North Sea over the rigs and the ships.

After an hour, we were back at Coningsby for two 'touch and gos' before landing for good. As the cockpit canopy came up, I offered an immediate confirmation for the grateful groundcrew that I was leaving the rear cockpit exactly as I had found it apart from a snarled up cassette. We retrieved it and I used the moment that it snagged in the documentary, adding 'actuality' from one of my pilot's earlier missions (with some bits blanked out for security reasons) to give the programme more atmosphere.

My Tornado for that flight had the serial number ZG734. Five years later it was leased to the Italian Air Force before being returned to the RAF in 2003 and stripped down for spares at RAF St Athan in South Wales. This powerful and graceful machine finally came to an undignified end in a scrap yard in Hitchin.

To complete a radio series I did on the Red Arrows in 1992, I joined that season's Red 2, Flt Lt Rob Last, on a singleton sortie to Norfolk and back. Pilots had to ensure that their solo skills were up to date and on this flight he would plan and execute a low level navigation exercise, perform some solo aerobatics and practice what to do in the event of a problem while in formation with the other Reds. After the standard ejection seat briefing and another 'fit to fly' medical, I settled into one of the famous red Hawks on the Scampton dispersal at 11.40am on 13 May.

Perfectly parked back at Scampton,
the Red Hawk XX306 and its back seat driver

Most of the flight was low level between 250 and 300 feet. The first 'target' was the sugar beet factory at Bardney, then it was down through the gap between Coningsby and Cranwell on a heading of 176 degrees. After a course change onto 069 degrees north of March in Cambridgeshire, we streaked through the sunny blue sky to the north of RAF Marham and onwards eastwards, Sculthorpe to the left of us and West Raynham to the right.

Then we were overhead Cromer Golf Club, near where Colin Curtis and his crew had their last sight of England as their Wellington climbed into the night sky 50 years earlier. There was brief pull-up and a short burst of smoke to say hello to the greenkeeper at my pilot's old club ('Don't mention that, please!') before calling up the tower at RAF Coltishall, a Jaguar base at the time and now silent and shut.

After the approach and overshoot on Coltishall's Runway 22, our Hawk headed east of Blakeney and turned onto 303 degrees to sweep across the mouth of the Wash. It was here that I got my hands on the joystick. 'You have control', said my pilot. 'I have control.' I nursed the Hawk along, making land just north of Skegness where Rob took over again. I suspect Rob's right hand was very close to the stick throughout my time in charge travelling at six miles a minute low level over the sea.

'Can you cope with a loop, Mike?' I was feeling very good actually. The Lincolnshire Wolds loomed up above me. What would the county's famous son Tennyson have made and written of this experience high above his birthplace? Indeed would the scientist Isaac Newton, who was born near Grantham in 1693, have grasped the concept and grace of powered flight. He died only ten years or so before the births of the Montgolfier Brothers, who pioneered the first manned ascent from earth in a hot air balloon.

Enough of these flights of fancy. Our Hawk was now back

in the Scampton overhead, pulling up sharply to replicate an engine failure or a bird strike. An hour after takeoff, we came in for a 'break and land' and it was all over. The tape recorder worked and feature went out the following week.

My aircraft for the flight (XX306) was one of the original Hawks delivered to the Red Arrows in 1980 and unveiled to the media at the press conference I attended at Kemble. The team used it for 32 years before it was retired in October 2012 – the same month and year that I retired from the BBC after 34 years. XX306 clocked up just over 7,378 flying hours and completed 13,007 landings including the one with me in the back seat. The aircraft got somewhat shabby in storage at Shawbury but was restored in 2015. To my delight, it is now on display as the 'gate guardian' at RAF Scampton and clearly visible from the A15.

—ᴡ—

Heading south west through the airspace where Colin Curtis learnt to fly the Wellington, the two Harriers powered down the Daventry radar corridor and on to the Welsh borders. The jump-jets, with callsigns Laser 1 and Laser 2, had done a rolling take-off on Wittering's Runway 26 on 99 per cent power and a 'bit of nozzle'. A student pilot who had recently completed his advanced pilot training on the Hawk was now learning how to operate the Harrier. He was tasked to lead his instructor in the second aircraft and find a bridge and a barn deep in rural Herefordshire and simulate attacks on both of them.

There had been some confusion in the crewroom of 20 (Reserve) Squadron as to whom I was going to fly with that day in July 1993. Some thought it was an afternoon trip as a singleton. Others wanted to be away at lunchtime for the school sports day. Squadron Leader Dave Poole was due to follow the student pilot that morning and was looking somewhat dubious about having a stranger in the back of his two-seater T4. He perked up when I said: 'If it helps, I have done this sort of thing before.'

It was a bumpy ride with more turbulence than the Red Arrows flight. Low level through the valleys of the Welsh borders was exciting but I reached for sick-bag. Dave Poole (callsign 'Poo') asked how I was doing in the back. 'Bit queasy. Got the bag out just in case.' He said there were about five more minutes at low level, then they would be pulling up to 11,000 feet for the flight home. I would feel better then, especially as he would let me fly it.

The student found his bridge and barn and the mission was deemed successful. The two Harriers gained altitude and headed back east in a very loose formation. Dave Poole handed me control and we ploughed on with a wary eye on the Harrier slightly ahead of us and higher up on the left. 'I think you've got the hang of this, Mike,' said Dave, which banished my last waves of queasiness. The trick is to be gentle with the joystick. Oh, and get someone else to look after the head-up display, rudder pedals, throttles, control surfaces, trim, instruments, airspeed, weather, maps, radio, oxygen, radars, warning lights and weapons. Piece of cake, as the chaps used to say.

Then we were into cloud and Dave took over again, easing our Harrier closer to the lead so that we remained 'visual' with him. Laser formation checked in with London Military air traffic controllers. 'Two Harriers inbound Wittering. One POB, the second two POB.' (Persons on board – sometime referred to as SOB for Souls on Board). The A1 slipped past below us as the Harriers decelerated towards the threshold of Runway 26. Dave executed a perfect vertical landing on one of the pads next to the runway.

The BBC cassette recorder plugged into the aircraft's communications system picked up everything said and heard on the flight and the feature on Harrier operations at Wittering was broadcast a few days later. It proved to be my last fast jet flight with the RAF but Harriers, in updated variants, continued with the service until controversially phased out in the 2010 Coalition defence cuts. Many were then sold to the United States Marine Corps for spares for their squadrons. However the registration of the one I flew in had a remarkable new lease of life.

ZD993 was later transferred to the Royal Navy and became a Sea Harrier T8 trainer. It was eventually grounded and ended up as an instructional air frame. However in 2014, an American entrepreneur and former Marine Corps pilot called Art Nalls bought another Sea Harrier T8 and shipped it from the UK to Maryland. He repainted it as the Royal Navy's ZD993 and is now in the process of restoring it to flying condition. Art has already got a single seat Sea Harrier back in the air and hopes to be flying both on the American air show circuit in due course.

We had a former RAF sergeant as a 'handyman' at Radio Lincolnshire for a couple of years. We fell into a daft dialogue as officer and NCO. As I escorted a BBC big-wig down a corridor, Frank snapped to attention with a barked 'Good morning, Sir' and an immaculate salute. I of course returned the salute and replied: 'All in control? Carry On! TACEVAL next week!' Out of his earshot, my BBC guest could only splutter: 'What the hell was that all about?' Welcome to Lincolnshire. Home of the Royal Air Force.

TACEVAL was RAF shorthand for the dreaded annual Tactical Evaluation, equivalent to a sort of Ofsted school inspection. It could last several days and had implications for everyone on the base in question. The lock-down affected media inquiries – no comments on anything until the TACEVAL was wrapped up. It was one of those words that needed an explanation if it was thrown out in an interview, like Q, squawk, TACAN, CAP, Hud and 'hairy legs' (aircraft's undercarriage fails to retract after take-off). Generally though, pilots and others did well to avoid the in-house jargon in radio interviews. We did broadcast an interview once with an aviation expert who, several times, talked about getting an aircraft with a problem into a 'ground situation' as soon as possible. He could not bring himself to say 'land'.

One RAF pilot who found himself in front of the microphone more than most was Rory Underwood. The England international rugby player regularly got called away from his squadron to turn out on the wing for the RAF and England from the mid-1980s through to 1996. He pitched up at the Lincolnshire county show one year and passed through our Radio Lincolnshire marquee for an interview. While he was waiting to be called to the microphone, he was given a drink and people hovered around him, making polite conversation. Someone called me in and said 'You know about sport – go and talk to him.'

My knowledge of international rugby was rudimentary but I *did* know a bit about the RAF. No doubt expecting a flaky surface-skimming conversation about England's rugby prospects, I think he was surprised to be engaged in a discussion about the handling qualities of the Hawk and how long he had been on Canberras at RAF Wyton.

Another visitor to our marquee at the Lincolnshire Show around 1990 was the Baroness Trumpington, Minister of State at the Department of Agriculture, Fisheries and Food. The Baroness was a guest at the show in her Government capacity and as such agreed to be interviewed by Radio Lincolnshire. As she descended on our marquee, she asked to have a breather before doing the interview with our farming reporter. In the private catering area at the back of the tent, the Baroness Trumpington – then nudging 70 – sat down and lit up a cigarette. After a long drag, she winked at me and said: 'They won't have me at Health, you know!'

Chapter 23

East of Ely

The flatlands to the east of Peterborough sweep up to the Wash and across to Wisbech and down to Ely and Mildenhall. On a grey bleak January afternoon in 2014, on the way to a few days on the Norfolk coast at Blakeney, we turned off the A47 at Thorney Fen and headed south then east down a single track, straight road that cut through the East Anglian arable expanses. I was looking for an isolated copse on the corner of a field that is forever America. Within it we found a small stone memorial and a flag pole flying a wind-battered and tattered Stars and Stripes.

There are 18 names on the memorial. They are the four crew and 14 passengers who were on a USAF C-141A Starlifter transport aircraft which broke up in the big grey skies above on a stormy night in August 1976. The Starlifter was nearing the end of a trans-Atlantic flight from McGuire Air Force Base in New Jersey into Mildenhall. Its weather radar was not working and the crew did not get the reports of developing storms. The wreckage of the aircraft (which had the capacity to carry up to 200 passengers) fell blazing into the fields around where this memorial now stands. No one on the ground was hurt.

The crash happened outside the editorial area of my

newspaper in south Lincolnshire but my friend Bob Whitaker, the freelance cameraman, was called by the *About Anglia* TV newsroom and despatched to the crash site. On his return he spoke of the terrible weather and the smouldering wreckage. The emergency services said that no one had survived. Nearly 40 years later, I sought out the memorial and paid my respects. I looked up into the grey drizzly huge sky and contemplated the terrible end of the lives of those 18 souls. We tidied up around the memorial as the flag whipped in the wind with its halyard rope beating against the metal pole surrounded by the bare winter trees. We continued on our way, deep in thought.

On the horizon, the elegant towers of Ely cathedral rise above the Fens. Within this 900 year old building, there is a memorial and dedication to the men of four Groups within wartime Bomber Command. Among the 19,000 names in the Roll of Honour is that of Pilot Officer Colin Curtis.

The road signs for Ely, Prickwillow and Queen Adelaide indicated you were on 'finals'. Shippea Hill railway station was another 'visual reference point' on the final approach from the north west. 'Somewhere in that misty mornin' light, there's another brand new start' sang Michael McDonald and the Doobie Brothers from the car stereo, as the hot air balloons rose from the dewy grass into the brightening sky.

Thousands of people streamed into 'little America' for the Mildenhall Air Fete on the Bank Holiday weekend at the end of every May. From the start, you were greeted with cries of 'A Burger and a Bud, Sir?' The smell of burgers with that special BBQ sauce was as familiar as kerosene at American air shows especially Mildenhall. The 'Bud' was cans of Budweiser beer which, along with Millers Lite and Coors, were swimming in vast dustbins of ice. One group of Air Fete fans set up camp every year with a small white chain link fence marking their 'home' for the day next to the runway crowd-line.

Ever since the Americans stayed in the UK after the Second World War, they put on public shows at many of their bases like Sculthorpe in Norfolk, Wethersfield in Essex, Alconbury in Cambridgeshire, and Upper Heyford in Oxfordshire. Some were relatively restrained affairs. At the Fairford show in 1981, the flying display did not start until 3pm and lasted only two hours and there were big gaps between each item. At the 1982 show, the flying display stopped between a Spitfire and the Red Arrows for a performance of 'Synchronised Marching by Majorettes'. God knows where they were on that vast airfield.

At Alconbury in 1984, in a scene reminiscent of a 1972 BBC television series called '*Clochemerle*', the Americans provided public male urinals comprising only a canvas 'fence' that covered the average male from his knees to his chest. Men moved to use this facility stared stoically ahead as families with young children streamed past on their way from the car parks to the static display. The sniggering that this unexpected sight provided was no doubt the main talking point for those who were not that interested in Warthogs, Phantoms and Tigers.

The 'Vintage Pair' collided at the Mildenhall Air Fete in 1986. On my way back to the Media Centre to get the bus over to the other side of the runway, I noticed one of the two jets heading down at an unusual angle. There was a huge flash of flame and a pall of smoke shot up. The other aircraft seemed to pitch upwards for a moment before plunging to earth. Then there were two parachutes. There should have been four.

The Vampire and the Meteor, which I had watched flying ahead of me in 'Pelican' formation from Leeming to Scampton just two years earlier, had collided performing a barrel roll. The Vampire had ejection seats and the two people in the jet escaped. The Meteor was not so equipped and the two on board had no time to get out. Both aircraft came down in fields on the south side of the airfield. Once again no one on the ground was hurt.

The two vintage jets were still based at RAF Scampton near Lincoln and, as the News Editor of BBC Radio Lincolnshire, I had a significant local story on my hands. I could ring my newsroom now and be 'on air' within minutes of the accident happening and before we knew if there were any survivors. I had no desire to be 'first with the news'. Most people at Scampton would know the crews and their support team. Someone would hear the 'newsflash' on Radio Lincolnshire which would shock the Scampton community and beyond.

The staff at Radio Lincolnshire nearly always included someone with strong family connections to the RAF. At one point, two of the team were wives of aircrew at Coningsby. Consequently every time we got a report on the wires in the newsroom that a military jet had come down somewhere, I would endeavour to tell our colleagues first before they heard it out of the radio speaker in their office.

In the Mildenhall media centre, I queued for a landline phone and rang the duty journalist at Radio Lincolnshire and explained what had happened. We needed to give someone at Scampton the time to get to the families with news of the accident before someone heard it on the radio. However there were a hundred thousand people at Mildenhall on that Sunday and many of them had seen the crash and indeed some had filmed it on their camcorders. This was still before mobile phones took off and social media was nowhere in sight, but the local Norfolk and Suffolk radio stations were at the Air Fete. They would 'go to air' with the story very soon and send it around the news wires.

I asked the journalist to try and get hold of the Community

Relations Officer at Scampton and also to keep in touch with the emergency services in Suffolk while I pulled together a report from Mildenhall to be used later. I delayed broadcasting my report as I balanced up the time it would take to alert the families of those involved with the time it would take for news of the accident to be broadcast on radio and television elsewhere. When the story started appearing in agency reports on the newsroom teleprinter seemed to be the appropriate time to make that decision. Later that evening on the national television news, I watched the chilling film of the tragedy, credited to an 'amateur cameraman' on the crowd-line.

The last Air Fete at Mildenhall was in May 2001. Four months later, the world changed and the base was never opened to the public again. It is the big UK airshow that enthusiasts miss the most, going misty-eyed over the recollection of rarities like the futuristic SR-71 Blackbird's thunderous display, trailing vortices from the wings and spewing fire from its afterburners. Today photographers continue to congregate in John's Field, a viewing point near the threshold of Mildenhall's runway 11, to capture the Stratotankers, Rivet Joints, Hercules, Ospreys and Extenders (Yes, it's an Extender!). Spoilt for choice, they can drive the short distance from the 'Hall' to the 'Heath' to watch the elegant F-15s leap out of Lakenheath.

The deal was done. A last minute check call to London confirmed that 95 million dollars had been transferred across the Atlantic and that the aircraft could leave Seattle. With interest on such a sum still calculable by the hour, it was worth hanging onto the money until the last minute. As a bonus, a deal for 70,000 dollars was also agreed to utilise the hold to move some cargo across the Atlantic.

The money was for a brand new Boeing 747-400 and was

moved from British Airways in London to Boeing in Seattle. The jumbo jet was signed off and powered out of Washington State, heading for Heathrow. Apart from the two pilots on the flight deck, there were just eight of us on board who predictably decided to decamp to the First Class section in the nose of the aircraft.

Walking around the empty rows of seats, upstairs and down, at 37,000 feet in mid-Atlantic was eerie and very special. There was no cabin crew but a BA executive was one of the eight on board. He ensured a spread of fresh salmon, numerous exotic meat dishes and salads and desserts – and a full bar from which you served yourself as and when. To cap an extraordinary experience, I was on the 'jump seat' on the flight deck for the dawn landing in the mist at Heathrow.

The idea of naming a British Airways aircraft after the City of Lincoln came from airline staff with Lincolnshire connections. They started a campaign, supported by the local media and the city council. British Airways, which was in the process of introducing the new and bigger 747-400s, agreed to the plan and the aircraft went on to lead several flypasts to underline its new association with Lincoln and Lincolnshire. At its official naming ceremony at RAF Coningsby on 16 May 1991, it flew in formation with the Lancaster. Another flight included a flypast over Lincoln with the Red Arrows.

The Boeing 747 emerged out of the dawn skies over London, rolled out along Heathrow's Runway 27 Left and turned off towards the British Airways engineering complex. Three days later, after being fitted out with all things BA, the aircraft went into commercial service with a flight to Bangkok. It had taken 18 months to put together at Boeing's vast complex in Seattle. It could take 400 passengers a third of the way around the world without stopping. G-BNLT was finally withdrawn from British Airways service on 1st April 2014 and later flown to Victorville in California, the civil aviation breaker's yard.

In the early 1990s, the Boeing assembly plant in Seattle was the biggest building in the world and covered 62 acres. An Air Force cadet, with time on his hands, worked out that Boeing could store nearly 94 million (exactly 93,792.000) beer cans in the building if they so wished. 8,000 workers were on the early shift and they were replaced by 7,000 for the late shift. The rush-hour change-over was staged mid-afternoon to stop Seattle traffic grinding to a halt. The building had no heating or air-conditioning. The lights, the machinery and the thousands of humans kept the temperature at 70 degrees Fahrenheit all year round. If it got too hot in high summer, they just opened the big doors.

There was another Boeing connection to Lincoln at the time which endures to this day. The ill-fated and scandalously expensive plan to convert Nimrod aircraft into airborne early warning platforms (Awacs) was finally scrapped. The government decided to buy American Boeing E-3Ds to do the job instead. The aircraft, called the Sentry, was also built in Seattle. The City of Lincoln Coat of Arms went on the nose of each aircraft as soon as the colour scheme was applied.

The 747 delivery flight and the Awacs production made a 30 minute documentary for Radio Lincolnshire, book-ended with a little exotic guitar from Seattle-born Jimi Hendrix. My wife Jo met Jimi Hendrix once. As a teenager, she was working at the Eastgate Hotel in Lincoln where Hendrix was staying during a package tour with other artists like the Walker Brothers, Engelbert Humperdinck and Cat Stevens. As she was delivering breakfasts one morning, she came across Jimi Hendrix sitting outside on a fire escape. He asked her to chat for a while and she produced her autograph book. He wrote: 'Stay sweet – Jimi Hendrix'.

—m—

There was no 'Citizen Journalism' in the 1970s. The public did not 'collect, disseminate and analyse news and information' because there was no internet. If someone took a photograph of something, it was off to Boots to wait the best part of a week to get it developed. If someone saw something unusual, you hoped they might mention it to one of us at the newspaper. If they had taken a photograph, they could bring their camera to our own photographers for a quick turn-round in the newspaper darkroom. That is why you nurtured your contacts in the hope that they would let you know what was happening in your patch. You respected 'off the record' briefings and tip-offs and kept your best contacts to yourself.

Driving down the Langrick Road at the end of Runway 25 at RAF Coningsby, I pulled over to see if anything was up and about on that winter afternoon. It was a good run out for me and my first car – my grandad's old Austin A40 which had the design characteristics of Richard Greene's hat in *The Adventures of Robin Hood* television series. I had been to interview someone for the paper and planned to go into work on the Saturday morning to write it up. I gave it five minutes of Friday afternoon inertia and decided to head for home when a distinctive distant drone drifted in from the east. An RAF Shackleton, developed from the same design as the Lancaster, emerged from the clouds on approach.

The elderly airborne early warning aircraft touched down with the big tyres of its main wheels throwing up a bit smoke as the rubber hit the asphalt. However when the tail wheel made contact with the runway, there was a shot of flame which turned into a small fireball. The Shackleton came to a halt with its tail wheel still ablaze. It was soon surrounded by fire trucks and the flames extinguished.

I put a call in to Coningsby on the Monday morning and the incident made a paragraph for the paper. 'An RAF Shackleton aircraft was surrounded by fire engines after its tail wheel caught fire when it landed at RAF Coningsby on Friday. No one was hurt and the aircraft sustained only minor damage. The Shackleton, from Lossiemouth in Scotland, is expected to be back in the air within a week'.

How would that have been treated and tweeted today? Someone would have snapped it on their iphone or tablet and uploaded the video. Someone would have called it a Lancaster, putting the whole of the Battle of Britain Memorial Flight in peril. 'Drama at Coningsby as plane catches fire – first pictures'… 'Fireball on the runway'… 'Tail wheels – should they be banned? Have your say!'… 'Were you in the vicinity when wheel went whoosh?'

With the explosion in digital technology and social media, 'citizen journalism' is often first with the news these days. There is no pause to consider the implications of rushing to publish or nail down the facts first. Whereas I agonised over when to go on-air with details of the 'Vintage Pair' crash at Mildenhall in 1986, today that news would be uploaded by thousands of people within a minute or so of it happening and retweeted round the world.

'Exercise Golden Eagle' was an ambitious project which took four Tornado F3s and their crews from 29 Squadron around the world. Accompanied by TriStars, VC10s and Hercules support aircraft, the whole trip lasted two and a half months and included exercises with their counterparts in Malaysia, Singapore, Australia and New Zealand. It all went exceptionally well, despite the chap at the airport in Pago Pago island half way between Australia and Hawaii initially forgetting they were on their way and switching off all the runway lights and heading for home.

Harrisburg is the state capital of Pennsylvania, not far

from where Abraham Lincoln gave the Gettysburg Address and near where Hershey chocolate bars are made. From the international airport, you can see the cooling towers of the Three Mile Island nuclear power station which was the scene of a partial nuclear meltdown in March 1979. The accident happened less than two weeks after the release of the film *The China Syndrome* starring Jane Fonda and Michael Douglas with a plot involving the secret filming of… a major accident at a nuclear power station.

At the Farnborough air show in 1988, I had fortuitously bumped into a Strike Command press officer in the media centre. He nonchalantly asked me if I was interested in a trip to Harrisburg the following month to hook up with the Golden Eagle Tornados from Coningsby on their last leg home. Oh, go on then.

A British Airways Boeing 747 flight got the small group of journalists from Heathrow to Washington Dulles followed by a drive in the rain to the Holiday Inn at Harrisburg East. Our 'minders' included the former pirate radio and original Radio 1 DJ Keith Skues who was also a Squadron Leader in the RAF's 7644 Squadron. This unit of part-time reservists was set up during the Second World War by Lord Beaverbrook to provide media support for the RAF across the world in times of peace and war. It was good for me to have Keith in the group as he understood exactly what a radio hack required from the trip. Another member of 7644 Squadron on the trip was the colourful character Colin Gower, a former RAF pilot and Fleet Street photographer.

The highlight of the show on both days was the US Navy's aerobatic team, 'The Blue Angels', flying F-18 Hornets. Their whole routine lasted an hour including engine start up and shut down, with lots of marching and saluting between the ground crew and the pilots. Once they got in the air, they demonstrated their speciality of extremely close formation flying. Their commentator played it seriously straight. 'These manoeuvres are not stunts nor daring feats but are refinements of basic techniques.'

The Sunday was declared 'Royal Air Force Day' by the organisers and was the cue for one of the Tornado F-3s to stage a noisy and tight display which moved the American commentator to repeatedly enthuse about 'this oorsome airplane' which he referred to as the 'Tor-nah-do'. For the rest of the trip, Colin Gower and myself went to ludicrous lengths to include the word 'awesome' in as many conversations as possible. He decided it would be my call-sign. Colin was a good mimic and had a huge repertoire of jokes and anecdotes. He checked out early in 2015 at the age of 81.

The weather over the Harrisburg weekend was not good and the rain leaked into the Tornado cockpit. The groundcrew managed to get most of it out but the navigator said he still got drenched when they first inverted the jet. Low cloud meant that the Tornado had to do a 'flat' display with no aerobatics. The organiser of the show was still impressed. 'It must have been like flying a helicopter around in a hangar.' I got the chance to sit in the right hand seat on the flight deck of a static C-5 Galaxy, one of the biggest military aircraft in the world. In my eagerness to 'play pilots', I failed to see that rain had also got into that cockpit and soaked the seat cushion. I spent the rest of the day slightly damp in the nether regions and affecting a Chaplinesque gait.

After more than 60 days on the road, 29 Squadron was ready for home. We all staged overnight through a freezing Goose Bay, the Canadian Air Force base in Newfoundland, before the last hop across the Atlantic. On board the TriStar, everything would go quiet and darker as the lights went off for the delicate task of air-refuelling the four Tornados on our wing. Nearly home after some 26,000 miles and the Golden Eagle formation was joined over the Mull of Kintyre by a VC10 carrying the Chief of the Air Staff. The *Daily Telegraph* carried a front page photograph of our TriStar and its four 'chicks' in stark silhouette before the final let-down into Coningsby and the family reunions. For me, there was a shed load of cassette recordings to be edited to quickly pull together some reports for the radio.

—✺—

'Get off! News priority!' was a familiar shout in radio production offices. Like my first years in local newspapers when you did not have a phone on every desk, so in my early radio days you could not edit your recording at your desk and on a screen. Several big Studer tape machines for editing were scattered around the office and were usually too few in number to handle demand, especially as news bulletin deadlines loomed.

Someone editing an interview with a gnarled old gardener rabbiting on about his radishes for the gardening slot would be bumped off by an urgent hack shouting 'News Priority'. Getting a tape machine at last, you would unleash a stream of vituperation when you realised that your predecessor had vacated with all the razor blades, splicing tape or yellow grease pencils. The profanities would be shriller and louder if you discovered there was just silence on your five inch spool or that the tape had run out just as the Bishop tearfully confessed to his liaison with the actress.

You always checked your Uher tape recorder before you went off on an assignment. Even so, you could still arrive at the location for an interview and realise that you have your machine and tape but have left the microphone back at the radio station. Or the work experience person who was asked to reclaim tape had left bits of yellow or red leader tape still in the spool that you snatched out the bin on the way out, meaning the interview missed words or even sentences.

Yellow leader marked the beginning of a piece ready for broadcast or the gaps between clips of audio. The appearance of red tape as the spool went round on the tape player indicated the end was nigh. Unless the presenter was 'self-opping' (doing it all him or herself), the Station Assistant (SA) on the other side of the glass would see the red tape appear and tell the presenter over the talk-back button 'Mic coming' and open the microphone fader. For the first couple of weeks at Radio Oxford, I would walk into a studio to hear the SA say 'mic coming' and treat it as 'Mike coming'. What were they trying to hide from the new boy?

Blood-stained editing machines were not uncommon at Radio Oxford. We were using razor blades (hopefully sharp but invariably blunted) to cut the tape and if someone was editing at speed to meet a deadline or had taken ale in the Dewdrop next door to gather inspiration for their radio piece, then carnage could prevail. The floor around these machines was littered with tape cuttings which everyone expected someone else to pick up. This was a dangerous dereliction of duty if the cuttings were allowed to accumulate. Many a time the best and most crucial clip from the interview would find its way round your neck for safe-keeping, only to slide off into the pile below. Cue more colourful colloquialisms.

The German-made Uher took five inch spools of quarter inch magnetic recording tape. It was quite heavy which meant reporters walked with one shoulder lower than the other and thus had a tendency to go round in circles. Gradually local radio started using considerably lighter pocket-sized cassettes and mini-discs before the full conversion to digital.

When you were set up and ready to roll with the interview, you would check that your tape machine was actually recording with a quick sound-bite to set the right recording levels. The interviewee was asked to introduce themselves and – standard question for some reason lost in time – state what they had for breakfast that morning. When I was a BBC local radio training instructor, one of my students went out to interview some protesting people who were staging a hunger strike and yes, he did ask that question. 'Nothing. I am on hunger strike. That's why you have come to interview me.'

Chapter 24

Death off Donegal 1942

Just over two weeks after Pilot Officer Colin Curtis and his crew were swallowed up by the North Sea, another RAF pilot with a family connection suffered a similar fate. The Curtis family of south Lincolnshire and the Smiths of Sunderland had not yet been introduced but after my parents met in Lincoln in the early 1950s, the two parallel stories emerged.

Francis Wilfred Smith was the son of my grandfather's brother, James Henry Smith and his wife Florence who emigrated to Vancouver in Canada in the 1920s. At the beginning of the war, young Francis returned from Canada to join the RAF. This young pilot (Service Number 41214) was posted to Coastal Command and rose to the rank of Flight Lieutenant. By August 1941, he was captain of the crew of a Sunderland flying boat with 201 Squadron in Northern Ireland. The 25 year old with Sunderland roots was fighting the war in an aircraft named after his home town.

Francis married Rhoda Mary Best from Leigh-on-Sea in Essex. They went onto have a young son who was also called Francis, like my mother's brother, my grandfather and his father. To be frank, there were a lot of Frank Smiths with Sunderland connections.

—ᨇ—

RAF Castle Archdale was located on the eastern shore of Lough Erne in Northern Ireland. The base, which was initially named after the Lough, was the most westerly of RAF units in the UK and was home to flying boat squadrons whose aircraft and crews operated far out in to the Atlantic. Their missions were to rescue downed airmen and ship-wrecked sailors, and protect the convoys from marauding German U-boat submarines. They could be in the air for 16 hours at a time.

To get to the Atlantic, the Sunderlands had to fly north-east past Londonderry to stay in UK airspace before turning west once over the sea. Ireland was a neutral country and the RAF was not permitted to fly over its territory. This long route to the ocean resulted in a serious gap in air coverage in mid-Atlantic where convoys were particularly vulnerable to the U-boats. This dangerous area was called 'The Black Gap' and was beyond the range of the flying boats based on Lough Erne.

In January 1941, the Irish Taoiseach, Eamon de Valera, agreed to a British government request to open a short aerial corridor from the western edge of Northern Ireland to the coast at Ballyshannon. This became known as The Donegal Corridor and allowed the Sunderlands and Catalinas to get from Lough Erne to the Atlantic very quickly. The initial agreement was for air sea rescue missions only but the rules soon changed and the flying boats lumbered down the corridor to chase the U-boats and cover that 'Black Gap'. The full extent of its use was kept secret until the end of the war.

On the afternoon of Thursday 5th February 1942, a Sunderland of 201 Squadron lifted off the waters of Lough Erne. Take-off time was 15.43. The aircraft's serial number was W3977 with the letters ZM-Q on the fuselage side. The Sunderland was powered by four Bristol Pegasus engines – the same type used in the Wellington. With those four engines at full power, it rose into the air and headed due west for The Donegal Corridor.

The Sunderland crew was tasked with a strike sortie, heading out into the Atlantic on an anti-submarine patrol. There were 12 on board – three of them with the surname of Smith. They were Pilot Officer John Barrett, Flying Officer Rodney Smith (an Australian from New South Wales), Flying Officer Henry Kitchin, Flight Sergeants Harold Mason, Norman Clare and John Smith, Sergeants Arnold Rolfe, Hugh Jones, Kenneth Nutt and Gordon Jacobson, and Aircraftsman Eric Hopkinson. The ranking officer was Flight Lieutenant Francis Smith, in the cockpit of the vast aircraft.

At 22.50, the crew radioed that they were returning to base with an estimated time of arrival at midnight. The last communication with the aircraft was at twenty minutes past midnight on Friday 6th February. Two hours later, RAF Castle Archdale was notified indirectly by the County Donegal police that an aircraft had crashed into the sea near the island of Rathlin O'Birne. A land search along the coast by the police and Irish Army personnel had found nothing. The RAF launched a Hudson and another Sunderland to scour the sea from the air but nothing was found.

Irish coastguards had reported 'explosions out at sea'. They estimated the point of impact was nine miles north of Rossan Point and twelve miles west of Dunmore Head. A few pieces of wooden wreckage were eventually washed up. Like those six souls on board Wellington Z1110 off the Dutch coast, none of the bodies of the 12 men on board were ever recovered.

A padre at RAF Castle Archdale, Squadron Leader I.R.Parsons, wrote to a relative of one of the crew five months later. 'With regard to Kenneth (Nutt), I can only answer your questions unofficially. Officially he and his comrades are still missing but I don't think there is a single person on the station who believes that anyone was saved. Nothing was found except a few pieces of wood and nothing has been found since. I said 'accident' because we all believe that to be the case. It was not enemy action. They were RETURNING home from operational duties and were nearly home when – silence – and nothing heard since.'

The 12 crew on board the Sunderland have no grave. The official Operations Record Book for 201 Squadron concluded its entry on W3977 thus: 'All the members of the crew had to be posted as missing. No conclusion could be reached of the cause of the accident.'

Flt Lt Francis Wilfred Smith, skipper of the Sunderland

Due to his parents' Canadian connections, Flight Lieutenant Smith is commemorated on the Memorial Arch at the West

Vancouver Memorial Park (WW II East Plinth). His name also appears in the Book of Remembrance held at the West Vancouver Memorial Library, the Honour Roll displayed at Branch 60 (BC/Yukon) of the Royal Canadian Legion, and also on a bronze plaque at St. Stephen's Anglican Church in West Vancouver. It can also be found on Panel 66 at the Air Forces Memorial at Runnymede, just three panels away from the name of Colin Curtis.

In his will, he left a letter to his parents and his sister, anticipating that he may not survive the war. It was read out at a memorial service in Vancouver in 1945. 'You must not grieve for me. After all, that is contrary to all our beliefs. Also it makes me feel so much better now if I know that my death is not going to make you unhappy, but on the contrary, proud that you have a son and brother that died for the cause. I know God is with me, and your thoughts and prayers are with me too.

'If I have not expressed sufficiently my love and affection in my letters to you, it must be by reason of my nature, I suppose, because I bear all the love and affection towards you that any son or brother could bear towards his parents and his sister. So now, goodbye and God bless you, Mother and Dad and Valerie. Love, Frank.'

Chapter 25

Contacts and Conversations

'The south transept has been badly damaged by the fire which is believed to have been started by a lightning strike.' My heart missed a beat after I switched on the bedside radio. There had been big storm over Lincoln overnight. No one had rung me about the Cathedral being struck by lightning. The newsroom had my temporary landline number in the rented property. I was the brand new news editor of Radio Lincolnshire and it looked as though I was blissfully unaware of the big news that morning.

Just as I reached the phone to ring the duty journalist, the story came round again. The fire was not at Lincoln but at York Minster. The storm had moved north. Three days earlier York Minster had been the venue for the consecration of the controversial David Jenkins as Bishop of Durham. Some said the fire indicated divine wrath at the appointment. It took four years to restore and cost well over two million pounds.

Radio stations and photographers had arrangements with the local fire brigade headquarters about being tipped off about significant incidents. Once the control room had got all the firefighters on their way to the scene, someone would ring a nominated person at certain media outlets and let them know what was happening. On numerous occasions over the years, the phone beside the bed would ring and the fire control operator would introduce herself and tell me staccato-style 'Pumps three, barn fire at Metheringham'. They called fire engines 'pumps'. It was down to me to decide if I should turn out the local reporter for the patch or staff up the newsroom in the middle of the night.

For a barn fire, I would leave a message on the newsroom voicemail for the early journalist to check out. Some tip-offs sounded big. After midnight I got a call to say that a nursing home near Spalding was on fire and up to 15 elderly people were 'unaccounted for'. I rang our south Lincolnshire reporter to get him on the road and prepared to leave home for the Lincoln newsroom. I also rang the BBC's main London newsroom to say there may be something significant underway. As I was going out the front door, the control room rang again. Their crews were now on site, everyone was accounted for and it was only a minor electrical fire.

My opposite number at BBC Radio York got a call from the fire service in the early hours to tell him York Minster was on fire. With no bedside phone (and of course no mobiles then), he went downstairs and answered the phone in the hall. 'Is that the news editor of Radio York?' said a voice. Confirming it was indeed the very same, this voice said: 'Fire at York Minister. Serious. Made pumps 20' and rang off. The Lincoln and York radio newsrooms often mused that their impressive Anglican buildings would feature in their biggest story in due course.

The Editor stomped back to bed, convinced it was a joke and thinking through which of his team would actually make such a call in the middle of the night. As he lay there, he started to wonder. What if…? And he started to grow nervous. He got up again and padded downstairs and rang the fire control room. 'Er, it's the News Editor at Radio York. Have you just rung me about a fire at York Minster?' The operator confirmed it, saying it was serious and she had to go. He said he just stood in the hall for a moment, trying to take in the enormity of what was actually happening.

From my experience, you emit more expletives than those found in the opening scene of *Four Weddings and a Funeral* while trying to get dressed with one hand and ringing your reporters with the other.

—ᛡᛡ—

The roof of the magnificent Lincoln Cathedral was destroyed by a fire in 1141. Forty years later, the building was almost destroyed by an earthquake. And 800 years later it was at the centre of an extraordinary saga for several years after the Thatcher appointment of Brandon Jackson as Dean of Lincoln. The Imp, set in stone by an angel in the 14th century, must have been grinning even more wildly in his elevated position high in the Cathedral's Angel Choir.

The Very Reverend and Honourable Oliver William Twisleton-Wykeham-Fiennes would occasionally stop by for a whisky in the manager's office at Radio Lincolnshire. Oliver, as we abbreviated him, was the Dean of Lincoln for 20 years, finally retiring in 1989. The outspoken Jackson succeeded him and fell out with the Bishop, the Sub Dean and The Chapter Canons over the ways in which things were run. At one point, he refused to enter Lincoln Cathedral and called for it to be exorcised and closed for six months. He was also cleared by a Consistory Court of sexual misconduct with a female verger. It gave us a long running saga to keep up with and it repeatedly made the national news as well.

Some journalists compared it all to the cloistered intrigues of Anthony Trollope's *Barchester Chronicles* but, for me, it was sadly nearer to the BBC comedy *All Gas and Gaiters*. The 'villain' in that generally thin clerical comedy of the late 1960s was usually the Dean. It was only enlivened by the actor Robertson Hare, playing the Archdeacon, who was always wondering where the next sherry was coming from.

—ɯ—

The daily assignments for a new young reporter at BBC Radio Oxford could include the housing estates of Blackbird Leys to the south of Oxford and the quiet academia of All Souls College. You could be sent to talk politics with Professor Vernon Bogdanor at Brasenose College, who later taught a young David Cameron. You could be chasing up Hughie Smith of the National Gypsy Council about the latest row over where travellers could pitch up or be sent to sum up the 'Englishness' of polo at Kirtlington or Regatta rowing at Henley-on-Thames.

One evening on the late shift at Radio Oxford I was sent to Lambourn to interview one of the great National Hunt trainers ahead of the Grand National. Fulke Walwyn, who had just got back from Wincanton races, had already had a snifter but gave this young journalist, who knew next to nothing about racing, a great interview and a gin and tonic. Despite huge success and training more than 2000 winners including horses for The Queen Mother, Fulke only got one Grand National victory as a trainer – in 1964 with 'Team Spirit'. He actually won the race as an amateur jockey in 1936.

Richard Nixon, the former US President who resigned in the wake of the Watergate scandal, was invited to speak to the Oxford Union in November 1978. It was his first public address since stepping down four years earlier. Security was tight in Oxford city centre and I was sent to get some atmosphere and ask the good people around the dreaming spires what they thought about having this man in their midst. Rather like the visit the following year of the Chinese leader Chairman Hua, the locals seemed more exercised by the traffic disruption. Having seen Nixon off after his session at the Union, I returned to the newsroom and picked up a ringing phone.

'Hi, it's KC (something) radio station in Tulsa, Oklahoma. You got Richard Nixon with you today?' Not sure if it was a question or a statement but I said indeed we had and I had just been at the scene. 'Hey, can we talk to you about it?' I said they could indeed, expecting a production conversation about the cue (introduction) and questions and indeed confirming my name and what I did. 'That's great, you're on now!' And I was, telling Tulsa about Nixon's historic visit to Oxford. They never asked my name or in what capacity I was being interviewed. They never rang me back to sort a payment and I had no idea which actual radio station it was but, hey, this was before the internet and I had been heard across Oklahoma.

Coming out of an Elvis Costello concert at the New Theatre in Oxford on 30th March 1981, we got in the car and heard on the radio that President Reagan had been shot. A few weeks later, Pope John Paul was shot in St Peter's Square in Rome. Global stories required local angles. We chased American academics in Oxford, spoke to USAF families at Upper Heyford, tracked down Catholic priests and Anglican bishops, edited down over-keen MPs, gathered vox-pops in Bicester, revisited archives and updated ready-to-roll tributes and obituaries.

BBC Radio Oxford went 'commercial' one Saturday morning in an elaborate April Fool. Spoof adverts were dropped into the output and the whole enterprise was given authority by the former Prime Minister Harold Wilson. The much-mimicked man had been in Oxford earlier in the week and the reporter who went to interview him asked if he would also be prepared to join in the fun. The 'pound in your pocket' politician agreed to record some statements along the lines of how pleased he was that the BBC was facing up to the commercial market. He was delighted that Radio Oxford had taken this brave step. Many listeners thought it was someone like the comedian Mike Yarwood, who was famous for his political impersonations, but it was the real Harold.

One of the presenters in the early days at Radio Oxford, Libby Purves, recalls a phone-in one morning. The riveting talking point for the programme was head lice. No-one rang in to contribute their views until, finally, the show had one caller. 'Well, it really annoys me when drivers do not dip them at night'.

One of the new Conservative MPs in the 1979 intake was John Patten, who won the Oxford seat from Labour. Patten, who was Education Secretary for a couple of years in the early 1990s, hosted a media reception at Hertford College each summer and served the assembled hacks a potent cocktail called White Lady (gin, triple sec and lemon juice). As we drained our glasses and proffered them for refills, the MP stayed on something that looked like the cocktail but obviously lacked the gin. Evidence of the impact of a number of White Ladies was clear with the sight of one tired and emotional representative of the Oxford media doing forward rolls across the width of the hallowed Hertford quad wearing a motorcycle helmet, before eschewing the Bridge of Sighs and The Turf Tavern and lurching into The Kings Arms.

—〰—

I loved Oxford pubs. The winter aroma of the rum punch at The Turf Tavern, which featured in Thomas Hardy's *Jude the Obscure*, hung in the air. The Eagle and Child, where the Oxford writer's group including C.S.Lewis and

Tolkien famously met each week, stood almost opposite St Giles from The Lamb and Flag where I once interviewed the monstrously moustachioed long distance runner David Bedford, who later went on to become the race director of the London Marathon.

Oh, to while away a summer's afternoon with Kate Bush beside the Thames in an Oxfordshire pub garden. Only four years younger than me, her sultry debut album came out three weeks before I joined Radio Oxford and was the soundtrack of my first few weeks with the BBC. Just over 12 months later I spent an evening with Kate, three rows from the front of her extraordinary and dramatic performance at the New Theatre in Oxford where she trilled out songs from her first two albums. It was the fifth concert on her one and only tour until she returned to the stage 35 years later.

There was a leaflet on each seat. 'Welcome to the Kate Bush concert which I am sure you are going to enjoy. A ten minute bell will be rung before the concert and seats should be taken at that time.' We all did as we were told. Before she went wuthering, there was another encore with her wearing something vaguely resembling an old flying helmet above Clara Bow eyes. 'Oh! England, my Lionheart! Dropped from my black Spitfire to my funeral barge. Give me one kiss in apple-blossom. Give me one wish and.........'

Leaflets were also distributed among the audience at a gig in Germany in the mid-1990s featuring the British band Latin Quarter. It was the final night of the tour and the audience were asked to follow the instructions in the leaflet during the concert. It drew attention to a traffic light system where you were asked *not* to clap if the light was red, to applaud wildly if it was green and just act normally if it was amber. Unfortunately for the band, they knew nothing about this arrangement.

Steve Skaith, the Lincoln-born co-founder of Latin Quarter, told me the story in another *Desert Island Discs* type show for BBC Radio Lincolnshire. While they went off to eat before the concert, their German road crew handed out the leaflets. Throughout the two hour gig, Steve and the band were mystified and increasingly irritated by the reaction of the audience. They would come to the end of a song they thought they had played rather well and there was no reaction at all. Half way through introducing the next song, the audience would burst into spontaneous and wild applause. It was not until near the end of the show that one of the musicians clocked what was going on and put everyone else out of their misery.

Latin Quarter continue to be far more popular in Germany and Sweden than in the UK where they had one big hit called 'Radio Africa' which got them an appearance on *Top of the Pops* in 1985.

At Radio Oxford, one of the first people I interviewed was Clive Jenkins who was general secretary of the Association of Scientific Workers. I remember thinking, as he babbled along, 'Thank God I am no longer in newspapers and having to write all this down.' There were interviews with Roy Hudd (another RAF National Serviceman in the mid-1950s), Henry Cooper, Yootha Joyce, Pam Ayres, Gerald Harper, Patrick Mower, Richard O'Brien (*Rocky Horror Show* creator), Sue Browne (the first female cox in the University Boat Race) and Desmond Morris (I had grown up with his television show *Zoo Time*). I chased round the centre of Oxford early in 1980 trying to track down Kris Kristofferson who, along with John

Hurt, was in town to film Michael Cimino's *Heaven's Gate*, the film that became better known for its vast overspend rather than its actors or storyline. I failed.

BBC Radio Oxford discovered Pam Ayres four years before I arrived in 1978. She was an Oxfordshire girl who was invited on-air to read her poems and she proved very popular. She first developed her love of entertaining while serving in the Women's Royal Air Force. After we moved to Witney, my wife and I occasionally went to the folk club in nearby Ducklington where I rashly offered to read some comedy poems by well-established writers in my best BBC voice. One evening I turned up and the girl on the door asked: 'Are you on tonight?' I said I had my book if they wanted a turn from me. 'Good, but don't do anything by Pam Ayres, will you? She's on the front row.'

In an Oxfordshire garden one summer's afternoon, I recorded an interview with Donald Swann who achieved fame in the late 1950s and early 1960s with his musical partner Michael Flanders. Donald Swann and his daughter were doing a concert in Oxford that evening and agreed to talk about what they were up to. I had treasured Flanders and Swann's two classic comedy LPs for years – *At the Drop of a Hat* and *At the Drop of Another Hat* which were recorded at the end of the 1950s. In 'Song of the Weather', they used the word 'bloody' to make a point about British weather. 'Sorry about the language! But we do think it's justified, don't you?' they said at the end. No advance Parental Advisory – Explicit Content. Crikey Moses again.

Bob Harris had an afternoon show on BBC Radio Oxford for a couple of years which coincided with my time there. I had grown up with 'Whisperin' Bob' on *The Old Grey Whistle Test* and was now working alongside him, going into the studio to read the news in his programme and lingering afterwards to discuss the merits of Steely Dan, Rickie Lee Jones, Jackson

Browne and Bruce Cockburn. Bob had interviewed many of the top music stars in the world and replayed some of those interviews (Bruce Springsteen, John Lennon among others) on his Oxford show.

When I first put my head round the door of the student union bar at Darlington Technical College in 1972, 'Come All Ye' by the fine folk-rock band Fairport Convention was coming out the speakers. Why do I remember that? In the month that I joined Radio Oxford six years later, the singer on 'Come All Ye' fell down some stairs at her parent's house in Cornwall and banged her head on the concrete floor. Within a month, 31 year old Sandy Denny was dead. She had left Fairport nearly ten years earlier but the band carried on until 1980. Two of them lived at Cropredy near Banbury including Dave Pegg whom I interviewed about the decision to call it a day. The main reason was that the remaining original member, Dave Swarbrick, had to stop playing loud electric music because of problems with his hearing. He was going to concentrate on quieter acoustic music from now on.

Dave Swarbrick was one of the most renowned folk fiddle players in the world. He also had the rare distinction of being one of the very few people who had been able to read his own national newspaper obituary. After being taken to hospital in Coventry with a chest infection in April 1999, word got to the *Daily Telegraph* that he had died. The paper published a long obituary on him and, needless to say, had to apologise profusely the next day. Swarbrick was quoted as saying: 'It's not the first time I've died in Coventry.' He lived for another 17 years, finally drawing his last breath in June 2016.

Two of the Monty Python team visited Oxford within two weeks of each other and I was tasked to catch up with them for a 'show biz' interview. Terry Jones was opening a student beer festival at Oxford Polytechnic (later Brookes University) and Michael Palin was at a charity event at the Randolph Hotel. After recording an interview, Terry Jones and I wandered around the festival introducing each other to brews we knew – my contribution to this bacchanalian extravaganza was Batemans of Wainfleet in Lincolnshire.

Two weeks later I was able to tell Michael Palin that I had already heard his humorous opening speech, involving a hovercraft. Terry Jones had used exactly the same one at the beer festival. Years later, Terry passed through BBC Birmingham on a tour to support his latest television show and book which was called *Barbarians*. He was reminded that I had interviewed him some 30 years earlier. Terry signed a copy of his book 'To Mike Curtis – Still at it.'

According to Terry, the very first sketch filmed for the *Monty Python* television series was about sheep nesting in the trees. It was originally written for *The Frost Report* and initially deemed too 'silly' for the Flying Circus by its early producer. It evolved into a discussion on flying sheep and the commercial possibilities of ovine aviation. The sketch even name-checked Brian Trubshaw who was the British test pilot for Concorde. Along with his French counterpart André Turcat, the two men had flown Concordes for the first time early in 1969. Ovine aviation made it to the small screen in October that year, leading the second programme in the first series before lurching off to the man with three buttocks.

—m—

When I was at Radio Oxford, there were still some rumblings about the idea of putting London's third airport in our editorial patch just north of Aylesbury. The old airfield at the appropriately named Wing in Buckinghamshire was recommended as the best site for an airport that would be three times bigger than Heathrow. In 1971, The Roskill Commission said the village of Cublington would have to be demolished. The locals started a huge campaign which was successful, but those in the area remained on their guard for years and found their way into my contacts book in 1978.

If you drove the Radio Oxford radio car onto the top of a multi-storey car park in Aylesbury, you could transmit a good strong signal back to the radio station for broadcast. Consequently, that was the place to go if any of us were covering a story in that bit of the patch. However when the radio car was upgraded, no-one told us that the height of the collapsed aerial mechanism on the roof was actually a bit higher. Blissfully unaware, one of the team drove into the familiar entrance of the multi-storey and ripped it off. No radio car 'live' broadcasts for a while after that.

Wrestling with the radio car was an occupational hazard for reporters who often handled it alone. You had to drive to the story, find a safe location and get the aerial pumped up to about 15 feet avoiding all electrical cables and telegraph wires. You had to assess the weather – the aerial would make a fine lightning conductor. Then you had to sort out the cables so that the microphone worked and that you could hear the radio station's output in your headphones. Inevitably a small crowd would gather, some of them wondering if it was a TV Licence detector van.

The radio car was regularly used out in the villages for a *Down Your Way* feature, highlighting the lives of the good people of Oxfordshire and beyond. It was usually done 'live' but occasionally it was pre-recorded. In those days, what they now call 'compliance' was not exactly observed with due diligence. We were famously caught out on one pre-recorded programme as an express train roared past the reporter and his interviewees. The switchboard lit up with enquiries about the train. A national strike by train drivers was leading our bulletins that morning.

A local radio colleague was sent out in the radio car to cover an ongoing operation to rescue some trapped miners at a Midlands colliery. The teatime presenter back at the radio station introduced the reporter at the scene with the words: 'It's getting dark now, how will that affect the rescue operation?' The nonplussed reporter struggled to find the appropriate words and solemn response that sunset made no difference half a mile underground.

'Live' radio interviews presented many challenges, not least mishearing someone or not understanding what they were on about. How about this Radio Cornwall interview about a charity stunt at the Elephant Fayre at the stately home of Port Eliot at St Germans? Cornish presenter Ted Gundry learnt from his interviewee that a group was going to raise money by washing as many 'kos' as possible within a certain time limit....'Clothes?', said Ted.....'No, Kos, washing Kos'.......'What's a Kos?', inquired Ted, presumably thinking this was some strange Cornish practice that even he had never heard of. 'Never heard of a Kos. What is a Kos?'.

'Well it's a thing with four wheels that you drive on the road.'...... 'Kos, describe a Kos', said Ted, digging deeper. 'Well, you drive to work don't you?'....'Yeah'....'Well, what do you drive in?'. The penny dropped, the laughter erupted and, there but for the Grace of God, goes everyone who has ever worked in 'live' radio.

A founder member of Radio Oxford back in 1970, Bill Rennells beautifully and accidently summed up the radio journalist's daily challenge of covering different and diverse stories within one day and also performing 'live' on the radio. He had been reporting on a cricket match in The Parks earlier in the afternoon and was now reading the news. In a preview piece for local elections, he said: 'It looks like a close struggle in the Headington ward where last year Labour regained the seat by 149 runs.'

Chapter 26

What's Going On

I ended up on both sides of the fence at Greenham Common for a while. The anti-nuclear protestors had the slogan 'Greenham Common – twinned with Moscow' but every two years this huge Berkshire airfield was 'twinned' with dozens of countries from around the world as aircraft flew in to take part in the International Air Tattoo.

Greenham Common became synonymous with a global anti-nuclear campaign and the women's peace camps, triggered by the decision to base cruise missiles there and at Molesworth in Cambridgeshire. Working at BBC Radio Oxford, Greenham Common was on the fringe of our editorial area but, like Reading and Swindon, was embraced into our coverage if the story was big enough. For a while there was a plan to base US Air Force KC-135 air refuelling tankers there but the protests prevailed with someone deciding that there were enough government 'assets' in the area like the Atomic Weapons Establishments at Aldermaston and Burghfield, and the Atomic Energy Research Establishment at Harwell. Like the air tattoo, the KC-135s went to Fairford.

I was one of the first reporters to go to the Women's Peace Camp after it was set up in September 1981. The group had marched from Cardiff to challenge the plan to site 96 cruise missiles in the Berkshire countryside, just south of Newbury's picturesque race course. There were only a few of them initially and they were living in primitive conditions. They attracted national and then international publicity when they chained themselves to the fence. The following year, 30,000 women formed a human chain round the perimeter of the air base.

The peace camp lasted for nearly 20 years and had an offshoot outside Upper Heyford air base north of Oxford. The Ground Launched Cruise Missiles arrived by C-5 Galaxy from November 1983 and were put into a huge new expensive facility on the south west corner of the base. Three years later, Reagan and Gorbachev agreed an anti-nuclear treaty for Europe and the last cruise missile was C-Fived out again in March 1991. The last RAF commander keeping an eye on the Americans at Greenham Common was Group Captain Andrew Brookes, a former 101 Squadron Vulcan pilot who wrote a book about life in 101 during the Second World War.

Despite my life-long love of military aviation, I never had any interest in the actual weapons that were slung under the wings, hung behind the bomb doors or sunk in silos. Many of those noisy, graceful flying machines at the International Air Tattoo were of course solely designed to deliver destruction. On the other side of the banner-draped fence, the Greenham Common women reminded you of that uncomfortable truth.

Seán Maffett, a former RAF navigator working as a freelance journalist at Radio Oxford, was the chief commentator for the International Air Tattoo (IAT). He invited me to join the commentary team covering the IAT at Greenham Common and an Army air show at Middle Wallop in Hampshire from 1979 to 1983. Most of the work was support duties, collecting information from pilots about their display routine and their family background. However I was let loose to commentate on the less dramatic items such as a helicopter display or the lost children announcements. It was the opposite to radio broadcasting in that you could see your audience (a quarter of a million over two days) and you could hear your voice reverberating back at you from the dozens of loud speakers dotted along the crowd line.

Home was a precarious-looking scaffolding tower next to Air Traffic Control and looming over the press centre. From there we could see both ends of the one and a half mile runway. We had a telephone link to the Tower team who could tell us what was coming next and from which direction. It was the best place to be at an air show but there was some hard work to be done. Like a good journalist, you were looking for interesting facts and gossip about the pilots displaying at the Tattoo. Most of the crowd were not interested in the all-up-weight of a Tornado but liked to hear unusual snippets about the flier flying before them.

There was Brian Lecomber who flew a Pitts Special with the four ship aerobatic team sponsored by the Rothmans tobacco company (tobacco companies sponsored everything back then). He started out as a motoring journalist, became a wing walker and then a pilot, winning many aerobatic championships as a solo. He was also a best-selling author and was called 'the Dick Francis of aviation.' Brian, who died in 2015, always remarked that actually Dick Francis was 'the Brian Lecomber of horse racing.'

There were commentary clichés to fall back on which wore very thin over the years. The Lancaster-lookalike, the Avro Shackleton, was routinely described as 10,000 or 40,000 or even 100,000 rivets flying in loose formation. The delta wing Vulcan was referred to by the Americans as 'the aluminium overcast' and sometimes in the static display provided a real umbrella rather than a nuclear one for crowds caught out in a summer shower. Aircrew humour was passed on to the crowd. The co-pilot of the Dutch F27 Troopship said: 'My captain is getting short-sighted so I tell him – if it is blue, we are going up. If it is green, we are going down.' It's the way you tell 'em.

We introduced music to accompany some of the displays. *The Dambusters* march was really too obvious for the arrival of the Lancaster but you needed to fade that down whenever the four mighty Merlins were growling in front of the crowd. As the Nimrod rolled in for its final flypast and pulled upwards and away on full power, Elgar's Nimrod from the Enigma Variations reached its climax. The Patrouille de France got a bit of Jean-Michel Jarre. David Gilmour's majestic notes from the Pink Floyd's 'Shine On, You Crazy Diamond' suited the hot air balloons and Peter Green's wistful 'From the Skies' complemented the gliders.

One of the columnists in *Flying Review* magazine highlighted the use of appropriate music as giving the show ' a touch of something that other displays lack' and hailed a 'new concept in commentating.' We proudly displayed this cutting until discovering that the writer was actually one of our support team who wrote under the pseudonym of Paul Humphreys. He confessed to us over a drink a year later and we said no more about it. Certainly to the man who claimed we ruined his 'display experience' because he wanted to record the actual sounds of the aircraft to listen to in his shed on winter evenings.

—◊◊—

The Royal International Air Tattoo moved to RAF Cottesmore in Rutland for a couple of years due to refurbishment work at Fairford. I was working for the BBC Asian Network in the Midlands at this time and offered to cover the media preview for BBC Radio Leicester as I knew a bit about 'RIAT'. One of the themes of that year's show was aimed at highlighting the activities of the Air Cadets.

Consequently the organisers had got the actor Warren Mitchell to support the media day as he was in the Air Cadets many moons beforehand. Like Richard Burton, Warren had joined the RAF in 1944 and completed his navigator training just as hostilities ended. He went on have a long and distinguished acting career but was still best known for playing Alf Garnett in the controversial BBC comedy *Till Death Us Do Part* in the 1960s. Garnett was played as a right wing bigot who supported West Ham, whereas Mitchell was actually left wing and followed Spurs. He was also Jewish.

At Cottesmore, a group of journalists surrounded Warren Mitchell, asking him about his time as an air cadet and what he thought about RIAT. At one point, someone helpfully stressed the truly international aspect of the Air Tattoo and rattled off a list of countries sending aircraft including Germany. At this, Warren Mitchell bristled and said he 'hated' Germans – while the Air Tattoo's Head of Public Relations visibly blanched in the background. His Jewish family had never forgiven the Nazis and he had joined the RAF as he 'wanted to bomb them.'

What the organisers had envisaged was a famous actor waxing lyrically on his memories in support of the Air Tattoo raising money for the RAF Benevolent Fund. However that was now potentially overshadowed by an outburst against one of the nations who had agreed to send some of its aircraft and crews in support. I had him on tape and on the record and drove back to the office wondering what to do with it.

The outburst was dramatic but was it new or relevant? Would it be too 'sensational' to make it the top line of my report? Would it in fact give the Air Tattoo even more publicity? As it was not relevant to the main event, would it be unfair to make a meal of it? How to balance it with everything else including interviews with the Station Commander at Cottesmore, the RIAT Director, and the current Air Cadets?

Warren Mitchell's views on Germans had been expressed before. The local media largely ignored his comments and just used his reminiscences of his air cadet experiences. And me? I said that Warren Mitchell praised the international aspect of the Air Tattoo but, in view of his Jewish background, made it emphatically clear that he did not intend to watch the German participation. To this day, I still do not know if I got it right. I wrote these few paragraphs about a month before the passing of Warren Mitchell was announced.

One aspect of a Cottesmore RIAT that *did* get some publicity were the cuts and burns sustained by some over enthusiastic photographers who gathered up against the security fence directly at the end of Runway 22. Chasing a dramatic shot when the B-1b Lancer opened up the reheat on its four engines, some were directly behind the aircraft as it started its take-off run. The incident was called 'Blown by the Bone', simply a reference to the Lancer's nickname. People scattered as the hot gases from the four engines blasted against them. The 'Bone' went on to give one of the most exciting display sequences ever seen by such a sizeable beast.

With airshow and television commentaries, you do not have to keep talking all the time. There are times when the crowd or the audience can see for themselves and, frankly, want you to shut up. However in radio, we feared 'dead air' when everything went quiet. An overlong pause by a newsreader or the failure of the play out system to burst forth with the opening bars of 'Dancing Queen' would have everyone in the production office staring at the speakers, immediately thinking there was a problem.

Many years ago a producer in the BBC World Service was overseeing a 'live' broadcast in Russian from Bush House. He did not actually understand the language and, confident that the presenter was burbling along happily and that the volume needles on the studio desk were wagging as they should, he buried his head in a book. Suddenly there was silence and the producer looked up to see the presenter leaving the studio. He rushed out into the corridor and shouted after her: 'What are you doing? You are broadcasting! Live! To Russia!'

The lady replied that she had forgotten her spectacles and was going back to the office to get them. The producer spluttered about the broadcast going quiet and what would the listeners in their flats and dachas make of the silence? 'Oh it's alright,' she smiled. 'I have told them what I am doing!'

Commentary is the most difficult of radio skills and I avoided it as much as I could. If there were two of you, you could bounce off each other but if you were on your own, it could be excruciating. In my first few months as News Editor at BBC Radio Lincolnshire, the new Bishop of Lincoln was enthroned. The radio station's religious affairs producer persuaded me against my better judgement to handle the commentary in Lincoln Cathedral, presumably because I used to live in a Vicarage. Despite all the notes spread around me in my eyrie in the organ loft, there were a couple of occasions where my mouth and brain disconnected. As the solemn procession edged up the nave, I tried to describe the Bishop's attire and accessories, ending up by saying 'and all those bishopy bits and pieces.' Oh lord, deliver me from all this evil......

At Christmas that year, I read a lesson at the Radio Lincolnshire carol service also in the Cathedral. As News Editor, the same religious affairs producer gave me the 'newsy' reading from the Book of Isaiah in which the prophet foretells Christ's birth and kingdom. The Cathedral was full and the service was being recorded by the BBC *Songs of Praise* programme complete with presenter Geoffrey Wheeler. Some nerves certainly but this time I had a definitive script, no requirement to 'ad lib' and it was all over in a couple of minutes. 'Here endeth the lesson'. (Thank God)

I made my commentary debut at the International Air Tattoo in 1979 which celebrated the 25th anniversary of the first flight of the C-130 Hercules and 21 years of the McDonnell Douglas F-4 Phantom. The air tattoo was the brainchild of Paul Bowen and Tim Prince, two air traffic controllers who had put on their first show at North Weald in Essex just eight years earlier. The event was now truly international and moved to the vast expanse of Greenham Common, a USAF stand-by airfield which could accommodate the biggest military aircraft and the vast numbers that the show now attracted.

Looking through the souvenir programme (price 50 pence) some 35 years on, you are reminded of how fast aviation has moved in a generation and how much variety there was at those shows. The aerobatic teams that year included The Sharks Navy helicopter team flying the Gazelle, The Asas de Portugal and their six T-37s and, belching flame and smoke, The Vikings, a pair of German Navy F-104 Starfighters. The Jordanian Falcons in their Pitts Specials were there – and seem to have been at the Tattoo ever since.

Another popular aerobatic team was The Blue Herons, four Hunters from the Fleet Requirements and Air Direction Unit at Yeovilton whose pilots were nearer to the end of their flying careers than the start. They were nick-named 'The Phyllosan Four' after the tonic available at the time that claimed to fortify the over forties. The following year, the show was called the Newbury Air Festival and hosted five Starfighters of the Canadian Air Force. Another long-time fixture on the IAT display list were The Grasshoppers, four Aérospatiale Alouette 111 helicopters from the Dutch air force.

The list of diversion airfields for crews at the 1983 IAT (the last one I worked at) included Brize Norton, Mildenhall, Lyneham, Bentwaters, Upper Heyford and Manston. Only Brize and Mildenhall are still active – and Mildenhall is due for closure in a few years. Indeed Greenham Common itself was eventually dug up and returned to common land, with only the control tower being preserved.

An information booklet for participants in the 1983 show had a photograph with the caption: 'There's always a pretty girl to keep visiting aircrew happy! Two of the Lloyds Bank hostesses enjoy the attentions of a crew of a French Nord 2501 Noratlas.' Obsolete aircraft and obsolete caption style.

Mixing with the military at shows such as the Air Tattoo meant you picked up numerous memorable anecdotes, many unrepeatable. A transport navigator told me the story of a colleague who had a heavy night during a stop-over in Malta and woke up in the early hours with a 'mouth like a badger's……'. He vaguely remembered seeing a glass of water in the room before the light went out and, not wanting to wake his room-mate, groped his way in the dark to find it. He had drained nearly all of it before coming across his colleague's false teeth. Bizarrely, a few years later I told this story to an RAF officer at a party in Cornwall and he confirmed its veracity. They were his false teeth.

The captain of an RAF Hastings transport aircraft liked to leave the flight deck for a stroll wearing dark glasses and tapping a white stick along the side of the seats in the aisle. Another tied two pieces of rope to something solid in the cockpit and trailed them down the fuselage and handed them to some unfortunate squaddie in an aisle seat. The soldier, facing backwards such was the layout of RAF transports, was asked to 'fly the plane' while the Captain headed off to the lavatory. Every so often, the co-pilot back on the flight deck would tug one of the ropes to add authenticity.

On the Friday of the 1981 show, I was standing on the outside balcony of one of the south side hangars with a bunch of other Tattoo volunteers. We had paused to watch yet another of the endless F-16 routines being rehearsed in front of the Flying Control Committee. Being airside and therefore on the other side of the runway to where the crowds would be on the following two days, we were almost directly underneath the display line of this fast jet jockey who was turning it on somewhat.

Beside me was a huge African-American crew man from the C-5 Galaxy which had earlier landed for the static display. Slowly chewing gum, he watched this F-16 for a couple of minutes before he turned round, kicked open the metal door behind him and almost sang, in lyrical hip-hop rap-style, this unforgettable urging: 'Wayne, justa come and look at this f**ker. He's a *really* kickin' sh*t!' Lordy Plonk, Mother.

Fast jet pilots arriving at Fairford from the east often make a 'run and break' down Runway 27. If they turn late into the left hand southern circuit, they will overfly the old airfield at Down Ampney. Disused since 1947, the airfield was home to some brave young women who, like the Bomber Command crews, were not formally recognised for nearly 70 years. They were The Flying Nightingales.

Marge Wilson was a WAAF nurse who helped to bring home more than 100,000 wounded servicemen from the European battlefields after the D-Day landings, flying back and forth across the English Channel in Dakota transports. From September 1944 until the end of the war, Marge would make around three trips a week from Down Ampney to numerous locations in western Europe. On the outbound trips, she would find herself sitting on boxes of ammunition and rations. Flying back, she would be looking after up to 24 stretcher cases or returning Prisoners of War.

If the aircraft was attacked on the way back, Marge was forbidden to use her parachute to escape. The nurses were ordered to stay with the casualties. They were the only women sent into war zones by the Government. As the outbound flights were not carrying casualties, the Dakotas could not display the Red Cross. They were regularly shot at and some were brought down. Marge got an extra 8 pence a day 'danger money' for the missions that she flew.

Interviewing her on an on-line video link from her home in Western Australia, Marge told me about her happiest flight, coming back to the UK on May 8th 1945 with a group of paratroopers who had been POWs. The captain came into the cabin to tell them that he had just heard on the radio that Germany had formally surrendered. 'I have never been kissed by so many men! Everybody was crying and laughing,' recalled Marge in 2015.

As a 17 year old nurse in London, she saw some terrible deaths and injuries during the Blitz. Three years later she became a WAAF nurse and a Flying Nightingale. Their work was not officially recognised until 2008 when, with the support of the Duchess of Cornwall, the surviving 'Nightingales' were each given a medal, a statute of Florence Nightingale and a lifetime achievement award signed by the Duchess. Like Bomber Command aircrew, they were all volunteers. And so young.

—⚊—

When the two Russian MIG-29s collided at Fairford in 1993, Seán Maffett handled the aftermath coolly and expertly. There was a basic script for such incidents but it was only a couple of paragraphs along the lines of 'You have seen what has happened. Please stay where you are' (although many away from the crowd line initially had no idea what had happened), 'Please make way for ambulances and rescue vehicles', 'We will bring you more details as soon as we can,' and later 'If you have any information, video, or photographs that may help the inquiry, please hand them in at any information point.'

The two MIGs, forming the Russian Flight Research Institute display team, got airborne mid-afternoon. Towards the end of their impressive routine, they collided at the eastern end of Fairford after one of the pilots lost sight of his colleague coming out of a manoeuvre. I saw the puff of smoke and flash of flame from a stand at the half-way point of the crowd line. There was an ominous silence immediately afterwards as two pieces of blazing wreckage tumbled out of the sky. Then there were some monosyllabic expletives from people around me. A woman screamed, followed by the click of cameras. One of the MIGs took an age to descend in a fiery flat spin. It crunched down behind some trees in an old woman's garden just outside the perimeter fence. Eventually two parachutes billowed up against the blue and white sky. Both pilots had ejected safely despite the impact and the low altitude. One was filmed shakily lighting a cigarette after parachuting down.

The wreckage from the other MIG fell within the airfield and damaged a Belgium C-130. To escape the blazing wreckage falling from the sky, one of the Belgium crew slid off the wing and down the side of the C-130 – some 15 feet on to concrete. The aircraft was stranded at Fairford for months until it was repaired. The newly restored Blenheim bomber was nearly hit. I found myself on the other side of the microphone, giving an eyewitness account to my news editor counterpart at BBC Radio Gloucestershire.

While the MIGs were displaying, the Swiss aerobatic team

Patrouille Suisse had fired up their six Hunters and taxied out to hold near the Runway 27 threshold. The collision happened above them but the wreckage missed them all. Not long afterwards, the steely Swiss got airborne. More than 40 years after test pilot Neville Duke displayed his Hunter just after his friend John Derry had died in the DH110 tragedy at Farnborough, the Hunter rose once again to settle the crowd. The whole Fairford display resumed, including a formation of 20 Hawks opening the RAF's 75th anniversary pageant.

No one on the ground was hurt. Twelve people were treated for shock after witnessing the crash. It was said the Swiss pilots did not have to buy any drinks at the pilot's party at the end of the Air Tattoo.

Chapter 27

Silent Contemplation 2017

75 years after Colin Curtis boarded his Vickers Wellington for the last time, I am standing on the flight deck of another product of the Vickers assembly line. The word I hear the most is 'Wow!' as parents bring their young children into the front of the aircraft. They can sit in the co-pilot's seat and pull back on the yoke and pretend they are taking off. Some of the youngsters are facing their first flight in the coming weeks so parents and grandparents want to introduce them to the principles of flying. They want to emphasize that it is normal and safe to climb into a long tube with wings and be launched into the dull grey overcast in pursuit of blues seas, waving palms, cloudless skies and distant relatives.

The aircraft is the nose section of a Vickers Vanguard. G-APES was delivered to British European Airways in 1962 and, after a few years in the passenger world, was converted into a freighter and renamed the Merchantman. It was finally grounded in 1995 after which the nose was cut off and donated to the Aeropark, now in the north west corner of East Midlands Airport. Parked alongside more than 30 other grounded relics of a bygone age, it offers a snapshot of aviation history and the chance, largely lost since 9/11, for young and old to get to see inside the business end of an airliner.

I try to judge the expertise of interested adults before going into my brief routine. On Thursday afternoons, some comment on the high volume of Ryanair flights leaving the airport. I gently point out that they are seeing the same aircraft, hammering the EMA circuit, training pilots to take-off and land. Some come on board for nostalgia having flown on a Vanguard as a passenger or worked on them on the other side of the airport.

A young man settles into the right hand seat and seems at home. He is a Ryanair pilot who says that, every time he lines up his 737 on Runway 09 to take off, he sees the Aeropark and promises himself a visit. Another has just come out of the RAF after twenty years flying the C-130 Hercules. The conversation upgrades from pointing out the basic controls to the idea that the over-powered Vanguard might have made a good maritime reconnaissance platform rather like the American's Lockheed P-3 Orion.

The Aeropark encourages youngsters to get interested in aviation. Hopefully a glimpse inside the Vanguard, the VC10 or the Nimrod will inspire them as I was by The Blue Diamonds and The Tigers in 1962. Wide-eyed youngsters gaze at the hundreds of dials, switches, buttons and levers. Teenagers wanting to be pilots bashfully point out throttles and altimeters to their siblings or grandparents. Some have a flight simulator on their PC or tablet and can take a Typhoon through the Mach Loop in Wales or fly a Vickers Wellington bomber from Oakington to Emden at night, with a practice diversion into Leeuwarden on the way back.

———⚍———

The Luftwaffe developed the airfield at Leeuwarden into its most important base in north west mainland Europe. It was close to the routes taken by RAF bombers heading for targets like Emden, Bremen and Wilhenshaven. By the end of 1941, its nightfighter pilots were benefitting from four radar stations like Tiger on Terschelling, which was never attacked by the Allies. Four years after the war ended, Leeuwarden became one of the main air bases for the Royal Netherlands Air Force. Today it houses F-16s and the new F-35.

During the war, a total of 260 aircraft based at RAF Oakington were lost. Z1110 was one of 16 Wellingtons, along with 113 Stirlings, 93 Lancasters, 36 Mosquitos and two Blenheims. Unlike many airfields built in haste, Oakington remained operational once the war ended. Dakotas based there flew missions in the Berlin airlift in 1948. Two years later it became a training base, subsequently operating the Harvard, Meteor, Vampire, Varsity and Jetstream over the years. In 1974 it was handed over to the Army and used as a base for Gazelle and Lynx helicopters.

A former driver with 657 Squadron of the Army Air Corps recalls being sent to lock up the control tower one night in 1984. He started at the top of the building and worked his way down, ensuring no one else was inside and locking rooms as he went. As he reached the ground floor, he became aware of footsteps on the lino floor above him. He called out but there was no reply.

'I felt very uncomfortable and I had to get out quickly,' he wrote. 'I told the duty NCO who said *he* was not going over there and he entered it in the duty log. I was asked about the incident by the CO the next day. I must admit that I had on several previous occasions felt the hair on the back of my neck rise and a discomfort in my stomach in certain areas of the tower.' Forty years on, was it someone in the tower still waiting for Z1110 to return home?

The Army finally moved out in 1991. Most of the runways had already been dug up. The domestic site later became an Immigration Holding Centre. Now there are plans for the airfield and surrounding area to be turned into a new town called Northstowe. Local people have ideas to ensure the RAF base is remembered somewhere and somehow in the development. There are suggestions that some of the new roads could be named after some of the men who flew from there in the war and never came back. Like so many wartime airfields, the ghosts of Oakington remain.

—⚹—

My father would raise a new enquiry about his brother with the RAF Records Office every few years. The photo on his desk was a persistent reminder of the family's loss and he always hoped for some news before he died. He contacted the Royal Netherlands Air Force who had an efficient Air Force History Section which monitored records of wartime crashes within its air space.

It had the basic details of Wellington Z1110 but could offer no more information. There was nothing new by 2016 when I checked again. Every so often, land reclamation or shifting tides off the Dutch coast reveal some wreckage of a downed aircraft. Seventy years after the war ended, aircraft parts and human bones are still being found across Europe. The only hope for a final resting place for Colin Curtis will be if the sea gives up its dead. During the war, 16,000 British airmen were lost at sea across the globe.

In November 1968, the Air Ministry replied to my father's latest enquiry. 'Although at the end of the war all possible investigations were made by the Royal Air Force Missing Research and Enquiry Service, unhappily no trace was found of your brother's aircraft. Should the aircraft in which your brother was flying as second pilot ever be found during the reclamation of land in Holland, we would of course be told and would communicate with you at once.'

Since 1950, the Dutch have been gradually draining the IJsselmeer, the vast inland sea due south of Terschelling. They have found dozens of aircraft wrecks, most of them dating back to World War Two. Between 1960 and 1985, 167 aircraft were found due to the draining project. Eighty of these were RAF aircraft and eleven contained human remains. In the summer of 2016, the Royal Netherlands Air Force Salvage and Identification Service retrieved wreckage and some human remains from a Wellington bomber flown by a Polish crew. It was shot down in May 1941 on its way from RAF Syerston near Newark to bomb Bremen.

Dozens of unknown Allied airmen are buried in cemeteries across the chain of the Frisian Islands. Over the years, they were recovered on land, from the tidal shores and sandbanks, from dykes or brought ashore by lifeboat crews or fishermen. These are the men who could not be identified. Some were reburied after the war. Some could be identified by their rank if their uniform was still intact. Some would have been in the sea for a long time or had lain unfound on land after falling from the sky. There is no evidence available to link any of these 'unknowns' to the crew of Z1110 but we will never know for sure.

Prompted by the 50th anniversary of the end of World War Two, I took up Colin's story in 1995. I wrote to the editor of *RAF News*, asking if he could run a short story about my search for information on Colin and his crew but he put it in the class-ads under the header of 'Where are they now?' The answer of course was somewhere in the North Sea but my disappointment at this somewhat indelicate way of handling it was soon forgotten by the two replies that it provoked.

One was from an amateur historian of the Second World

War called Chris Ward who lived in Berkshire. He was immediately telling me things that I did not know such as Colin's Wellington was one of 25 detailed to attack Emden that night and that Z1110 was the only one without a known crash site. He also had photographs of the German fighter pilot (Ludwig Becker) who shot him down.

The second reply came from a current member of 101 Squadron, Simon Ludlow, who was flying VC10 tankers out of Brize Norton. Not only did he have the squadron contact and access to its history room, his aunt was Colin's fiancée Doris Fines. Simon's mother Gwen was one of two sisters of Doris, who had fond memories of Colin and still found his death upsetting.

Doris Fines was engaged to
Colin Curtis when he was killed in January 1942

Simon sent me copies of the Battle Orders involving Colin as well as the operational record of his short time with 101 Squadron. There was also 101 Squadron's casualty record which showed that, after Z1110 was lost, more squadron Wellingtons failed to return on 9th March, 2nd April and 15 April. All the crews were killed.

He pointed me to the book *Bomber Squadron at War* by Andrew Brookes, the aerospace analyst and aviation author, who published it in 1983. Brookes, who was a pilot with 101 Squadron in its Vulcan era, wrote up the war-time history of 101 Squadron and devoted a chapter to Wellington operations.

All this information, along with Colin's RAF diary, wings and cap badge, were pulled together in a folder for my father who died three years later in 1998. There they remained untouched, awaiting the time when I could explore it more and pull it all together as a logical narrative and a proper tribute.

A few months after Colin Curtis was killed, 101 Squadron had a particularly tragic period. Between July and September 1942, the squadron lost 20 Wellingtons and 86 lives. Crews from 101 flew on more raids than any other bomber squadron during the war and lost the most aircrew. Colin was one of 1,176 who were killed. The youngest was 19 year old Pilot Officer William Hardie.

The number of Royal Air Force airmen who served during the Second World War and who have no known grave is 20,456. Their names are commemorated at the Air Forces Memorial at Runnymede which overlooks the Thames and the riverside meadow where Magna Carta, enshrining man's basic freedoms under law, was sealed by King John in June 1215. Colin's name is recorded there on Panel 69.

His name can also be found in the RAF Church of St

Clement Danes in London and the Bomber Command Memorial in Ely Cathedral. The war memorial in the village of Holbeach St Johns also remembers the son of the former parish priest there, and his name, along with that of his father, is on a small brass plaque on a processional cross in the church. It can also be found on memorials in the sports pavilion at Moulton (on the site of the former grammar school) and in St Leodegar's church in Wyberton.

From June 1943 until the end of the war, 101 Squadron was based at RAF Ludford Magna, a few miles south of Binbrook. To this day, the village church holds the old squadron standard and its Roll of Honour which includes Colin's name. A squadron reunion is held there every year.

The captain of Z1110 on its last flight, Sgt Peter Chapman, is remembered on the restored war memorial near St Mary's church in Ware in Hertfordshire. The name of air gunner Herbert Mantle is inscribed on a memorial plaque which was displayed at the Bowater paper and pulp mill at Kemsley Mill near his parent's home of Sittingbourne in Kent. The company commissioned the plaque to remember its 91 employees who died during the war. The plaque was later moved to the Kemsley Arms pub, which closed in 2013. The Royal British Legion found a new home for it in Holy Trinity church in Milton Regis where it was formally unveiled again with a commemoration service in March 2017.

Just south of Lincoln, a new Bomber Command Memorial is taking shape on Canwick Hill. Initially this will be a tribute to those who flew from the 27 bomber airfields in Lincolnshire in the war and those in Numbers 1 and 5 Groups. Eventually it will record all 55,573 Bomber Command losses, including Colin's crew from Oakington which was part of Number 3 Group at the time they were lost. Aircrew from 60 nations flew with Bomber Command during the war, including men from China, Peru and Nigeria.

At the ANZAC Memorial in Sydney, there is a brief ceremony at 11am every day to remember the war dead. Ten thousand Australians served with RAF Bomber Command and about a third of them were killed. There is a plinth with the powerful inscription: 'Let Silent Contemplation Be Your Offering'.

—⁂—

At the end of hostilities, Campaign Stars, Clasps and Medals were issued in recognition of service in the 1939-1945 war. The Under-Secretary of State for Air presented his compliments to Colin's mother and, by Command of the Air Council, had 'the honour to transmit the enclosed Awards granted for service in the war.' The Council shared her sorrow that Pilot Officer C.H.Curtis did not live to receive them. He posthumously received the medals that all UK aircrew in Europe were entitled to – the War Medal 1939-1945, the 1939-45 Star and the Air Crew Europe Star Campaign medal.

At the height of the Battle of Britain in September 1940, Winston Churchill said: 'The fighters are our salvation but the bombers alone provide the means of victory.' However in his Victory speech five years later, there was virtually no mention of Bomber Command operations.

Despite what British cities had faced in the Blitz, towards the end of the war there was growing unease among the Allies about the bombing of German cities, typified by Dresden. The Commander-in-Chief of Bomber Command, Arthur Harris, was criticised for the strategy of bombing civilians which was introduced in the months after Colin had died. The argument was that such action might weaken the resolve of the German nation and bring an early end to the war. There was no campaign medal and no national memorial for the men of Bomber Command.

Over the years, the campaign to recognise their sacrifice gathered pace. It took nearly 70 years but in 2012 a special memorial featuring the bronze figures of a bomber crew was unveiled by the Queen in Green Park in London. The roof of the memorial was designed to evoke the geodesic structure of the Wellington bomber's fuselage. The following year, the government announced that the Bomber Command Clasp would be awarded to aircrew in recognition of their bravery and service. Relatives of those who lost their lives could also apply and in due course I received a Clasp in the name of C.H.Curtis to add to the other collected memorabilia of the man who never made it.

My generation in the UK missed conscription and rationing, and benefitted from huge advances in medicine and travel. We rode a cultural revolution which opened up new worlds of music, films and fashion. We never wore a collar and tie when we went on a seaside holiday.

The day before Colin died, the actor and singer Michael Crawford was born. Muhammed Ali was born three days earlier. The day after he died, Alfred Hawthorne Hill (better known as Benny) celebrated his 18th birthday before his call-up into the Army. Telly Savalas (tv cop *Kojak*) hit 20. Four days later, the Portuguese football legend Eusebio was born. Among the others making their debut in 1942 were Paul McCartney, Martin Scorsese, Carole King, Billy Connelly, Aretha Franklin, Stephen Hawking, Barbra Streisand, Jimi Hendrix, Harrison Ford, Nobby Stiles and Muammar Gaddafi.

The American painter Edward Hopper actually completed his most famous work on 21st January 1942. That was the date that he declared *Nighthawks* was finished. It became one of the most recognisable paintings in American art and influenced many working in literature, music, film, opera and television. Its depiction of late night loneliness has crept into television's *CSI*, a production of Verdi's *Rigoletta*, the musical *Pennies from Heaven* and the music of Tom Waits.

I went to see the Terence Rattigan play *Flare Path* in 2011. It centres around a love triangle but the whole mood underlining it was defined by war and by men flying off each night into the jaws of death. It is set in a hotel near a Wellington bomber base and has a character called Doris. Rattigan wrote it in 1941 and it was first performed on a London stage in 1942 – something else Colin would not live to see.

Colin did not make his 23rd birthday. He did not get the chance to marry his fiancée and have children. He did not share adulthood with his brothers and sisters or reunions with his squadron mates. His travel experience was limited to the training in Canada, two overnight returns to Cherbourg and Wilhelmshaven and the final fatal one-way trip to Emden. He never walked on a Goan beach, swam off Bondi, rode a vaporetto in Venice, dozed beneath the palms of Batu Ferringhi, strolled the Las Vegas Strip or coveted the super-yachts in Antigua's English Harbour. He never drank a glass of wine while silently contemplating life and 'tasting the pleasure of remembering' as the sun set over the Greek islands.

'The sky is a pale translucent blue, fading further where it reaches down to merge into the thick, grey mist which hugs the far horizon. Out of this mist, thin grey trees appear, scattered across the distant fields: nearer, they stand out like black silhouettes. The rising sun is a blinding white haze low in the sky. Already the air is warm with a promise of heat later in the day when the clear summer sky will become criss-crossed with its usual maze of vapour trails.

'A broad, green field, the green that can only be seen in England, stretches away into the distance and across it rolls a vast white ribbon of concrete, scarred at each end with long black streaks of rubber. From the unmistakeable ribbon lead other, narrower ribbons, curving and turning towards a focal point, a short wide platform of concrete behind which stand vast towering buildings whose glass walls blindingly reflect the sun's light. The buildings are aircraft hangars; the concrete before them, the Flight Line.

'Between one of the hangars and the Flight Line is a large area of well-mown grass surrounding a small concrete building – the line hut where the ground crews are gathered, drinking coffee, joking, laughing, yawning and reading yesterday's papers for a second time. Two of them wander outside to test the warmth of the morning and escape the fug and glance at the sky. Overhead at tremendous height, a gleaming sliver of silver cuts its way steadily through the blue, heading towards the sea; obviously an early riser. The two airmen watch its progress, vaguely annoyed at being unable to identify the exact cause of the contrail.'

These three paragraphs were among the first words written for adults to capture my imagination. They appeared at the beginning of a writing competition entry for the *RAF Battle of Britain Souvenir Book* of 1962. The writer (a Corporal M.J.Wood) won second prize. The article went on to unpick one day in the life of modern fighter squadron involved in an exercise over the North Sea and was illustrated by sketches of Javelins.

I was eight and new to the exciting world of aeroplanes. Narnia, the *Ladybird* books and the antics of Pooh Bear, Ratty and Mole were all very well but these three paragraphs drew me in. They described a wide scene and then narrowed it all down to two figures staring up into the sky – something which

I was increasingly prone to do. I now knew what it was like to be 'vaguely annoyed' at not knowing what aircraft was creating that white line across the sky at 'tremendous height.'

It was a world away from Mr Pastry, Bill and Ben the Flowerpotmen and their monosyllabic mate Little Weed, Andy Pandy who lived in a picnic basket with his moll Looby Loo and a teddy bear, The Woodentops and *Crackerjack* with Leslie Crowther, Peter Glaze and their pencil prizes.

The brilliant summer morning described by Corporal Wood contrasted bluntly with that cold dawn of 21st January 1942. Snow flurries swirled across the Cambridgeshire fens. It was freezing out on Oakington airfield. The groundcrew stamped their feet to keep warm and clutched mugs of cocoa. There would have been no desire for laughing and joking that morning. Two of the Z1110 groundcrew wandered outside to test the chill of the morning and escape the fug and glance at the sky, still hoping.

Their trains of thought would have been interrupted by a shout from the Flight Sergeant. They have been re-allocated to look after another Wellington which, if all the fog lifts, should arrive at lunchtime. Another crew fresh out of training will pitch up at 101 Squadron tomorrow.

Life goes on. There is a war to be won. Young lives are being lost every day. Get used to it. You do not dwell on death. Live for the moment. Somewhere another squadron adjutant is dictating the lines of another telegram. A squadron commander is searching for fresh words to pay tribute to yet another young man shot out of the night sky and who has 'Failed to Return'.

Debrief

The recollections of a young local journalist are really the sub-plot in this book. This was no searing account of a foreign correspondent in exotic locations or a news anchor under fire from the world's trouble spots. This was the humdrum day-to-day stuff of life in the 1970s and 1980s from the editorial front line in England. It is close to home for many young journalists of that era who will have similar and better tales to tell.

The story of the unremarkable life of Colin Curtis with its exceptional and tragic end is more important and significant. It was going to be at the beginning of the book and then at the end. Eventually I decided to integrate it with other tragedies, heroes and reminders that death catches up with us all. Colin was a war hero without medals for gallantry or documented stories of valour and heroism. He never got the time for those, disappearing on his third mission.

If he had survived, where would he have gone next? He would have certainly captained his own crew in a Wellington before long. He would almost certainly have transferred onto Lancasters as the big four engine bombers started to enter service later in 1942. By all accounts, his character was one of reliability, determination and a strong sense of duty. As his reputation spread, could he have got a call-up for a special operation such as 'Chastise' in 1943? Would his name ever have come to the attention of people like Guy Gibson or

Leonard Cheshire? Might he have stayed in the RAF at the end of the war and gone on to command a Cold War Vulcan squadron like 101? Or would he just have collected his demob suit and gone back into teaching?

Colin was typical of the vast majority of those 55,573 men who died in service with Bomber Command during the Second World War. Their individual exploits have not been laid out for all to see in magazine articles, books and films because they either simply never got the time to have those exploits or because they just got on with their terrifying job until their number was up and their luck ran out.

There are many books which have helped me try to understand what life was like for a young airman in Bomber Command in the early years of the war. They include *Aircrew* by Bruce Lewis, *Bomber Boys* by Patrick Bishop, *Bomber Crew* by James Taylor and Martin Davidson, *Bomber Squadron at War* by Andrew Brookes, *Damned Good Show* by Derek Robinson, *Flights into the Night* by L. Anthony Leicester, *Guy Gibson* by Richard Morris, *Looking into Hell* by Mel Rolfe, and *A Wing and a Prayer* by Harry Crosby. This last one is an American perspective from personal experience with the USAAF 'Bloody' 100th Group which suffered heavy losses in daylight bombing missions flown from airfields scattered across East Anglia.

Bruce Barrymore Halpenny maintained that all airfields were haunted. He started collecting the stories and publishing them under the *Ghost Stations* series. The Binbrook and Kelstern ghost stories are to be found in the first *Ghost Stations* book from 1986. There are many more. Bruce died in 2015.

Graham Hurley is a film maker and thriller writer with many novels to his name. His best known creation is Detective Inspector Joe Faraday whose beat is around Portsmouth. In a rare move away from fiction, Graham spent a year with the team organising the 1998 Royal International Air Tattoo. The result was *Airshow* (Orion Publishing), a fascinating look at the trials and triumphs of pulling together the biggest military air show in the world. Fifteen years after my spell with the IAT (before it became Royal and before it moved to Fairford), the book reminded me what a privilege it was to climb that commentary tower and wear that 'access all areas' pass that took me backstage to aviation ecstasy.

Airshow starts with the arrival of the bat-like B-2 Spirit bomber at the 1997 show. Graham writes of the 'extraordinary hush' in the face of 'an intruder so alien that it silenced even conversation'. I remember it well, along with Seán Maffet's measured tones reflecting the awe of the huge crowd on that hot summer's day. The B-2 and the sheer scale of the show prompted Graham to ask Paul Bowen and Tim Prince if he could write a book about it all.

Other aviation books that inspire include *Empire of the Clouds* by James Hamilton-Paterson, *Farnborough – 100 Years of British Aviation* by Peter J Cooper and two Rowland White books – *Phoenix Squadron* and *Vulcan 607*.

The latter is the true gripping story behind the first 'Black Buck' mission in which a 101 Squadron crew took their Vulcan to bomb Port Stanley airfield during the Falklands war in 1982. They were actually the reserve crew and were bumped up to 'primary' after take off when the lead Vulcan developed a problem with cockpit pressurisation. A hugely complicated endeavour that required skill, determination, courage and luck got the Vulcan from Ascension Island to the Falklands and back. It involved an awesome choreography of shuffling eleven Victor tankers in the dark amidst the unforgiving weather many miles from landfall high above the South Atlantic.

—⁓—

Derek Lambert did his national service with the RAF. He then embarked on a long career in print journalism. He started on the *Dartmouth Chronicle* from which he was fired on his 21st birthday after reporting an outbreak of chickenpox as smallpox. He worked on the *Eastern Daily Press* at Kings Lynn and the *Sheffield Star* before joining the *Daily Mirror.* He later became a foreign correspondent with the *Daily Express*, working in Africa and Moscow.

He was also an acclaimed author, publishing his first thriller in 1969 and continuing to write until a year before his death in 2001. In 1979 and 1980 he wrote two wonderful books about his early career as a young newspaper reporter. The tales he told all resonated with me and prompted me at the time, just a year or so out of newspapers myself, to wonder if I could attempt to do the same one day. Derek's local paper reminiscences were covered in *Don't quote me...But* , followed by his arrival in Fleet Street with *...And I quote* (both Arlington Books). Like my era, they were the days before mobile phones, 24 hour rolling news and social media.

Denis Pannett is a respected artist and a Fellow of the Guild of Aviation Artists. I was drawn to his fine paintings of the Wellington, flying low and alone or in a pair. 'Moonlight over Norfolk' struck me as particularly apposite. Colin's Wellington would have flown over Norfolk on its way to Emden on that final fateful night. Denis has generously allowed me to use his work to illustrate the Wellington and indeed a Sunderland flying boat like the one which crashed off Donegal a mere two weeks after Colin was killed. Denis is also renowned for his wider art covering golf, landscapes, railways and seascapes. You can find out more about him and his wide body of work at denispannett.co.uk

—m—

Some chapter titles explained…

'Son of a Preacher Man' is a song by Dusty Springfield (written by Hurley & Wilkins) from her acclaimed album recorded in Memphis in 1968 and released the following year. The song was quite helpful in my youth. Colin Curtis was also the son of a preacher man and I have used the song title for the chapter that covers his life up to the edge of going to war. The actor John Hurt, who went to school in Lincoln and who was also the son of a preacher man, said in 2009: 'You're automatically an outsider if you're the son of a vicar'.

'Life Short Call Now' is a song and album title by the Canadian singer Bruce Cockburn. I first picked up on his music in 1980 with an album called *Humans*, although he had already been recording for ten years. His work covers human rights, politics and environmental issues but he also writes very evocative personal songs like 'Lovers in a Dangerous Time' and 'Live On My Mind'. I borrowed *Life Short Call Now* for the title of a chapter about those cub reporter experiences that introduce you to the fragility of life. Bruce Cockburn should be as well-known as his Canadian counterparts Neil Young, Joni Mitchell, Gordon Lightfoot and Leonard Cohen.

'Glamour Profession' is a song by the American rock band Steely Dan, formed by Donald Fagen and Walter Becker in New York in 1972. The song, which has nothing to do with journalism, association football or being a fighter pilot, would be on the shortlist for my *Desert Island Discs* selections. Of course the name Becker is part of the Colin Curtis story. I wonder…

'Riders on the Storm' is the last track on the last album by The Doors before Jim Morrison died. Sequentially it is the last track across six studio albums in which Morrison's voice is heard, sinking into nightmare with an echoed whisper against the sound of rain and rolling thunder.

'Postcards of Scarborough' is a song by the British guitarist

Michael Chapman. The lyrics relate how Paradise, an actual place on the cliff top behind Scarborough castle, and the harbour down below are not the places that they used to be since his lover left. The two postcards he has remind him of 'time past and time passing', repeated three times. The song appeared on his 1970 album called 'Fully Qualified Survivor'. In 2017 at the age of 76, Michael Chapman produced one of his finest pieces of work, an album called simply '50'.

'Time of No Reply' is a song by the English singer Nick Drake, who died aged only 26 in 1974. His grave can be found in the churchyard of Tanworth-in-Arden in Warwickshire. A couple of lines out of his song 'From The Morning' are inscribed on the head stone. 'Now we rise. And we are everywhere'.

This book had its genesis in the 'Picture in a Frame' but the inspiration for the title of the first chapter was triggered by the Tom Waits song of the same name.

'What's Going On' is the title of the Marvin Gaye album which is deservedly ranked as one of the greatest landmarks in modern popular music.

Cotswold Radar was the name given to the area radar at RAF Brize Norton for five years up the end of 1980.

Thank you…

Simon Ludlow replied to my initial call for help and then extracted relevant material from the official records of 101 Squadron. Those records at Brize Norton offered a wealth of information, including the Battle Orders for the squadron in January 1942. Simon also offered information about his family including Colin's fiancée Doris Fines. Along with the 101 Squadron Association, Simon is in touch with Longstanton Parish Council about possible street names on the new development which will engulf the old Oakington airfield. He has suggested celebrating the lives of five 101 crew members who have no known grave – Frederick Craig (who was mentioned in despatches), William Hardie (the youngest 101 crewman to die) and Colin Curtis, Peter Chapman and Herbert Mantle of the Z1110 Wellington crew.

The Dutch aviation researcher Willem de Jong lives a few miles from Leeuwarden air base in The Netherlands. Willem has done exhaustive research into the wartime history of the Frisian Islands and beyond. The information that he has gathered over the years into the Allied aircraft that crashed in the area and the fate of the crews on board is fascinating and compelling. I am grateful for his generosity in allowing me to use some of his findings around the evening of 20 January 1942. A link to his web pages can be found on this book's website.

Other aviation historians kindly responded to my emails. They included Chris Ward in Berkshire back in 1995 and more recently Dennis Burke in County Sligo and Garth Barnard in Northamptonshire.

The late Roland Beamont generously gave his time for a wide-ranging radio interview about test flying back in 1988. My documentary 'Life with the Lightning' is still available from the Lightning Preservation Group at Bruntingthorpe airfield in Leicestershire. All of the money goes to the group who keep a couple of Lightnings in taxiable condition and have now successfully housed them in the old QRA sheds from RAF Wattisham. You can buy the cd from the Lightning Preservation Group – link on the deadlines101 website.

Paul McDaid-Smith is the grandson of my mother's brother Frank Smith, whose bomb disposal exploits are outlined in Chapter 20. Paul unearthed some tapes which Frank recorded many years ago and which shed new light on both his career and how he was injured in Korea.

My brother Chris Curtis grilled the Spalding Chutney Mafia about the Curtis family history some years ago and extracted some valuable information from them. The SCM – Joyce and Mary Curtis – were the sisters of Hugh, Colin and Wilfrid. Boxes of family photographs and documents lay in cupboards and drawers for years after much loved members of the family passed on. There was a lot of material from my Mum and Dad, Sheila and Wilfrid Curtis as well as Joyce and Mary. My eldest son Tom Curtis lent his photographic expertise to the project.

There are so many photographs in my archives relating to times with the RAF. Some are my own ancient grainy snaps. Others are the sharp clear professional shots taken by RAF photographers from the back seats of fast jets as they fought the weight of their camera as the g-forces kicked in. Examples of all of these images, plus other relics, reminders and links to related websites can be found at: www.deadlines101.com

Time past and time passing. So far so good. Mind over Matter. Where are you on the family tree? Who do you think you are? A fully qualified survivor?

Will the sea ever give up the wreckage of Wellington Z1110? Does one of those 'unknown' graves in the Frisian Islands host one of the lost souls on board? How many spokes *were* there on a bicycle wheel in 1944? Did the Reginald Simpson Trio offer Mrs Simpson a gig? Indeed, is Mrs Simpson still playing the organ somewhere celestial? When the music's over, turn out the light…

Who knows where the time goes? So many questions and so little time.

www.deadlines101.com